Praises For:

Understanding the Revelation

Understanding the Revelation is an easy-to-read and easy-to-understand summary of Revelation that is both informative and encouraging. Geographical and historical details engage readers, while biblical reminders inspire them to make the most of every evangelistic opportunity. Rather than brashly pushing a single perspective, Dr. Keith Kunda carefully and thoughtfully addresses different eschatological views with an overarching emphasis on Jesus. I encourage you to read this book.

-**Dr. Nate Herbst**, Team Coordinator, *Great Commission Alliance.*

***

As a certified professional life coach, my objective is to help others find their identity in Christ as a primary tool for overcoming obstacles. It is often a challenge because many people are afraid of the Bible due to a lack of understanding. This is especially true for relatively new believers or those who have not been properly disciplined in the Word of God. Keith takes one of the most feared books in the Bible that even many seasoned believers are afraid to crack open, The Revelation, and helps make it understandable to the masses. He does so without compromising the text of Scripture. He digs deep into the historical perspective of the Word, and he works diligently to steer completely clear of man-made doctrine and/or false teachings about The Revelation. He helps to reveal what God intended for His children... a true and biblically sound understanding of The Revelation. As you read this book, you will walk away from each lesson wanting more. You'll walk away not confused, but enlightened; not fearing, but hopeful; not defeated, but encouraged to live fully alive in Christ, and not condemned, but victorious! This is a book on discipleship. A book of love. A book of hope! I look forward to reading it again and again!"

-**Doug Hartle**, BGS, CPC, Professional Life Coach.

***

Oh, what becomes The Revelation of Jesus Christ? How does one understand such a magnificent confluence of living concepts? As a Preterist? As a historicist? As an Idealist? As a Futurist? Or some combination thereof? Pastor Kunda does a magnificent inter-weaving of what is and what is to come of the glorious return of our Lord Jesus Christ at His long-awaited, but certain, second coming. His series of sermons on the book of The Revelation of Jesus Christ does a superb job of inter-connecting the once hidden, now visible, truths about Jesus Christ and His final victory in His glory.

This very thought-provoking, heart-searching investigation of eschatology that Pastor Kunda shares with the reader on the doctrine of last things pose many questions and answers, including the last battle of defiance of human history with the ultimate, and never questioned defeat of the antichrist. Buy it, read it, and meditate on the truth of Jesus Christ and the truths of our risen and glorified Son of God and what is to come!

-**Terry McIntosh**, Omnibus Instructor, *The Classical Academy*, and Home School College Credit Consultant.

***

Dr. Keith Kunda's book, ***Understanding the Revelation*** is obviously well-researched and presented on the basis of expository teaching (verse by verse). I very much enjoyed this instructive and inspirational study of the last book of the New Testament. I found it to be relevant, practical, and easy to read.

-**Dr. Steven D. Emery**, District Superintendent Emeritus of *The Wesleyan Church*.

***

Many readers shy away from the last book of the Bible because of its strange visions and scary predictions. Keith Kunda helps us view Revelation in a more positive light. If we read God's Word with an open heart and a humble attitude, there is much we can learn from John's grand vision.

With the skill of a teacher and the perspective of a shepherd, Keith helps us to recognize: (1) *Revelation is a practical book* leading to action steps that "Apply To Me" (ATM). (2) *Revelation doesn't have to be a divisive book.* Even when we disagree about the details, our different views shouldn't produce quarrels and divisions. (3) Above all, *Revelation is a Christ-centered book*, for Jesus Christ, is its source, theme, and main character. Thank you, Keith, for reminding us, "If we study only to satisfy our curiosity, but miss Jesus, our study will have been in vain. This book is about Jesus Christ."

-**Dr. David Faust**, former president, Cincinnati Christian University.

Understanding the Revelation

Dr. Keith Kunda

Published by KHARIS PUBLISHING, an imprint of KHARIS MEDIA LLC.

Copyright © 2021 Dr. Keith Kunda

ISBN-13: 978-1-63746-071-9
ISBN-10: 1-63746-071-6

Library of Congress Control Number: 2021939911

All KHARIS PUBLISHING products are available at special quantity discounts for bulk purchase for sales promotions, premiums, fund-raising, and educational needs. For details, contact:

Kharis Media LLC
Tel: 1-479-599-8657

support@kharispublishing.com
www.kharispublishing.com

KHARIS
PUBLISHING

Foreword

The lessons in this book are based on a sermon series I preached in 2020 on the entire book of The Revelation. Although the series was interrupted for three months by the global pandemic, I was able to resume the series at the exact spot I left off in March of that year. (You will notice several references to the pandemic starting with Lesson 7.) The motivation to publish the sermons in commentary form came from the encouragement of many church members who said, "I never understood The Revelation before your series."

Each chapter of this book is labeled a *Lesson* in order to avoid confusion with the word *Chapter*. I only use *Chapter* to identify a chapter in Scripture, mostly chapters in The Revelation itself.

I have chosen the title *Understanding the Revelation* because I believe God gave this book, not to confuse, but to reveal. The Revelation is meant to be *understood*. There are many complex themes and symbols, and I have done my best to explain everything clearly, recognizing that there are a few verses where we must honestly say, "I don't know the meaning or the reason." Although there are multiple methods used to approach this great prophetic book, I have chosen to study it chapter by chapter and, for the most part, verse by verse. The material within a few of the lessons is organized thematically because that is the most appropriate approach for certain chapters.

I believe that Chapter 6 begins a long series of prophecies of *future* events which begin with the opening of seven scroll seals of judgment. Out of the seventh seal come seven trumpets of judgment, and from the seventh trumpet come seven bowls of wrath. I believe those three "sevens" comprise a chronological series of events that will take place on earth over the course of seven years of tribulation. I also believe The Revelation contains interludes, parentheses, and supplemental material; I have been very clear to identify such sections in our study, for they "interrupt" the overall chronology.

My theology and therefore my approach to the book is pre-millennial. I believe Christ will return to earth and that He will reign for 1000 years while Satan is bound. After that Satan will be loosed for a brief time before he meets his final doom in the Lake of Fire. So, this book is not post-millennial or amillennial in its approach.

I want to thank Kathy Starling, Nancy Cornacchione, and Beverly Flick for their assistance in transcribing my sermons in order to prepare this material, as I do not preach from manuscripts. Their many hours of work are very much appreciated. I also want to thank the many people who encouraged me in this endeavor. If the Bible's 66th book has confused you in the past, I hope this set of lessons brings clarity to its meaning.

Dr. Keith Kunda,

August 2021.

CONTENTS

Introduction

Our Journey Begun: What Is This Book About?

First Things First (Actually 11 Things First)

Before we begin our chapter-by-chapter study of The Revelation, it is important that we look at the book as a whole so we know where we are going. I want to emphasize 11 things.

First, this book is about Jesus Christ. Yes, it is a book of prophecy, and yes there are evil beings that show up. But above all it is a book about Jesus Christ:

He is the source of the book.
He is the theme of the book.
He is the main character of the book.
He is the climax of the book.
He is the Judge in the book.
He is the Victor in the book.
He is the Ruler in the book.

If we study only to satisfy our curiosity but miss Jesus, our study will have been in vain. This book is about Jesus Christ.

Second, this book fulfills an essential component of the Christian faith: Jesus must return.

❖ The return of Jesus Christ is mentioned 318 times in the New Testament. If He does not return, that would render untrue a high percentage of the New Testament.
❖ He must return to marry His bride (The Church).
❖ He must return to judge the world.
❖ He must return to rule the world.

Third, it is a blessing book. It starts with a blessing: **Blessed is he who reads and those who hear the words of the prophecy, and heed the things which are written in it (1:3).**[1] It ends with a similar blessing: **Blessed is he who heeds the words of the prophecy of this book (22:7).** In between are five other blessings:

**Blessed are the dead who die in the Lord from now on (14:13).
Blessed is the one who stays awake and keeps his garments
(16:15).
Blessed are those who are invited to the marriage supper of the
Lamb (19:9).
Blessed and holy is the one who has a part in the first resurrection
(20:6).
Blessed are those who wash their robes, that they may have the
right to the tree of life (22:14).**

Fourth, this book is a controversial book. Charles Swindoll says:

No other book of the Bible has provoked greater fascination or led to
more controversy than Revelation. Its profound mysteries, elusive symbolism, powerful predictions, and colorful language are unparalleled in the rest
of Scripture. Attempts to interpret its details have spanned the extremes
from the sublime to the ridiculous. Throughout my life of ministry, I've
seen the book of Revelation drive fanatics to set dates for the return of
Christ, frighten believers who find themselves overwhelmed by its judgment and wrath, and turn off skeptics who already think the Bible is filled
with indecipherable nonsense.[2]

I want to say at the outset that not everyone will agree with some things
I say, and probably very few people will agree with everything I say. That is
fine. But we should not let different interpretations keep us from studying
and doing our best to understand this great book, leading us to apply it to
our lives today.

Fifth, it is a life-changing book. Hear again what Charles Swindoll says:

We all must study this book with humility, seeking to balance careful
reading, restrained and reasonable interpretation, and practical application.
The purpose of Revelation is to change us, not simply to inform us.[3]

If study of this book does not change me, once again I am only a curiosity seeker. Warren Wiersbe echoes this sentiment:

No believer should study prophecy merely to satisfy his curiosity. We
need to approach this book as wonderers and worshippers, not as academic
students.[4]

Sixth, it is a "sevens" book. The number seven occurs 54 times. Specifically we see:

Seven blessings
Seven seals

Seven trumpets
Seven bowls
Seven stars
Seven lampstands
Seven churches
Seven angels
Seven plagues
Seven kings
Seven peals of thunder
Seven I AM's (just as in the Gospel of John)

Seventh, it is an Old Testament-related book. There are nearly 300 quotations from or allusions to the Old Testament.

Eighth, it is a Genesis-contrasted book. By that I mean there are many themes that are polar opposites from what we read in Genesis:

In Genesis there is the first heaven and earth; in The Revelation there is the new heaven and earth.
In Genesis there is the tree of life lost; in The Revelation the tree of life returns.
In Genesis the first man (Adam) is given authority over creation; in The Revelation the second Man (Jesus Christ) and His bride rule over a redeemed creation.
In Genesis there is the beginning of sin; in The Revelation there is the end of sin.
In Genesis the serpent-devil is active; in The Revelation the devil is thrown into the lake of fire.
In Genesis there is the first city of man; in The Revelation there is the city of God.
In Genesis there is darkness and light; in The Revelation there is no more night.
In Genesis the curse is pronounced; in The Revelation the curse is removed.
In Genesis there is the beginning of sorrow and suffering; in The Revelation there is the end of sorrow and suffering.
In Genesis there is the first death; in The Revelation there is the end of death.

Ninth, it is **the** consummation book. Harry Ironside says: "It is like the headstone that completes and crowns the whole wondrous pyramid of truth."[5] The consummation of history and prophecy are contained in this book.

Dr. Keith Kunda

Tenth, it is a revealing book. The Greek word is *apokalupsis*, from which we get our word apocalypse. In our vocabulary that word has mostly come to mean catastrophe, but the Greek word means *revealing*. The book was not written to puzzle or confuse or hide: it was written to *reveal*.

Eleventh, it is a symbolic book. The Greek word *homoios*, which means *like*, *resembling*, or *similar*, occurs 21 times. David Jeremiah notes:

This book is filled with mystery. It portrays things seen and unseen. It portrays things in the body and out of the body. It portrays things of the world and things of the world to come. It symbolically portrays angels and demons and principalities in the heavenlies. It speaks of agents and of nations and of potentates, and sometimes the symbols represent people.[6]

Because of the symbolism, there can be disagreements about what things mean. Many of the symbols are interpreted for us in the book itself, and some others can be understood from other Scripture. But that is not always true, and that is where interpretive differences occur. So why did God choose to use so many symbols? There are three reasons. Symbolism is timeless, symbolism arouses emotions, and symbolism protected the early Church during days of intense persecution, when those outside the Church would not understand the full meaning of what was written and use it against believers.

Interpretive Differences: 2 Key Issues

I also want to say two things about interpretation systems that have been used through the years. Some have said that The Revelation is a collection of myths that teach only the triumph of good over evil. (They often call the book *Revelations*, which is incorrect. The title is singular: *Revelation*.) I reject this interpretation system. Others believe the book was entirely fulfilled during Roman times. Again I reject that interpretation system. Still others argue that its fulfillment has been going on continually since it was written. I believe that is only true for Chapters 2 and 3. My understanding of this book—and the one I will use throughout our study together—is that (starting with Chapter 4 of The Revelation), it is a prophetic book, telling events which have not yet happened.

The other interpretive difference (and probably the biggest reason scholars don't agree about many parts of the book) has to do with chronology. Some believe the book is 100% chronological. Others believe it is almost exclusively thematic. An example would be the 7 scroll seals, the 7 trumpets, and the 7 bowls of judgment. Chronological interpreters believe these are consecutive. Thematic interpreters would argue that these are all symbols of the same events: i.e., they are concurrent. I fall between the

xii

chronological interpreters and the thematic interpreters. I believe that the book is *primarily* chronological, but that it includes some flashbacks, some parentheses or interludes, some zooming in, and some big picture zooming out. I will be very clear about where I believe those non-chronological portions occur.

Conclusion

I believe we must study this book. It is often neglected in pulpits, and that is very unfortunate. Yes, it can be hard to understand at times, and some passages are open to different interpretations. But The Revelation is Holy Scripture, and as such we dare not ignore it. At the very least everyone should study it—even if only one time—to remind us of Who wins! Finally, let us remember that Satan is defeated in this book, and he hates it when people study that truth. I conclude this introduction with a brilliant observation by Louis Talbot:

Many people treat the Book of Revelation like the priest and the Levite treated the man who was beaten and robbed in the story of the Good Samaritan…they pass by on the other side. The devil has turned thousands of people away from this portion of God's Word. He does not want anyone to read a book that tells of his being cast out of heaven… Nor is he anxious for us to read of the ultimate triumph of his number one enemy, Jesus Christ. The more you study the Book of Revelation, the more you understand why Satan fights so hard to keep God's people away from it.[7]

Lesson 1

Read 1:1 – 8

A Glorious Beginning

One nice thing about studying Revelation is it's easy to find in the Bible. It's not like finding the book of Haggai. It's the last book in the Bible, number 66, and it will be very important to *read* the indicated passage before reading a lesson in this book.

Preface

The first three verses form the preface of the book. The source of the information that we are receiving is God, and we are told that it has come from God the Father to God the Son to an angel to John (the human author) to the bond-servants of God. This is easier to see in graphic form:

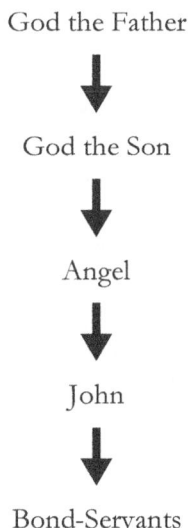

God the Father

↓

God the Son

↓

Angel

↓

John

↓

Bond-Servants

The information started with God and was ultimately received by bond servants, and those bond servants are in seven churches to whom this book was originally written. They are the recipients of the information. You probably know that the Apostle John gave us five books of the Bible. In his Gospel his message is "Be saved." He said, **These things have been written so that you may believe that Jesus is the Christ, the Son of God; and that believing you may have life in His name** (John 20:31). So his message is "Be saved." In his epistles (First, Second, Third John), his mes-

1

sage is "Be certain." *Know* that you have eternal life. Here in The Revelation his message is "Be ready."

The purpose of the book is to show—not tell—but show. It was given to John in pictures, in images. Throughout the book he says *I saw, I saw, I saw, I saw.* It was to *show* what *must* take place. There is no question: this must happen. There are two important words to understand here: near and shortly. The time is near: what must shortly take place. Near is an indication that from the time of John until however long it is before Christ returns, the Church must always be ready. It could happen at any time. Be ready. *Shortly* has to deal with the truth that once it starts, once these events begin to happen starting with Chapter 6, it will be one event right after the other after the other. It will be short.

Later on we will find out that throughout the book God used multiple channels of communication: sometimes Christ, sometimes an angel, sometimes an elder, sometimes a voice from heaven. So the diagram on the previous page (from God the Father to God the Son to an Angel to John to his bond servants who are in the churches) is the preface of the book.

Greeting and Triune Author

In v. 4 and the first half of v. 5 we have the greeting and the Triune author. The greeting is *grace and peace*. I think members of the early Church must have greeted one another with the words *grace and peace* when they gathered together. We find it in Paul's letters; we find it here in The Revelation: grace and peace. First we must experience the grace of God in our lives. We must come to the cross and admit we cannot save ourselves. We must throw ourselves on the mercy of the Lord Jesus Christ and accept His substitutionary death on our behalf. Once we experience the grace of God, we have peace with God, and finally we have peace with one another. Grace and peace *is* the gospel.

Now we see who the Divine author is: ...**from Him who is and who was and who is to come** (v. 4). I believe God the Father is implied. The other named author is the seven spirits. Now don't be confused about the seven spirits. It means the Holy Spirit. Some translations will say the seven-fold Spirit. Where does this come from? This symbolism comes from back in the Old Testament, Isaiah 11:1- 2, where the Holy Spirit is called ...**the spirit of the Lord, the spirit of wisdom, the spirit of understanding, the spirit of counsel, the spirit of strength, the spirit of knowledge, the spirit of the fear of the Lord.** Seven characteristics of the Holy Spirit. That's what is meant here. So, the book is from God the Father, it is from God the Holy Spirit, and it is from Jesus Christ who is God the Son (v. 5).

The Trinity shows up right here at the beginning. It is from the Triune God. God the Father, God the Spirit, God the Son.

As noted in my Introduction, the book is *about* Jesus. In the first half of v. 5 we learn that He is the faithful witness, meaning this: did He ever tell a lie? No, He did not. Whenever He spoke, He spoke truth. Most importantly when He said, **"I am the way, the truth and the life; no one comes to the Father but through me"** (John 14:6), He spoke truth. Is there another way to eternal life? No! If you believe strongly enough in Transcendental Meditation, will that get you into heaven? No. If you are a really good Muslim and you pray to Mecca three times a day, will that get you into heaven? No. He spoke the truth. He is the faithful witness. Everything He said is true. He is the first born from the dead. He is alive. If He is not alive, he cannot come again because He's dead. That's pretty simple, isn't it? He must be risen from the dead. In celebrating the Lord's Supper we read, **As often as you eat the bread and drink the cup you proclaim the Lord's death *until he comes*** (I Corinthians 11:26). He cannot come again if He is dead. He has to be risen, and He is the ruler of the earth and the kings of the earth. Vladimir Putin is not in charge of the kings of the earth. The Ayatollah is not in charge of the kings of the earth. Donald Trump is not in charge of the kings of the earth; Joseph Biden is not in charge of the kings of the earth. Jesus Christ is in charge of the kings of the earth; He is the ruler over the kings of the earth. He has the earth in His hand and He will never let go. By the way, faithful witness, first born from the dead, ruler of the kings of the earth—all three of those titles are found in Psalm 89—three of those many references from the Old Testament.

Two Doxologies

All these things that John has said led him to burst out in not one but two doxologies of praise. He says, **To Him** [Jesus] **who loves** [not loved, but loves]**, us and released us from our sins** [how did He do that?] **by His blood** [without the shedding of blood there is no remission of sins]. **He has made us a Kingdom** [not an earthly kingdom, but a heavenly Kingdom] **and made us priests to His God** (1:5b-6). We do not have to go through a human priest in order to confess sins and be forgiven. The priesthood of all believers is a fundamental doctrine of The Reformation and of true Christian faith. We don't have to go through a priest. In the Old Testament when people brought their sacrifices they had to go through a priest. John says He's made us priests to His God. When we sin we go to Him. We don't come to Keith, we don't go to the elders, we go to Him in confession. By the blood of Jesus Christ we are forgiven. John uses "to Him" twice and adds **be the glory and the dominion forever and ever**

3

(1:6), and he concludes with a powerful *Amen*. That's one doxology of praise.

Then in the next verse John starts over. He says Jesus is coming with the clouds, and every eye will see Him. How will that happen? Because if He comes where I live, I'd see Him. But what about the rest of the world? He is going to come in such a way supernaturally—I don't know how it will happen—but every eye will see Him. John said even those who pierced Him. John was there at the cross. Most of the rest of the apostles were in hiding, but he was there and he saw that awful moment when they pierced the side of his Lord and our Lord. He never, never forgot that horrible sight, and he includes it here. All tribes will mourn over Him because the earth will be filled with tribes who missed Him. *They will mourn.* Once again John says *Amen*.

The Sovereignty of God

Finally, in v. 8 we find the total sovereignty of God, and I believe that here we are talking about the triune God: Father, Son, and Holy Spirit. He says, "I am the Alpha and the Omega," which are the first and last letters of the Greek alphabet. We would say the A and the Z. The first word is Alpha, spelled out in Greek. But for Omega there is just the letter; the word is *not* spelled out. Is there significance to why Alpha is spelled out and why Omega is not? Vernon McGee believes it is because the beginning has already happened, but the end (the last) hasn't happened yet.[8] It's still future, and so we don't have it spelled out because it's not complete yet. Perhaps under the inspiration of the Holy Spirit John wrote it that way for that reason.

No matter what, we know that He's the God who is, He's the God who was, and He's the God who is to come. The present is His, the past is His, and the future is His. He alone sits on the throne. Do you know how many times the word throne is used in the book of The Revelation? 46 times. That should tell you something about this book. This book is not about the suffering servant Jesus who died for our sins as we find in the Gospels. This is the reign of the King of kings and Lord of lords. The word king is used 37 times in this book. God is in control. Have I whetted your appetite for more? Read on!

ATM (Apply to Me)

1. Jesus is coming again. Never forget it: Jesus is coming again.

2. God's victorious, glorious Son is worthy of worship. When churches gather together each Sunday in His name, part of what we do is give glory to Him because He is worthy of worship. He is the first born from the dead: the faithful witness.

3. God's sovereign plan replaces fear with hope. So, I must ask this question: do I know personally the Lord Jesus as He is described in these verses? I don't mean some milquetoast, watered down Jesus. Do I know the risen victorious Lord? Have I surrendered my life to Him and Him alone as Lord and Savior? Do I know Him personally as He is described in these verses, or have I made up my own version of Jesus. *Well, I sort of kind of believe in a good teacher.* That's not the Jesus of the Scriptures and it's not the Jesus of The Revelation!

4. Am I ready to encounter Jesus in this amazing book? We must come with humility, and we must come with submission. We must come with open hearts to see what He has to say, not just to the seven churches of Asia, but to you and your church today. Am I ready to encounter Him?

5. Finally, am I ready for His return? If He returned this afternoon, would I miss Him? If you can't answer that question with confidence, then the Holy Spirit is speaking to you and saying you need to surrender your life to Christ now. I can't wait to go through this book with you. Let's prepare our hearts to see what the Spirit says to your church and to each one of us.

Lesson 2

Read 1:9 – 2:17

Christat and His Churches

T he Revelation is about Jesus Christ and His return. It is called The Revelation, no "s." Some of you might have an older Bible that titles it *The Revelation of St. John the Divine.* That would be inaccurate. You might have a Bible that titles the book *The Revelation of Jesus Christ.* That would be accurate. It is His Revelation. A complete title might be *The Revelation of Jesus Christ Which He Gave Through an Angel to His Apostle John.* That's probably too long of a title! But it is not The Revelation *of* John; it is a Revelation *to* John given *by* Jesus Christ.

The Revelation completes a critical set of verses that are found in Philippians 2:8-9. I am sure you are familiar with this passage: **He [Jesus] humbled Himself by becoming obedient to the point of death, even death on a cross. Therefore also God highly exalted Him, and bestowed on Him the name which is above every name.** All of that has happened. But the rest of it has not yet happened (Philippians 2:10): **that at the name of Jesus every knee shall bow, of those who are in heaven, and on earth, and under the earth, and that every tongue shall confess that Jesus Christ is Lord, to the glory of God the father.** That is yet future, when every tongue will confess and every knee will bow. There will be no question that He is the risen Lord of Glory, and The Revelation provides the complete story of how that will happen. We noted that John is the human author and that the chain of communication is from God the Father to God the Son, through an angel to John to bond-servants, specifically bond-servants in seven churches. Beginning with Chapter 2 the churches are actually named.

Who Is John?

What do we know about John? We know that here in v. 9, just like in v. 1, he identifies himself. (I love letters in the Bible. I don't like the way we write letters today (when we still write them!). You have to go through the whole letter and then at the end you find out who wrote the letter. Sincerely, Very truly, Love, Mildred or Mortimer or whoever it is. For New Testament writers the tradition of that day was that the writer said upfront "here's who I am." I, Paul or in this case, I, John. He identifies himself as their brother. He does not call himself the apostle. He could have. He had that authority; he was an apostle. He was the last living apostle at that point in time (about 95 A.D.), but he identifies with them as their brother. He

6

was well-known to the churches in Asia. He had served in Ephesus, and they would know exactly who he was. He said, "**I was on Patmos because of the word of God**" (1:9). Patmos was a place where people who were enemies of the state were exiled and sentenced to hard labor. Previously he had been the pastor at the church in Ephesus, and before his exile he was probably also something of a circuit riding pastor who traveled to these other churches in Asia Minor.

There is also a legend about John. (When I say legend I want to emphasize that word. We do not know whether this is true.) The legend tells us that Roman authorities attempted to boil John in oil, but that he was miraculously preserved, which baffled and frightened the superstitious officials. John was then exiled to Patmos because of his testimony of Jesus Christ. Sir William Ramsey, the noted historian, reports truth that exile was preceded by scourging, marked by perpetual fetters, scanty clothing, insufficient food, sleep on the bare ground in a dark prison, and work under the lash of military overseers.[9]

The emperor at this time was named Domitian, and (the legend continues) he was afraid of the kingdom of God and wanted to rid the world of any threats to his own power. So, he sought out any known descendants of King David. He questioned two grandsons of Jesus' half-brother Jude regarding the nature of Christ's kingdom and whether they were heirs to the throne. To Domitian's surprise these Jewish Christians, relatives of Jesus, explained that the kingdom they proclaimed was not earthly but heavenly and that it was to be established at the end of the world. Additionally, they had little monetary worth. After they showed the emperor their empty pockets, he released them from custody. The result was that John was soon released and returned from exile. He then directed the churches of Asia until his death in 98 A.D. This legend has John on Patmos for about a year and a half. Little did he know when he was sent there (we *know* that much is true: his exile on Patmos) that it was a part of God's greatest mission for him: the writing of the 66th and last book of the Bible.

John's Remarkable Experience

John tells us that he was in the spirit. That is, he was "spiritized" on the Lord's Day. I know that's not a word, but that's a good description of what happened. His body was on earth, but in the spirit he was able to move between earth and heaven and see both scenes on earth and scenes in heaven. He was able to move through time and see things that were yet to come in the future. Remember that this is a book of pictures. John constantly says, "I saw, I saw, I saw."

There are questions about the meaning of the Lord's Day. Some say it means he was taking time off. They allowed him to take time out from his labor there while he was in exile, and on what we know as the first day of the week he was having a time of communion and worship with his Lord. Others say this refers to the Lord's Day at the end of time: *I saw these events that were going to happen on the Day of the Lord.* Whatever it was, he was able to have a vision of the future that no one else had. And he was told he should write what he saw; that's very important. This wasn't a secret vision for John. This is a book that was to be *written*. It was to be sent to the seven churches, and it has been preserved as part of God's Word for us through today. That means God meant for *us* to read it, to study it, and understand it. It is not to be some mystery. *God meant for us to understand it.*

What was John to write and to whom was he to send it? The church recipients are named: Ephesus, Smyrna, Pergamum, Thyatira, Sardis, Philadelphia, and Laodicea. If you look at the list, you might notice that only one of them was the recipient of a letter from the Apostle Paul. Paul sent letters to the church in Galatia, the churches in Colossae and Philippi, and two letters to Thessalonica, two letters to Corinth, one letter to Rome, and one letter to Ephesus. Ephesus is the only church that received one of the seven Revelation letters as well as a letter from the Apostle Paul. So why this order of the churches? It's easy to understand if we look at a map.

You can see Ephesus almost right in the center of the map. Then if you travel northward and follow those stars around clockwise you will see that is the order in which the churches are listed after Ephesus: north to Smyrna up north to Pergamum and then down southeast to Thyatira, Sardis, Philadelphia, and finally Laodicea, forming a sort of circle. Patmos was of course close by; Ephesus was the closest church to Patmos. So it makes sense that it would be listed first. We will say more in Lesson 4 about the reason for choosing these churches and not Paul's epistle recipients.

God's Outline

One of the very wonderful things about the book of The Revelation is that God Himself provides the outline. If you look in commentaries (Romans, 1st Corinthians, 1st Peter, or Old Testament books like Exodus, Judges, etc.), you can find all different ways that scholars have outlined those books. But here the outline is given by God Himself, so we don't have to debate how the book is organized. John is told to write three things. First he is told to write the things he has seen. What things are those? The things described in Chapter 1, and John has done that for us. Next he is told to write those things which are. Those are the things John writes to the seven churches. In this lesson we will be looking at three of those churches and in the next lesson the other four. That's Chapters 2 and 3. Then Jesus said to write the things which will take place after these things, as stated in Chapter 4 to the end. How do we know that? Look at 4:1. **Come up here and I will show you what must take place *after these things*** (italics mine). So Chapter 4 is the beginning of the third section. Therefore, the outline is the things you have seen, the things which are, and the things which will take place after these things. If we keep that in mind, the God-given outline, it will be much easier for us to understand The Revelation as we study.

A Vision of Jesus

What are the things *that John has seen* besides what we saw in Lesson 1? What did John see? First, he didn't actually see, he *heard*. It was a voice that sounded like a trumpet. I have a pretty big mouth, but I don't have a voice like a trumpet. I play the trumpet, but I don't have a voice like a trumpet. This was a loud voice that commanded attention. The voice was behind John. How do we know it was behind him? He says, *I turned around when I heard the voice*, and he tells us what he saw: **"I saw seven golden lamp stands"** (1:12). Presumably they had lamps or lights on them; they weren't just empty stands *for* light. He says that Jesus is standing in their midst. How do we know it was Jesus? As this man talks with him, it becomes very clear. John sees a vision of Jesus the judge. Everything here speaks of the fact that

9

Jesus will stand as Judge of all the earth at the end of the age. His robe reaches to his feet; that is a sign of His greatness. His golden girdle is a sign of the righteousness of a King/Judge. His head and hair were like white wool, even white as snow. John says he's searching for just the right words to describe how His head and hair were such a bright, white color. This is a sign of the purity of judgment.

If you were to go back to the book of Daniel (7:9), you would find that Daniel had a similar vision. He said, **I kept looking until thrones were set up, and the Ancient of Days...** (I love that title for God; it is only used there). **...the Ancient of Days took his seat. His head was like white snow and the hair of His head like pure wool.** Daniel's vision was a picture of God Almighty. Here in The Revelation is a picture of the glorified Lord Jesus Christ. It is more evidence of the deity of Christ, that He Is God Incarnate. His eyes were like a flame of fire: nothing was hidden from Him. His feet were like glowing bronze, showing the power of His judgment. His voice was like waters: a voice that was going to be heard everywhere. A two-edged sword proceeded from His mouth. The basis upon which men and women will be judged is the Word of God. His face was glowing like the sun, showing the glory of the resurrected Son of God. He held seven stars in His right hand. I will say some more about those in a moment. John's response? **I fell at His feet as a dead man** (1:17).

John's Reaction

When he catches a glimpse of Jesus, he falls at His feet. This is the same apostle who lay on Jesus' breast at the Last Supper. He had known Jesus as God Incarnate in human form. He had seen the resurrected Jesus. He came back from fishing and there on the shore was the resurrected Jesus. But now he encounters the glorified Jesus, and his response is not, "Hey buddy, how are You doing?" His response is "I fell at His feet." Jesus reaches out with his hand and touches him and says, **"Do not be afraid...I was dead...I am alive"** (1:17-18). For how long? **"FOREVERMORE"** (my capitals). And He says, **"I have the keys of death and of Hades"** (1:18). That's why it's so important that we have a living, risen Savior. He has the keys of death and of Hades. Warren Wiersbe says:

> *We need not fear life, because He is The Living One. We need not fear death, because He died and is alive, having conquered death. And we need not fear eternity because He holds the keys of Hades and of death.*[10]

I love that, oh I love that.

Jesus' Explanations

Then Jesus explains some things. The seven lamp stands symbolically represent the seven churches that John named. The seven stars are the angels (literally messengers) of the seven churches. The word can mean heavenly messenger, called an angel. It can also mean a human messenger. The instruction to these messengers in several of these letters is to repent, which would be a sign that they should be interpreted in the context as human messengers or leaders (angels do not repent). These are letters to the human leaders, the pastors of these churches.

Overview of the Letters

Each of the letters follows the same outline. First it says, **"To the messenger of the church in…"** (2:1, 8, etc.) and the city is named. Then there is a particular description of Jesus. Each one of these is unique to that church and is taken from what we have read and seen in Chapter 1. He then says; **"I know…"** (2:2, 9, etc.) and He describes what He knows about that church. How does He know? Because He stands in the midst of the churches. He's in the midst of every church just as He promised: **"Where two or three are gathered there am I in the midst of them"** (Matthew 18:20). When He was resurrected and the apostles were gathered together behind locked doors, He came and stood in the midst of them. He is in the midst of the churches and He knows. Then there are commendations for each of the churches, except for two. One receives no commendation; one receives only an acknowledgement that there are a few people who are doing what is right. The other five have good things that are going on. Next there is condemnation, except for two of the churches, one of which we examine in this lesson—things that are not right in the churches. Then there's a correction: *Here's what you need to do to fix what's wrong.* Then there is the phrase, **"He who has an ear to hear…"** (2:7, 11, etc.). In other words, don't ignore this. Jesus says it would be fruitless for Me to give a diagnosis to your church and then you ignore it. He who has ears to hear, *listen*. Finally comes the phrase **"He who overcomes…"** (2:7, 11, etc.). Not that there would be some Christians who would overcome and some who would not. All believers are overcomers. In the fifth chapter of his first epistle John wrote how we are overcomers through Jesus Christ. What will be the blessing for the overcomer? Each church hears a different blessing. So, Jesus is demonstrating His authority to give blessing. Now those last two phrases ("He who has ears to hear" and "He who overcomes") are switched in churches four, five, six, and seven. The order I gave is for churches one, two, and three, but in four, five, six, and seven it's reversed. We will see that in our next lesson. As He demonstrates His authority, He is saying that He is the One who is allowed to judge what is happening in the Church. *I died*

11

for the Church. The Church is My bride. I am in the midst of all the churches. So He knows and sees everything about us. He is present in your church today. He sees our worship. He knows when the offering plate is passed who is being faithful in giving. When we serve each other and love each other and reach out and help each other, He sees and He observes that and He smiles. He sees and knows everything.

Ephesus

Now let's get to the physician exam for each church. The first church was in Ephesus. It was the most prominent city in Asia Minor. It was not the capital, but it had a large population of 200,000. The Temple of Diana or Artemis seated 24,000 people. Think of what kind of worship there was for this pagan goddess. The Temple of Diana was four times larger than the Parthenon in Athens. It was 425 feet long and 260 feet wide with 130 columns, 37 of which were studded with precious jewels. It was made completely of marble. It contained a lewd image of Diana, goddess of fertility. The temple was one of the seven wonders of the ancient world. It included the bank for all of Asia Minor as well as a magnificent art gallery. The sale of images of Diana was a great source of money for merchants in the city of Ephesus. About the worship Vernon McGee says:

> ***Around the temple of Diana were performed the grossest forms of immorality. She was worshipped by probably more people than was any other idol. The worshipers indulged in the basest religious rights of sensuality in the wildest orgies that were excessive and vicious.***[11]

Much of the trade from the East came through Ephesus. There was a large emperor cult, that is, worship of Caesar himself. To that city the Apostle Paul had gone boldly and had started a church. Later Paul had put Timothy in charge of the church in Ephesus; we know that from his two epistles to Timothy. It is likely that John was arrested there when he was sent to exile on Patmos. So how was the church doing? Well it was a deed-filled church—good deeds. Jesus says first that He knows their good deeds, and then He says He knows their hard work. What is the difference? *Good deeds* refers to normal work; hard work is toil to the point of exhaustion. So they were committed. They were a persevering church. Nothing stopped them from what they were doing. They were also doctrinally true, with no false apostle. There were people who were saying that a certain Apostle had commissioned them and given them his apostolic authority. They claimed a doctrine of apostolic succession, which has no basis in Scripture. The office of Apostle was limited to a small group of men especially commissioned by Jesus who were eyewitnesses of the resurrected Christ. The Apostle Paul said in I Corinthians 15 that he was almost born too late to be an apostle because there were no more apostles. These heretics claimed to be second generation apostles. There is no such thing as apostolic succession. That was a false doctrine, and the church in Ephesus challenged those who claimed it. They stated clearly that these were not true apostles. They endured whatever kind of criticism they got for Christ's sake, and they did not grow weary. Paul had written in Galatians 6:9, **Do not grow weary in well-doing.** They lived it.

What if I saw these things listed about a church, and that church asked if I wanted to come and be their pastor? You know, I'd be thinking this is a great church. Look at this list of good doctrine and good practice. But then we come to the next word: **but**. Read on in v. 4: **"I have this against you. You have left your first love."** In right teaching and in good works you're great, but you left your first love. David Jeremiah says:

> *Leaving one's first love means losing the excitement and devotion a new believer experiences when first born again. It's getting over the honeymoon and allowing Christianity to become a religion instead of a relationship.*[12]

They have left their first love. So, the prescription from the physician is this: fix it! How should they fix it? They should repent: Remember your first love and live the way you used to. Otherwise, I will remove your lamp stand. What did the lamp stand symbolize? That church itself. He's saying you've got to fix this or you're going to cease to exist as a church. That's how serious Jesus is about this problem of having left their first love: they will lose their lamp stand. There won't be a church anymore. Does He have authority to do that? He's in their midst. He died for the Church. Yes, He has that authority.

Then He nicely turns back to the positive. He says they hate the deeds of the Nicolaitans, and that's a good thing. Who are the Nicolaitans? We're not entirely sure. There are two explanations. One is that these were people who were followers of Nicholas and a cancerous teaching known as syncretism. Syncretism is simply combining elements of some other religion with a relationship with Christ. In this case pagan temple worship + the worship of the true God. It always leads to idolatry and always leads to immorality. He says you hate those people—followers of Nicholas. That's one possible interpretation. Another is that the word means lording it over the people. You see the word laity there in "Nicolaitans." Nico means lording over, so lording over the laity, an unnatural division between clergy and laity where the clergy were superior. You might have attended such a church at some point: *The reverend says this, the right proper, very Reverend is superior to the laity who are the peons.* Well, the reverend is a sinner, saved by grace just like everyone else. People ask me what they should call me. Keith, that's my name. God help us if we ever develop some kind of unnatural division between leadership and laity. So, the Nicolaitans were teaching one of those two things, and Jesus says the Church was doing great in resisting it.

Finally, He says that he who overcomes will eat from the Tree of Life. The Tree of Life was in the Garden of Eden, but The Garden of Eden was blocked after Adam and Eve sinned so they could not eat from the Tree of Life. We presume that the Garden of Eden was destroyed in the flood. But in The Revelation, the Tree of Life comes back. For the overcomer, for the true believer in Jesus Christ, there is the Tree of Life which gives eternal life.

What ultimately happened to the Church of Ephesus? The same thing that happened to the whole city. Today the city of Ephesus is a heap of ruins. Nothing is left.

Smyrna

Go 35 miles to the north and you come to Smyrna. Smyrna was a unique city. It was founded about 1,000 B.C. and it was destroyed in 600 B.C. Then it was rebuilt by one of Alexander the Great's generals whose name was Lysimachus. Over the course of 20 years it was rebuilt, and it was the most beautiful city the Greeks ever built. Because it was being rebuilt, they developed a master plan where the original city had stood, and the city came to be called *The Glory of Asia*. Its resurrection and beauty were a great source of civic pride. There were temples to Zeus, Diana, Aphrodite, Apollo, and others. They had a street that was called the street of the gods because there were so many temples. There was a huge amphitheater that seated 20,000 people. There was a music center with a stadium; it was the center of emperor worship. The city's cry was *Caesar is Lord*. That was obviously an issue for believers.

John says there were also problems from the Synagogue of Satan. What does he mean by that? There was a Jewish synagogue there, made up of people who had rejected their Messiah—The One who was long awaited for centuries, the One prophesied about going all the way back to the Garden of Eden and, more specifically, promised to Abraham, and then later through David, and then through the prophets and finally all the way to Malachi. Then during 400 silent years between Malachi and the New Testament the Jews waited. Here comes Jesus on the scene, the long-awaited Messiah. The Jewish Messiah. Jesus came and they rejected Him and they crucified Him and He is risen from the dead. And they still rejected Him, and they have become a Synagogue of Satan because they have missed their Messiah. Between the persecutors who insisted that the Christians say *Cae-

sar is lord and the persecution from those of the Synagogue of Satan, it was a really rough time and place for believers.

The chief industry there was myrrh, which sounds like Smyrna. The city got its name from myrrh. In the New Testament it is a sign of suffering, and that's what was happening to the Christians there. This is the shortest of the seven letters, and John says, **"I know your tribulation"** (2:9)—pressure that comes from the emperor worship cult. The word describes lying on your back and having a large stone put on your chest so that it gets harder and harder to breathe. The weight of that stone gets heavier and heavier and heavier until you finally die because you can't take a breath anymore. That's what the word is describing. That was the kind of pressure they got from the emperor cult. And they were poor. He says that He knows their poverty, but they are rich spiritually. Their poverty wasn't just *not wealthy*. It wasn't not-super-rich-like-Bill Gates poverty. This was a word that means destitute, starving, wondering where every next meal will come from. Along with the pressure from the emperor worship cult and the slander that came from the Synagogue of Satan, these people were excluded from commerce, making any kind of vocation extremely difficult. Jesus says to them two things: **"Don't fear"** and **"Be faithful unto death"** (2:10)—death if it comes through martyrdom or death if it comes through the end of your natural life—*be faithful.*

He warns them there is even more intense persecution ahead. It will last for ten days. That's probably a symbol saying it will be a short time and not ten literal days. It will be super intense, but by being faithful unto death they will receive the crown of life. One person who was faithful unto death was a man named Polycarp. Some fifty years later, Polycarp, in his eighties, had served the Lord there in Smyrna for a very long time. He is recorded as saying on the day of his death:

> *Eighty and six years have I served Him, [Jesus], and He has done me no wrong. How then can I blaspheme my King and Savior? You threaten me with a fire that burns for a season, and after a little while is quenched; but you are ignorant of the fire of everlasting punishment that is prepared for the wicked.*[13]

Polycarp was burned at the stake for refusing to burn incense to the Roman emperor. On his farewell he said: "I bless You, Father, for judging me worthy of this hour, so that in the company of the martyrs I may share the cup of Christ."[14] He was faithful unto death, and I guarantee you he received the Crown of Life.

The people there in Smyrna were key participants in the annual athletic games. They would have understood the meaning of crown. This is far better than a crown for winning a race; it is the Crown of Life for endurance in the face of persecution. Then the text says *I have this against you...* Wait, no it doesn't say that; no condemnation is given to this church! They are only commended for their faithfulness and encouraged to continue to be faithful. Again, Jesus identifies Himself. Did you notice the beginning of this letter? Jesus described Himself as **the first and the last who was dead and has come to life** (2:8). Why does He use that description? Remember that this was a city that was dead and had come to life. This is specific to this church. And He says, **"He who overcomes will not be hurt by the second death"** (2:11). The second death refers to a dead soul who has died without Jesus Christ and is raised to judgment at the last day. He/she appears before the great white throne and dies a second time, cast forever away from the Lord, judged unforgiven because that person rejected the only way to eternal life. The judgment of Christ is what the second death refers to. It's something Christians need not fear.

It has been rightly said that a man who is born once (physical birth) dies twice, (once physically and at the end of time dies spiritually). But a man who is born twice (physically and then born again spiritually) only dies once. When physical death comes, he doesn't have to fear the second (spiritual) death.

Today the city is called Izmir. It's in Turkey. It's still functioning as a city.

Pergamum

That takes us to Pergamum another 70 miles north. It was the capital of the Roman government in Asia, and it served in that role for almost 400 years. Its library was second only to that of Alexandria, Egypt. If you saw the movie *National Treasure*, you know that some of those scrolls from that library in Alexandria were beneath Trinity Church in New York. But not in real life! However, the movie rightly emphasized the vastness and value of Alexandria's library. Pergamum was second. There were 200,000 scrolls kept in Pergamum. In fact, the name Pergamum came from the word for parchment, which is what the scrolls were made of. It was the medical center of Asia. Some of the medical practices were very questionable, but people came from all around to try to be healed. It had a temple to Caesar Augustus. There were large temples to Athena and to other gods, and there was a 90-foot square 40-foot high altar to Zeus. There was a large gymnasium and a grand theater. The city of Pergamum still stands today.

What about the letter? Jesus says that He knows they live where Satan's throne is. He was probably referring to that altar to Zeus. He says you didn't deny me even when Antipas, my faithful witness, was martyred. He uses the same word to describe Antipas as he used to describe Himself in

Chapter 1: *my faithful witness*. There's a legend that Antipas was slowly roasted to death for his testimony of Jesus Christ. Jesus says that Satan was dwelling in their city. I believe that for periods of time Satan took up residence in specific places so that he could personally oversee the trouble. That's what John is telling us: he knows that Satan lives there. I believe Satan took up residence in Germany in the 1930's and at other places throughout history. He is not omnipresent, and in John's day he took up residence there in Pergamum. Jesus says, **"I have a few things against you"** (2:14), including the teaching of Balaam. In the Old Testament Balaam got the people of Israel to worship idols along with worshiping their Lord God, Jehovah/Yahweh. Mixing in idol worship in Pergamum was similar to what happened in Balaam's day. They were also pursuing the Nicolaitans' teachings, unlike Ephesus where the people refuted it. So, what was happening? The Church was getting married to the world. They were compromising their testimony and their lifestyle. Jesus says to fix it and repent. I'll come to you with the sword of My mouth, which is the Word of God. The Word of God will judge all the ways you are contradicting the will of God. To the overcomers there will be hidden manna—that would be heavenly food not available to unbelievers.

Jesus also says He will give a white stone with a name known only to the recipient. There are many symbols in the Book of Revelation, and most of them are explained. Many others, as we noted in the Introduction, can be interpreted from the Old Testament. I would love to be able to say what the white stone is, but I can't find it. I don't know. One commentator said there are more than ten different explanations for the white stone. That doesn't narrow it down very much, does it? We don't know what this is. Here are some of what I believe to be the best explanations.

1. A white stone was used by a judge and jury to indicate an acquittal. A vote for guilty was a black stone.

2. A white stone was used to gain admission to a feast.

3. Those first two do not explain what was written on the stone however, so consider this: the people of Asia Minor had a custom of giving to intimate friends a cube or rectangular block of stone or ivory with words or symbols engraved on it. It was a secret, private possession of the one who received it. I like this explanation the best.

Conclusion

As we compare and contrast the three letters, we see there were good things in each church. Two of the churches had issues that they needed to deal with. Ephesus was the lost love church; Smyrna was the persecuted church; Pergamum the compromising church. The church that was suffering the most was the one that received no word of condemnation. But all needed to hear what the Holy Spirit was saying to the churches. These are specific messages for each church, but they were also for all the churches.

Vernon McGee sums it all up:

We need to break the shell of self-sufficiency, the crust of conceit, the shield of sophistication, the veneer of vanity, get rid of the false face of porosity, and stop this business of everlastingly polishing our halo is if we were some great saint.[15]

That's his word of encouragement and need for repentance for churches today. What does it all mean to us?

ATM (Apply to Me)

1. Have I fallen at the feet of the glorified Jesus Christ recently (or ever)? Does your church do that in worship? Do you do that symbolically in worship? A great hymn says, "Praise, my soul, the King of heaven, to His feet thy tribute bring; ransomed, healed, restored, forgiven, evermore His praises sing."[16] We also need to be careful about the music that we select, that it honors and accurately portrays the glorified Jesus Christ.

2. Here's a personal question for each one to answer. I can't answer this for you. You have to answer this individually. Is there any way that I have left my first love? Have I gotten complacent in my faith? I need to remember when I first met Jesus.

3. That sword of the spirit is now the complete Scripture, the complete canon of 66 books of the Bible, by which we must judge every endeavor of our lives and of our churches.

4. Finally, Jesus is present in your church every week. He is watching how we worship, how we teach, how we serve, how we give, how we love and live. Jesus is in our midst, and He will one day give us His personal verdict. I think of that church in Ephesus. Can you imagine going to the doctor and the doctor says, "You've been to your ENT doctor, and I see your ears are good. I see you've been to your eye doctor, and I see your eyes are good. I see your kidneys are good, liver is good, your blood pressure is really good, and your breathing is good. That's all the good news. But I'm sorry I have to tell you that you have some heart disease that's getting rapidly worse, and if you don't get a heart transplant in the next six months you are going to be dead." That's a good diagnosis until the "but." If we have left our

18

first love in any way, spiritual life has become drudgery. If it's become a burden to serve, a burden to give, a burden to worship, we need a heart transplant. So, friends, keep on keeping on in the name of Jesus, and don't leave your first love!

Lesson 3

Read 2:18 – 3:22

Four More Churches

We looked at Jesus' letters to the first three churches in our last lesson, and here we're looking at the other four churches.

One of the things we noted in our last lesson is that this is a book for which God Himself provided the outline in 1:19. Jesus told John to write the things that *are*. That's Chapters 2 and 3. They were happening in the seven churches in Asia. We noted that John was in exile on the isle of Patmos. He was sent there on account of being a believer and teaching and preaching the Word of God and teaching that Jesus Christ is the Savior of the world. At Jesus' instruction he sent letters to the seven churches of Asia Minor. The four churches we are looking at in this lesson are Thyatira, Sardis, Philadelphia, and Laodicea.

We noted previously that each letter follows the same outline. It says **To the angel... [messenger]** (2:1, 8, etc.). The word can mean heavenly messenger, which would be an angel. But it can also mean an earthly messenger, which seems to be the best way to understand it in this context. The messenger would be the pastor or the leader of each of these churches. Then it gives a particular description of Jesus. Almost all of those come from the vision of Chapter 1, and each one is particular to that church. Next He says that He knows certain things about each church. He gives commendation to them (except for two of the churches), and He has words of condemnation (except for two other churches). Then there is a word of correction: here is what you need to do to fix what is wrong. Next He says, **"He who has ears to hear, let him hear what the Spirit says to the churches"** (2:7, 11, etc.), and He says, **"He who overcomes...."** (2:7, 11). Now that particular order was for the first three churches. In these last four churches, the last two items are reversed. I cannot find any theological reason for that or any reason to start a new denomination over why that is, but in churches four through seven *overcoming* is first, and then each letter concludes with **"He who has ears to hear let him hear what the spirit says to the churches"** (2:29, 3:6, etc.).

We know that Jesus has the authority to do all of this because in Chapter 1 we saw Him standing in the midst of the churches. He is the one who has the right to judge the churches. We noted in the last lesson that Ephesus was a church that had lost its first love; Smyrna was a church of poor, persecuted people just barely able to get by, but they were rich in what mattered. It's one of two churches that received no word of condemnation. And we saw that Pergamum was a compromised church where they had taken truth and mixed it with error.

Thyatira

That takes us to Thyatira, the first of the four churches we will look at in this lesson. This city and the three remaining cities are inland. The first three were coastal cities, but now we have moved inland. Thyatira was not a grand city like some of the others. It did not have a great place of prominence. It was located, however, on a major Asian trade route, and because of that there was great wealth and tourism and trade that went through the city of Thyatira. It was founded as a shrine to Tyrimnus who was the *sun god*. It was known for its commerce and its many trade guilds. There were guilds for every type of trade imaginable. They were sort of the forerunners of our unions today, and that would seem to be harmless. But membership in a trade guild came with pagan religious obligations. So, refusing to be part of a guild because it was contrary to God's Word (forbidding idol worship) might mean difficulties in making a living, and that was problematic for people in the Church. Thyatira was essentially a blue-collar city. It was also the center of the dyeing industry—not dying as in becoming dead—but dyeing as in dyeing of material. You might remember from the book of Acts that Lydia, Paul's first convert in Philippi, was from Thyatira. She sold purple fabric; she was part of that industry. Today there are only a few ruins that remain of Thyatira.

The letter itself is the longest of the seven letters. Jesus starts out by calling Himself the Son of God. Why? Because He is contrasting Himself with the sun god, which was the focal point of worship for founding the city. This is the only church where He uses the title Son of God.

Good things were happening there. He says, **"I know your deeds and your love and faith, and service and perseverance"** (2:19), and **"Your deeds of late are greater than at first"** (2:19). Their lifestyles were continually becoming godlier. This is a strong word of commendation for this church in Thyatira. Sounds really good to be part of that church, right? Love, faith, service, perseverance, and more and more as the days went by.

"But I have this against you," He says. **"You tolerate the woman Jezebel, who calls herself a prophetess."** (2:20). Although He calls her Jezebel, it is likely that that was not her real name, but that's the kind of person she was. Do you know anybody named Jezebel? Do you know why you don't know anyone named Jezebel? Jezebel in the Old Testament was the wife of Ahab, the most wicked king Israel ever had. Along with her husband she led the nation into the worst immorality and idolatry ever. She was just a horrible, horrible person. That is the kind of person this false prophet was there in Thyatira, so she is given the same (symbolic) name. She was leading believers into immorality. She was leading them to eat things offered to idols. The implication is that they were not just eating the food, but they were also offering sacrifices to idols. It is likely that Jezebel was encouraging Christians to go along with the idolatrous and immoral practices of the trade guilds. These people were proud of what they were doing, and they called them the deep things of Satan. This was happening in the church! You see why Jesus says, **"I have this against you"** (2:20).

Notice also that this church is the opposite of Ephesus. There they had good doctrine—they would not tolerate the teaching of the Nicolaitans— but they had left their first love. This church has good love, and it's getting better and better, but they have bad doctrine. They're tolerating the false teaching of Jezebel. In the Church we need always to have both right doctrine and strong love for others. We must have both. Charles Swindoll warns, "It's always alluring to justify immorality in the name of grace, and then grace becomes a license for sin."16

Paul had written to the Ephesians (4:15) that they should speak the truth in love; the two need to go together. Paul had written about it to Timothy (I Timothy 1:5). (I heard of this often in the church I grew up in, but they only quoted the first few words [in the KJV]: **The aim of our charge is love** [NASB says **The goal of our instruction is love**], and they stopped right there.) Look at the whole verse. **The goal of our instruction is love from a pure heart and a *good conscience* and a *sincere faith*** (italics mine). Love and doctrine must always be present together. Ephesus had one, Thyatira had the other, but neither church had both.

Now of Jezebel herself Jesus said she's had time to repent (3:21), but she likes her life the way it is. Have you known people like that? Because she liked her life the way it was, Jesus says her future was bleak. She was going to be cast on a sick bed, whoever she was. Those who followed her were to suffer the same fate. They would all die from pestilence. But always, always the hand of grace is extended, always to the end of a person's life. The hand of grace of Jesus Christ was extended there. He says it's not too late for them and for her to repent. She just won't do it.

Jesus has also identified Himself as not just the Son of God, but also as one **who has eyes like a flame of fire, and His feet are like burnished bronze** (2:19). Those are symbols of One who sees all and One who has the authority to judge (specifically Jezebel and her followers). Jesus also says, **"...to you, the rest who are in Tyatira, ...who have not known the deep things of Satan..."** (2:24) [you've not gotten mixed up with this tolerance of sin...]. We don't know what percentage had not compromised, but He told them He had no word of correction for them; they were to just keep on doing what they were doing. They were to keep on holding fast until Jesus' return. Overcomers would receive authority over the nations. That's in the millennial Kingdom.

They would also receive the morning star. At the very end of The Revelation Jesus calls Himself the Morning Star (22:16). The reference here in Chapter 3 is to participation with Him in the new forever Kingdom. Since He had said that He was the one with eyes like a flame of fire, He knew who the faithful were. He knew to whom He was talking.

Are there Jezebels today? I think of famous people, singers, actors, and athletes who say, "Yes, I am a Christian." Then when you look at their lifestyles, have you ever scratched your head and wondered what the Judge, the one with the eyes like flame of fire, is thinking? What does that do to the witness of the Church—those who talk the talk but don't walk the walk? It damages our message; it damages our witness, and possibly also forces other people to compromise. Charles Swindoll says this about those in the Church who are Jezebels today, who want us to compromise with culture:

A culture that tolerates evil calls disagreement "phobia." Taking a stand is considered hate. Conviction is seen as bigoted fanaticism. Centuries-old Christian doctrine is regarded as discrimination.[17]

There are Jezebels everywhere and there is danger. Thyatira was the church that was tolerant of sin, and Jesus uses very harsh words in warning them of judgment to come.

Sardis

That takes us to Sardis; it was inland about 50 miles east of Ephesus. It was 1500 feet above the valley floor. It had sheer cliffs on three sides that could not be scaled. There was a narrow isthmus on the fourth side. It was a very secure city, and it was the first city to mint gold and silver coins. Woolen garments and carpets were made there. It was impregnable, or so the people who lived there thought. But twice it was conquered by surprise attack, long before Jesus wrote this letter. Cyrus the king of Persia offered a reward to any of his soldiers who could figure out a way into the Fortress of Sardis. By chance, a Persian soldier noticed a Sardinian soldier drop his helmet accidentally over the city wall. When the Sardinian appeared briefly at the bottom of the wall to retrieve his helmet, the Persian soldier knew there had to be a passageway into the city. Under the cover of darkness, a Persian raiding party found the opening, made their way into the city and opened the gates from the inside. The Sardinians were asleep when the Persians came like a thief and conquered the city. A century later, the city was conquered in exactly the same way.

Before Jesus had occasion to tell John what to write, the city had previously been ruled by the Persians, by Alexander, by Antiochus the Great, and then by the Romans. In 17 A.D. the city was devastated by an earthquake. Though it was somewhat rebuilt after that, the city's reputation was based on its former life. But it was mostly dead. It is fascinating to look at that history of Sardis and now hear what Jesus says to this church. He starts with no word of commendation. He says, **"I know your deeds, that you have a name that you are alive, but you are dead"** (3:1). It was just like the city. Their deeds were not complete. What did they have to do? They had to wake up and strengthen what remained, what was about to die. He says, **"Repent...I will come like a thief"** (3:3), just like the invaders had come against the city in the past.

However, Jesus did note that there was a faithful remnant. He had introduced Himself as the one who has the seven Spirits of God (that is the Holy Spirit and His seven-fold ministry) and the seven stars. The seven stars are the pastors or the messengers of the churches. He says, **"You have a few people in Sardis who have not soiled their garments"** (3:4). He knew who those people were. I think the implication here is that the leader (the pastor) there was probably one who was not dead but was still alive in the faith. John says the unsoiled would walk with Him in white because they were worthy.

Then he says these overcomers will not have their names erased from the book of life. Far too much has been made of that verse when it comes to salvation about the possibility of a name being erased from the book of life. We need to understand something about ancient cities in that area. They kept registers of all their citizens. If a citizen was convicted of a crime, he was punished, and his name was erased from the book of the city registry. Jesus is simply saying that overcomers, those who have faith in Jesus, can't have their names erased from the book of life. It is different from the city registry, when you can have your name erased. It would be foolish to try to build a whole theological system about the idea of security of salvation on this one verse. He's just saying, *It's different with Me. It's different from the way cities do this*. He said that He would confess the faithful remnant before the Father and His angels. What a wonderful thing to know that Jesus will confess the faithful before the Father.

What causes a church to die like this? Dr. Vance Havner says:

A church often is a man, movement, machine and monument. It starts with a man with a vision. Next is a movement of people. After that it just becomes a well-oiled machine and everybody just thinks about keeping the machine going. And then it finally becomes a monument to the past.[18]

24

Dead churches worship their past. Dead churches have carnal and/or lazy leadership. Dead churches neglect children and youth—the next generation. Dead churches lack missionary zeal, and dead churches neglect their mission and their message. Charles Swindoll has written with tongue in cheek a description of what a dead church might be like:

> *Maybe it means that the sanctuary is a morgue with a steeple. It's a congregation of corpses with undertakers for ushers, embalmers for elders and morticians for ministers. Their pastor graduated from a theological cemetery. The choir director is the local coroner. They sing Embalmed in Gilead and Amazing Grave, How Sweet the Ground. You might describe their worship as stiff. At the rapture they'll be the first church taken up because the Bible says, "The dead in Christ shall rise first." They drive to church in one long line with their headlights on. Whenever someone joins their membership the church office immediately notifies the next to kin. Each week they put an ad in the obituaries. The church van is a black hearse, and the church sign is a tombstone. Their motto is "Many are cold, and few are frozen."[19]*

We can laugh at all of that, but if you've ever been part of a church that felt lifeless, it's not a funny thing. David Jeremiah says he has been questioned about why church membership is such a serious thing for him, and he says:

> *I occasionally have people question the need for membership of the local church, suggesting that we let anyone who wants to 'join' just do so by their attendance and involvement. But church membership, and the examination process which accompanies it, is an attempt to keep a good church from going bad over time. It is a way to keep the focus on the truth and on spiritual life so that false teaching or sin doesn't creep in unawares…. A church full of people who are full of the Holy Spirit will be a church that is full of the Holy Spirit.[20]*

I would add this: to have church members who do not know the Lord and therefore do not have the Holy Spirit will gradually suck the life out of any church. Sardis thought they were alive, but they were dead.

Philadelphia

That takes us to Philadelphia, literally meaning—you might have heard it so-called—City of Brotherly Love, or the city of one who loves his brother. Where does that come from? The city was founded in 140 B.C. by a man by the name of Attalus II. Attalus II had great love for his dying brother Eumenes. Eumenes was king of Pergamum until he died. In fact, when Eumenes died, Attalus II himself became king of Pergamum. So, when he founded a new city in the last years before his brother died, he named the city after him, literally *who loves his brother*. It was the key or the gateway to the central part of Asia Minor, and it was actually called the gateway to the east. The same earthquake that destroyed Sardis in 17 A.D. destroyed Philadelphia. Conquerors also destroyed it over time, but it was always rebuilt. Philadelphia still stands today under a different name as a prosperous Turkish town of about 36,000 people.

In the letter to the church Jesus says He has the key of David. What in the world is the key of David? In the Old Testament under the reign of good King Hezekiah, a man named Eliakim served us the royal treasurer; he alone had the authority and responsibility of guarding the royal treasury. He alone possessed the key to those riches, and it was called the Key of David. Here it is symbolic of the riches of the kingdom that are given to those who know Christ, the One who is descended from David. He says, **"I have put before you an open door which no one can shut"** (3:8). It was a door of opportunity for evangelism in a place that was the *key* or gateway to central Asia. They were to use that key to spread the gospel. He says, **"You have a little power"** (3:8). Don't overemphasize the *little*. Yes, it was little, but it was *power*. The Greek word is *dunamis*; we get our word for dynamite from that. You have power. It might not be much but it's real and it's genuine. A little bit of it will be enough. *You kept My word, you've not denied My name, but I have this against you...*

If you're following along in your Bible, you're looking for that. And again, you won't find it, will you? He doesn't say it. Like Smyrna we looked at in the previous lesson, this is the second church where he does not say, "I have this against you." He does not say anything against the church in Philadelphia. He gives them nothing but encouragement and praise. He says the synagogue of Satan will bow down to you—those who call themselves Jews but they have rejected their Messiah. One day they're going to recognize that Jesus, the One who was killed by the Jewish leaders, is the Messiah. He says, **"I will keep you from the hour of testing"** (3:10), which seems to be a reference to tribulation that is someday going to come on the whole world. We'll talk more in a future lesson about how God might do that. He says, **"Hold fast what you have"** (3:11). Hold on. You have a little power; keep holding on. It will grow into more and more power. Keep holding on.

For the overcomers He says, **"I will make him a pillar in the temple of My God"** (3:12). Ancient cities often honored great leaders by erecting pillars with their names inscribed on them. That's what Jesus is saying to the heroes of Philadelphia: *I will erect pillars with the name of the heroes, spiritual pillars with the names of faithful people. I will write upon the pillars who is the hero—*

the faithful, the overcomer—the name of my God and the name of the city of my God, the New Jerusalem. The name is going to be some new name that we don't know; only Jesus Christ knows.

Philadelphia was the church with opportunity. Do you have opportunity today? "No I can't, I can't. I don't have opportunity, I'm too busy, too tired, I'm too sick, I don't have opportunity, it's just not there." Charles Swindoll has some advice for you:

> *Are you in a place where sharing your faith is beset with difficulties or living your faith has unique challenges? By place I don't necessarily mean your physical location, though that can play a significant role. Sometimes our place in life can feel limiting. You might work at a job where your boss puts the kibosh on anything religious. You may attend to school where every perspective is tolerated except the Christian one. You may be a stay-at-home mom with a talkative toddler running around your feet all day. You may feel limited by physical disabilities, financial constraints, or a tyrannical schedule. Whatever the circumstances that appear to limit your opportunities are and close the door in your prospects for fruitful ministry, Christ's words to the church in Philadelphia have something to say to you today. I have put before you an open door which no one can shut.*[21]

That was the opportunity for the church in Philadelphia.

Laodicea

Finally, the church in Laodicea. It was one of three cities that were relatively close together; the other two were Colossae, ten miles to the east, and Hierapolis, six miles to the north. Laodicea was a wealthy city. It was noted for its glossy black wool cloth and for Tephra Phrygia. Tephra Phrygia was a pill that was crushed and used for eye salve all over the Roman Empire. The city was a center of banking and medicine. The worship of Zeus was popular. Its name meant *justice of the people* or *right of the people*—the right to do whatever they wanted in that city. Not true justice, but the right to do anything. Today only ruins remain of Laodicea.

Jesus says, **"I know your deeds"** (3:15), and it is not good deeds. He only says, **"I know your deeds."** Because there are no good deeds. You're not hot, you're not cold, you're lukewarm. We need to understand something about Laodicea and those other two cities. In nearby Hierapolis, which was six miles to the north, there were hot springs. Ten miles to the east in Colossae there were wonderful cold springs. Aqueducts were built to transport the water from both places to Laodicea, but by the time it reached Laodicea, the hot water had cooled, and the cold water had warmed, so that

27

all they ever got was lukewarm water. On the day I preached on this passage I put a cup of water inside the pulpit an hour before the service. I also had someone bring me a bottle of water from the refrigerator right when I got to Laodicea in my sermon. Now which one of these two do you think was better? You probably know that public speaking can make your throat dry and make you thirsty. Cold water is what I drank. I didn't want that lukewarm water; I would have spit that out of my mouth. That's what Jesus is saying: *I wish that you were cold or hot, not lukewarm.*

The church said, *I am rich, and have become wealthy. I have need of nothing.* Do you know churches like that today? God help us that your church never becomes like that. He says you're not truly wealthy. You're wretched and miserable and poor and blind and naked. Notice that this is the opposite of the church in Smyrna. They seemed to have nothing. They were poor, but spiritually they were rich. This church thought it was rich, but spiritually they were poor. He says you need gold refined by fire (probably the fire of persecution). You need spiritual white garments (not like the physical black wool clothes that were made there). You need spiritual eye salve (not like what was sold all around the empire for physical eye needs). In the midst of all of this He says to them, *I love you, I love you, I haven't given up on you, but you need to be zealous and repent.*

And He says, **"I stand at the door and knock"** (3:20). Now, we know that this verse is used many times in evangelism: Jesus knocking on the door of an individual's heart seeking entry. Some of you might be familiar with the painting of Jesus knocking on a door. There's no latch on the outside. It has to be opened from the inside, and that is certainly true about each individual's need to receive Christ. But in context here this refers to Christ who has been locked out of His own **Church**! How sad it is that the Church in some places has become nothing more than a social institution to meet needs, sort of like Goodwill. Christ has been locked out. He says, *Let me in, let me in.*

Overcomers will sit down with Jesus on His throne. At the beginning Jesus had described Himself to this church as the Amen (that is, the final truth) and the beginning of creation. Why is that relevant? There are many churches today that are proud to say, *Oh, God created the world through evolution; that's how He did it.* They don't want to believe in the power of God. They don't want to be viewed as: *If you believe God created the world by speaking it into existence, you must be a fanatic,* so they compromise. Jesus identifies Himself to misguided churches like that as the beginning of creation. *I'm the One who made all things.*

How does a church get to that point? The word of God is denied. The miraculous is denied, morality is compromised, and traditions, culture, or convenience/experience supersede biblical authority. Entertainment supersedes worship. Deeds of charity, as good as they are, replace salvation from sin as the primary mission of the church. It is what Paul warned Timothy about—people with itching ears who want preaching to just tickle their ears. They don't want solid Bible preaching, so the Word of God is neglected or ignored, and the church becomes what Vernon McGee says is a nice church. That's where there is a nice group of people, with a nice pastor, and every week the nice people get together and they have a nice little service and the nice pastor gets up and tells the nice people to be even nicer.[22]

We have the message of salvation for the world, and Oh that we would not lock Christ out of our churches. So, Laodicea is the lukewarm church.

Summary

To sum up the four letters: one church had no words of condemnation (that was Philadelphia); one church had no commendation (Laodicea); one church had very little that was good (just a faithful remnant: Sardis); and the other church (Thyatira) was mixed. It had good love and good deeds, but it had doctrinal issues because of Jezebel. The richest church financially was the poorest spiritually. That was Laodicea. At the end of each letter Jesus said that everyone with an ear needed/needs to hear what the Spirit says to the churches. These letters were written not just for their instruction, but for ours also.

ATM (Apply to Me)

This application section is different from other lessons because I have some questions for you which only you can answer. What would Jesus say to your church? Is it faithful in worship, mission, prayer, and service? Does it have missionary zeal? Are people faithful in giving? Is the Word of God preached faithfully as the whole truth of God? Is it compromised by false teaching? Has it lost its first love? What diagnosis would Doctor Jesus give *your* church?

I believe He'd advise all of us in any church to not lose our first love; not to be lukewarm; not to tolerate false teaching; not to become dead while looking alive; and not to lose the joy of serving. He who has an ear let him hear what the Spirit says to the churches.

Lesson 4

Reread 2:1 – 3:22

Church History 701 (as Revealed to John)

Our lessons in the book of The Revelation have brought us to a short pause. Before we continue to Chapter 4, there is further study that we need to do in Chapters 2 and 3. I know we studied all seven churches. But there is something else we want to look at in regard to those two chapters. You will recall that at the end of the message (letter) to each church Jesus said, **"He who has an ear let him hear what the Spirit says to the churches"** (2:7, 11, etc.). So, we want to ask some questions. What is it that Jesus meant when He said the churches? Is it just those seven churches? Is it churches today? Is it churches throughout the ages?

You will recall that in 1:19 God provided an outline for the entire book of The Revelation. He told John to write the things which he had seen. That was the vision of the risen Lord Christ, the glorified Lord Christ in heaven. Then He told John to write the things which are. That's the letters to the churches of Chapters 2 and 3. Third He told John to write the things which shall take place after these things. That's Chapter 4 to the end, and in our next lesson we will begin to study those things that are yet in the future.

I believe John was told to write each of these letters to a real first century church with specific commendations and/or condemnations. As we studied them, we have also been able to make practical applications for us today, because the things that the Spirit says to the churches apply to us as well. However, there is a strong possibility that there is also a prophetic application that the seven churches are not just the literal churches of Asia at the end of the first century, but they also represent the Church throughout the ages. Yes, Jesus wrote to seven specific churches, but He was also writing to seven Church ages, i.e., seven periods in history. This is the view that was held by Harry Ironside 100 years ago.[23] It is a view that was held by Vernon McGee 50 years ago.[24] It is a view that is also held by David Jeremiah today.[25] Three brilliant scholars: they all agree that this is what the Spirit was saying to the Church *ages*. Does everyone believe that, you might ask? I must honestly say no. This is not a viewpoint that is held universally by Bible scholars. Some consider it a possibility. There is a smaller number who reject it outright. But I stand with the three men I mentioned in believing it is very probable that this is exactly what Jesus was doing. He was writing to seven literal churches at the end of the first century, and He was also prophesying what would happen in the Church for the next two thousand years and more.

Now one objection to this particular point of view is that since these were literal churches in that day, that's the only way we should take the message. We should leave it at that. Ephesus, Smyrna, Pergamum, Thyatira, Sardis, Philadelphia, and Laodicea. However, if you know Old Testament prophecy, you know that often in the Old Testament when something was spoken or written, there was both an immediate or soon to happen fulfillment of a prophecy, and then there was a double—a second—fulfillment, something that refers to a later time or to the end time that is yet future for us. An example would be the prophecy in Daniel (11:21-45) about a horrible, horrible tyrant who would arise and be totally cruel to Israel. In history that man is known as Antiochus Epiphanes. But the prophecy also refers to a future tyrant who is far worse. That is Antichrist.

Another objection to this point of view is that the same good and bad that we find in those churches can be found in many churches during the last two thousand years. That is also true. In response to that objection I would say that the overall descriptions are too generally accurate in evaluating the Church through the ages to ignore the church-age interpretation. I would also point out once again the outline of the book—the things which you have seen, the things which are, the things which will take place after these things. After these things is the tribulation at the end of time, which would argue for the things which are in Chapters 2 and 3 not just presenting a point-in-time local snapshot but also a complete prophetic history of the Church until the tribulation. Furthermore, I must return to a question we asked in Lesson 2: why these seven churches? Because they were close to John and he couldn't get these letters to anywhere else? Oh, please. Paul sent letters all over the Roman Empire. And if you were picking seven churches just to see how they're doing, why not pick the seven churches to which Paul wrote: churches in Corinth, Rome, Thessalonica, Galatia, Ephesus, Colossae, and Philippi? Why these seven churches? Because they represent seven church ages.

This is where it gets really fascinating. I have titled this lesson Church History 701. It's graduate level study, so it's 701, not 101. I chose seven, of course, because of the seven churches as revealed to John. So we will examine the seven churches again and what was said about them in John's day, and we will see what period of history each represents.

Ephesus

First was the church at Ephesus. Recall that this is the church that had left its first love. It seems to represent the church from 33 to 100 A.D. or somewhere around that time, a period from the resurrection and ascension of our Lord until the end of the first century. They had, like the church at Ephesus, good deeds and toil and perseverance and endurance and exposing false apostles, all of which were very important in the first century. They dealt with evil men, but there was a problem. The church at Ephesus had left their first love. So, it also happened in the first century as time passed. As the first generation died out and was promoted to heaven, new leaders took their place. The burning passion to take the gospel message to the whole world was fading. The apostle Paul had been martyred, and what began as a movement was becoming rote and automatic. I noted in our last lesson what Vance Havner said about a dying church or a dead church. It goes through four phases.[26] First there was a man with a vision, followed by a movement when people got excited and got on board. Then everything became so homogenized, sterilized, and processed that the church just became a machine. Then eventually it became spiritually dead and just became a building as a monument. The church was becoming *machine*. Of the original apostles only John remained. By the end of the first century missionary zeal was waning. It had been there with Peter, James, John, Andrew, Philip, and all of the apostles, and then Paul who was added to their number. But that flame was burning out. They had left their first love. Ephesus represents the Church at the end of the first century.

Smyrna

The second church was a persecuted church in Smyrna. It was a church that was suffering greatly, and Jesus had no criticism for this church. The church was rich in what mattered even though they were not rich materially. It represents the Church from 100 to 313 A.D. Again, nothing negative was said to the original church at Smyrna. They and their members were not just poor—they were dirt poor. Because of persecution (probably many of them could not even participate in commerce), many of the members of that church wondered where their next meal was coming from. Jesus said ten days of persecution are about to come upon you. Ten days probably represents a short period of extreme persecution. But scholars have also noted that those ten days could possibly apply to ten periods of persecution of the Church by Rome up to the year 313 AD. Emperors would not be persecutors of the Church through their entire reign. Persecution would go through waves when an emperor would decide, *They have a King Jesus, but I'm the king and I have to do something about it.* A great persecution would arise, but then it would subside. Then the same thing would happen with another emperor. So through ten emperors (ten days) ten waves of persecution came upon the Church. The first had already happened. That was by Nero, which was when Paul was murdered. Second was Domitian; he was the one who had John exiled to the Isle of Patmos. The third was Trajan at the beginning of the second century. Then in the middle of that century was Marcus Aurelius; and in the third century were Severus, Maximinius, Decius, Valerian, Aurelian. Finally moving to the fourth century there was Diocletian. Here is a list:

64-68	Nero (Paul)
95-96	Domitian (John)
104-117	Trajan
161-180	Marcus Aurelius
200-211	Severus
235-237	Maximinius
250-253	Decius
257-260	Valerian
270-275	Aurelian
303-313	Diocletian

You can see that these are not dates of their reigns; these dates don't connect. These are periods (waves) of persecution that went through the Church *within* the reigns of the various emperors. They devised dreadful things that they used to torture Christians. Some were boiled in oil, some were put on a rack and pulled limb from limb, some were burned at the stake, some were slowly roasted to death over a flame, some were fed to wild beasts, and of course others were crucified. What was it that Jesus had said to the church at Smyrna? He said, **"Be faithful unto death"** (2:10), and many were. The death of martyrdom. Now the ending year of 313 seems awfully specific as an end date. Why isn't that rounded off to 300 or 310 or something like that. Why 313? As we look at the next church we will understand why.

Pergamum

The next church on the list of The Revelation was the church at Pergamum. We saw that it was the compromised church; they compromised with the teaching of Balaam. It represents the time from 313 to 500 AD. In the Old Testament Balaam was one who encouraged people to intermarry with pagans and add worship of their spouse's idols to the worship of God. In the New Testament there was compromise in Pergamum with the teaching of the Nicolaitans. It was either more idol worship or unscriptural division of clergy and laity. What does all that have to do with the year 313? If you know Roman history, you know the name Constantine, who became emperor. He is said to have seen a vision of a cross of fire and to have heard a voice saying, "In this sign, conquer."[27] He was told the cross was the sign of the Christian Church, and that it must mean that the God of the Christians was calling him to be the champion of Christianity; that if he obeyed the voice, he would be victor over the army of Maxentius and become emperor of the world. He called for Christian leaders and asked them to tell him what they believed. He said that he accepted their beliefs and declared himself to be its God-appointed patron and protector. He did win a victory over his opponents, and in the Edict of Milan he stopped all persecution of Christians. When was the Edict of Milan? 313 AD. Church bishops now sat on thrones with the nobles of the empire. What a change from the persecution of the previous two centuries, and you might say, *Hallelujah, this is great—no more persecution.*

But Christianity became Rome's state religion! Let me ask you, is that the way Jesus wants people to come to Him? Because the state says this is now your religion? Bad idea. Pagan temples became Christian churches. Pagan priests became Christian priests. Christian worship became tainted by the practices of pagan worship. At some point Constantine had mass baptisms of the army: *You're in the army, you're all going to be baptized in the name of Jesus.* "Aye, aye sir!" Is that the way Jesus wants people to be baptized? No, baptism is a public profession of *personal* faith in Jesus Christ. Another disastrous thing that happened was that teaching about the second coming of Christ faded away. People said, *Why, the millennium has come, the Emperor is a Christian, we did it, we won!* At what cost? Just like the church in Pergamum, the cost was compromise. Many scholars question the authenticity of Constantine's conversion. I don't know. Only God knows Constantine's heart, only God knows your heart, only God knows my heart. I don't know how genuine it was, but I do know that it was a disaster for the Church. As horrible as the days of persecution were during the two previous centuries, the Church was much purer during that time. If being a Christian means maybe tomorrow I die, there's no place for compromise. But the emperor, he's a Christian now; it's cool, and in fact it's the state religion. Pergamum, the third church, represents the period from 313 to 500: a time of compromise.

Thyatira

The fourth church that Jesus wrote to was the Church of Thyatira. It was a church that was tolerant of sin. You might remember it mentioned the woman Jezebel. That was probably not her real name but was symbolic. She was *like* Jezebel of the Old Testament who led her husband Ahab to be the worst king in the entire history of Israel. The church in Thyatira was tolerating sin. In the history of the Church it represents a thousand years—the period we call the Dark Ages. David Jeremiah says this about it: "The union of church with Rome in the previous period initiated a thousand-year period of time in which the institutionalized, politicized version of the church [was] headquartered in Rome."[28]

If you know your European history, you know this to be true: Rome became the power behind the thrones in Europe. The divine right of kings. In fact the king was *appointed by God*, and therefore he could not sin. He could do whatever he wanted, and it wasn't sin because he was appointed by God. Tolerant of sin, and not just tolerant of it but promoter of it! During this time, Jesus became known as the son of Mary, and worship of her (capitalized Virgin Mary) was instituted. (It is not insignificant that Jesus had introduced Himself to the church in Thyatira as the Son of God.)

Ultimately, the Inquisition came from within the Church during this time. The Inquisition was a powerful office set up within the Catholic Church to root out and punish "heresy" throughout Europe and later the Americas. Beginning in the 12th century and continuing for hundreds of years, the Inquisition is infamous for the severity of its tortures and its persecution of "heretics": Protestants (i.e., pre-Luther), Jews, and Muslims. When a suspect was convicted of unrepentant heresy, the inquisition tribunal was required by law to hand the person over to secular authorities for final sentencing, at which point a magistrate would determine the penalty, which was usually burning at the stake. One historian described it this way: "The annals of church had become the annals of hell."[29]

This was the era of John Wickliffe. He attacked the privileged status of the clergy, which had bolstered their powerful role in England. He then attacked the luxury and pomp of local parishes and their ceremonies. He was not martyred. He died when he suffered a stroke in 1384. In the years before his death he increasingly argued for Scripture as the authoritative center of Christianity, that the claims of the papacy were unhistorical, that monasticism was irredeemably corrupt, and that the moral unworthiness of priests invalidated their office in sacraments. That didn't make him real popular with the Catholic Church of the day! In fact, long after his death (30 years) the Council of Constance declared Wycliffe a heretic. They banned his writings, effectively both excommunicating him retroactively and making him an early forerunner of Protestantism. The Council decreed that Wycliffe's work should be burned. They hated him so much that they had his body removed from consecrated ground. His corpse was burned and the ashes cast into the river. Overall it was the time that gradually brought all the corruptions of the Church of the Dark Ages that would lead to The Reformation.

Sardis

The fifth period of time in history is represented by the church in Sardis. They were a church that had a name that they were alive, but they were dead. In history that represents the period from 1500 to 1700 A.D. But isn't that the time of Reformation? Martin Luther's 95 theses (1517) recently celebrated their 500th anniversary! Yes, and good things happened during that time. But Jesus said to the original church in Sardis that they had a name that they were alive. They were dead. Why would you say that about these two centuries? State Protestant churches replaced state Roman churches. Luther initially rejected infant "baptism," but he changed his mind when he saw how it could combine citizenship with church roles. Is that how people become part of the Church? Because they're born citizens of that country where there's a state church? Was that a good thing?

The Scriptures were translated into multiple languages for study, and that helped set the stage for revival of the doctrine of justification by faith (not works) which had been lost for centuries. Much doctrinal error was repudiated. There were good things but think overall about what happened within these state churches. Then ask yourself this question: The Church of England, was that a reformation or just a king who wanted a divorce? It had nothing to do with doctrinal error. Furthermore, the Catholic Church itself responded with what is now called the Counter Reformation, in which they reaffirmed all of their errors and all the things that they had been teaching for over a thousand years.

The doctrine of Christ's return was still neglected. You find very little written by the reformers about the return of Christ. Paul had written to the church at Thessalonica, describing their conversion:

You turned to God from idols to serve a living and true God, and to wait for His Son from Heaven, whom He raised from the dead, that is Jesus, who delivers us from the wrath to come (I Thessalonians 1:9-10).

The church in the Sardis era turned from the living and true God, but they missed waiting for His Son from heaven. Very little was said and written. A *name* that they were alive was true of the church with some individuals who were really alive; that was the situation in that original church in Sardis. It was the same from 1500 to 1700: individuals who were powerful witnesses for Christ, but overall there was still much dead religion.

Philadelphia

That takes us to the sixth church, the sixth age, which is the church in Philadelphia. This is the second church about which Jesus said nothing negative. We call it the church of opportunity, and it represents the church from 1700 to 1900. Remembering that there was no criticism or condemnation of this church, consider what Jesus said to them: **"I have put before you an *open door* which no one can shut"** (3:7, italics mine). That is exactly what happened around the world between 1700 and 1900. Great mission movements began. You might recognize these names: William Carey (India), Hudson Taylor (China), David Livingstone (Africa), and Adoniram Judson (Burma). Men with a vision saw an open door, and they knew that no one could shut it. The gospel was taken around the world. It was the time of the first and second great awakenings, the time of D. L. Moody, Charles Spurgeon, George Whitefield, John and Charles Wesley, and Charles Finney. It is said of George Whitefield that when he would stop preaching, the crowds would cry out, "More, preach to us more, Mr. Whitfield." An open door that no one could shut. Along with that there was finally a revival of second coming teaching and scholarship. Social ills inside society were also addressed: slave trade was stopped in various places, ungodly child labor was stopped, and there was a new concern for the poor and on reaching out and helping those in need. Some of you might know about George Mueller's work with orphans in which thousands of orphans were cared for because he had faith to trust God. It was a gospel with feet that went to the world—those who put their faith right where the people were. It made a difference in the world around them. It is the second most exciting period in the history of the church. Only the time of the apostles in the book of Acts is more exciting. 1700 to 1900. It was an open door, and throughout the world people saw the open door that Jesus had set before them. They heard the call, they answered the call, and the gospel was spread with great missionary fervor.

Laodicea

That brings us to the seventh and final church, the church in Laodicea. Jesus said, **"You are neither cold nor hot....you are lukewarm"** (3:15-16). In history it sadly represents a period from 1900 to today. Many churches, many pastors, many professors, many seminaries developed a "smarter than God" theology. They deny the miraculous. *That thing about Jonah and the fish? That could not possibly have happened. I mean, really, do you believe that someone could get swallowed by a fish and survive? We know those kind of things just don't happen.* Well, they might not happen in your world, but they happen in mine. Your problem is not about the fish, your problem is that your God is too small.

Leaders and teachers rejected the authority of Scripture, saying, *Well, the Bible isn't the word of God, the Bible <u>contains</u> the Word of God.* And we as the smart ones have to figure it out: which are the actual parts that are the word of God? When you do that, who is the final authority, God or man? They miss the fact that Christianity has always been (Judeo-Christianity has always been) a faith of revelation. Some even claim that the literal resurrection of Jesus wasn't important. It doesn't matter if Jesus actually rose from the dead. It just means if you believe that He could have risen from the dead, or *maybe* He rose from the dead, then you believe in a brighter tomorrow. And if you do that then all will be well. Just believe in a brighter tomorrow. The "smarter than God" people embrace evolution over God's Word. Even in seminaries there are people who will tell you exactly how the world came into being (evolution). I always have one question for them: were you there? Because I've got a Book. It's a Book written by Someone who was there, and He tells me how it happened.

Once again the second coming is neglected or worse yet denied! Or they redefine it: *Oh, I believe in the second coming of Jesus. He comes again when we experience him anew in our lives.* And I'm not making that up. That's the teaching in some seminaries and pulpits today. Even Bible-believing churches (so-called) have sermon series like *At the Movies*. The Lord's Supper in many churches is rarely celebrated or in some cases is absent altogether.

Giving is sometimes poverty level. What do I mean by that? Sadly, I served in one church where our youth pastor looked at the total giving one year. He looked at the number of giving units, and he divided total giving by the number of giving units to see what the average giving unit was contributing to the church. He said if that was 10% of their income, that meant the average person in that church was making so little that they were all eligible for food stamps. Poverty level giving.

Missionary zeal has also declined in many churches. Many churches never even tell people how they can know that they have eternal life because the teaching of repentance and the necessity of being born again has been replaced by *be a better person*.

David Jeremiah says of a good portion of the church in our day:

> **Nauseating, sickening, poor, wretched, blind, torn by false cults, ripped apart by offbeat theologies, incapable because too weak, it could not deal with the problems of today's world, and the Laodicean church is a weak church that has tried to be both in the world and out of the world...it is powerless to deal with the issues of today.'[30]**

Author Stanley High has some advice for the Church:

> **The church has failed to tell me that I am a sinner. The church has failed to deal with me as a lost individual. The church has failed to offer me salvation in Jesus Christ alone. The church has failed to tell me of the horrible consequences of sin, the certainty of hell, and the fact that Jesus Christ alone can save. We need more of the last judgment and less of the Golden Rule; more of the living God and the living devil as well; more of heaven to gain and**

a hell to shun. The church must bring me not a message of culti-
vation but a message of rebirth. I might fail that kind of church,
but that kind of church will not fail me.'[31]

That's his prescription for a lukewarm church.

I recently walked past a church sign that read, "[I won't give the name] Church is a congregation with open hearts, open minds, and open arms. We welcome and affirm you in the name of Jesus Christ, our Savior, regardless of your race, ethnicity, age, gender identity, sexual orientation, social or economic status, physical and mental ability, or religious affiliation. We are all God's beloved children."[32] That sign is displayed prominently on the side of their building, and they openly approve of same-sex relations. You can't miss it as you walk by. Jesus stands outside the church today and He knocks, asking to be let in, asking to let Him be the Lord of His Church.

Conclusion

I want to say one more thing because I'm sure you've thought about this. Are some of these things continuing today? Yes. The Roman Church of the Dark Ages still exists today. My dad grew up in one of those church-es. He was in church every Sunday, one of ten children. They all went to church every Sunday. He told me this: *Keith, I was there every week. I never heard that I had to be born again, I never heard that I needed to have a personal relationship with Jesus Christ, I never heard that I could know for certain that I was going to heaven, never.* Does the church that has a name of being alive but is dead still exist today? The church that has come from the Reformation? Yes. My mom grew up in one of those situations—a Protestant church. She never heard the gospel either. Oh, I am so thankful that by God's grace they both came to know Jesus Christ later in life. When Dad was promoted to heaven and six years later Mom was promoted after him, I know that the minute they took their last breath, the second they took their last breath on earth, they were in the glorious presence of Jesus. Today they walk the streets of gold with Him by God's grace. But the message of truth didn't come from those churches they grew up in.

But does a church like Philadelphia still exist today? Oh yes it does. Some of you might be familiar with what's going on in South Korea. The outreach that is going on there far exceeds anything anywhere else in the world. They are teaching their missionaries how to witness to their exe-cutioners if they are martyred for their faith in Muslim countries. There are mission societies around the world that are still making an impact. All of these coexist today along with the lukewarm church.

ATM (Apply to Me)

1. Keith, does everybody believe this teaching? I said at the outset: no. But as we have gone through this lesson, I hope you see why I have taken time to present it. I believe these parallels are so clear that we see Jesus was indeed speaking to the seven church *ages* as well as to seven literal churches. But I must hold this teaching with humility and grace toward others who disagree. If you disagree, it's okay—I love you, God loves you, and Jesus saves us both. If you believe it and you discuss this with someone, encourage him/her to check it out, to investigate, to research and see where the Bible and the study of Church history leads.

2. I must do everything in my power to pray for, give to, and serve a Philadelphia kind of church.

3. Individually, what open door has God set before me, before you? A friend, neighbor, co-worker, relative, someone who cuts your hair, whoever it might be. Is there an open door that God has set before you?

4. Finally I'm reminded of the story of a little boy who liked to listen to the clock chiming; he would count the chimes on the hour. One day it was noon, and the clock was chiming, and he counted 1 2 3 4 5 6 7 8 9 10 11 12. Then it chimed again. He became very concerned, went running upstairs and he said to his mom, "There's a problem; it's later than it's ever been." I must tell you whether or not we are in the last Church age, we know this for a fact: the return of Christ is nearer now than it has ever been. It's later than it's ever been. Am I ready? Are you ready? If Jesus came this afternoon, are you ready? Do you know Him personally? That's the biggest ATM of all. He who has an ear let him hear what the Spirit says to all of us.

Lesson 5

Read 4:1 – 5:7

Who Is Worthy?

Chapter 4 to the end of the book is the last and by far the longest division of The Revelation. It describes future events. We know that we have entered that third section because 4:1 says, **"I will show you what must take place after these things,"** the exact same wording as in 1:19 in both Greek and in English. And notice the use of the words *must take place*. These are things that have to happen because unless these things take place, there is no final justice in the universe. These things *must* happen in order for anything to make sense about good, evil, reward, justice, and punishment. They *must take place*.

You might have noticed that in this chapter there was a change of geography. John is no longer on Patmos. At the beginning of the chapter he has gone through an open door into heaven. The invitation to go through that door was from the very first voice he heard. That was back in 1:10—a voice that sounded like a trumpet. We saw that the voice is clearly the Lord Jesus Christ Himself. So, the Lord invites him to come to heaven and he says immediately he was in the spirit; that is he was again "spiritized" (See Lesson 2).

As we look at Chapter 4, we will answer the question of what he saw. We will find out that this is one of the most glorious chapters in all of the 66 books of the Bible. John does his best to describe it in words that we can understand, but it is almost beyond description; it truly is indescribable. Harry Ironside says:

> *We are carried far above the shifting scenes of this poor world and permitted to gaze with awestruck eyes upon a scene of glory indescribable and to hear things that have been kept secret from the foundation of the world.*[33]

This is a glorious opportunity for John and ultimately for us.

So, what did he see? First, we are told that he saw a throne, and then he saw 24 other thrones. *Throne* is the key to understanding this entire chapter. John uses the word 12 times just in this chapter. The Revelation uses the word *throne* 46 times. There are 27 books in the New Testament, and the other 26 books combined use the word *throne* 15 times, an average of less than one per book. So throne is very important in The Revelation and particularly in this chapter. Because it is so important, it forms the outline of how we understand this chapter. (I am indebted to David Jeremiah for providing the idea for the following approach to this study). We won't study verse by verse; instead we will study topically. There are five themes, and they will help us understand the importance of the throne:

On the throne
Before the throne
Around the throne
From the throne
Toward the throne

On the throne

Whom did John see? He says he saw one sitting on that main throne and describes Him as One like a jasper stone and sardius in appearance. I would never use any kind of words like this to describe a person, would you? That tells us that the One sitting on the throne is so indescribable, the only thing John can come up with *He's like jasper and sardius*. The Jew reading this would have immediately understood the symbolism of jasper and sardius because they are the last and the first stones on the high priest's breast piece in the book of Exodus. There were 12 jewels on the breastplate that the high priest wore, one for each of the 12 tribes of Israel. The last one was jasper, and the first one was a ruby, which is what John calls a sardius.

Later on in Chapter 21 of The Revelation John would describe the jasper that he saw as clear as crystal. That's not the jasper that we know today, for our jasper is not clear like crystal. This is something very different, so many scholars believe that this is actually referring to a perfect, clear diamond. Whatever it is represents God's glory, and I'm sure you can guess what the red stone represents: the blood of sacrifice. So, this description is of a Person seated on the throne, and it is totally different from any person you would ever see described. Human words cannot fully describe the nature or image of God. That's why John uses the word *like* so many times. He says, *It was like this* or *It was like that*, because he can't find words to fully describe this vision in our language. From all of this we see that God is powerful and God is glorious. Of course, the red stone is a reminder of His mercy and His love—what happened on Calvary. So that is *on the throne*.

Before the throne

Before means in front of the throne. What did he see? Something that looked like a sea of crystal glass. Again, he doesn't say it *was* a sea of crystal glass. He says **as it were** (4:6). That means it *looked like* a sea of crystal glass. That's the best description he can come up with, and it most likely represents God's holiness and His righteousness. Some speculate that it represents God's Word, His perfect eternal Word because later the martyred saints who refuse the mark of the beast are standing on this sea that was *like* crystal glass. Before the throne he also sees seven lamps of burning fire, and he is told that they are the spirit, i.e. the Holy Spirit. We looked at the beginning of our study about seven lamps representing the Holy Spirit. We said that is a reference to Isaiah Chapter 11, where the Holy Spirit is described as the Spirit of the Lord, wisdom, understanding, counsel, strength, knowledge, and fear of the Lord: the seven-fold ministry of the Holy Spirit. There are not seven Holy Spirits; there is one Holy Spirit with a seven-fold ministry represented by these seven lamps of burning fire. So that's what he saw *before the throne.*

Around the throne

What and whom did John see around the throne? He saw 24 other thrones, and there were 24 elders seated on those thrones. They were wearing white garments, representing purity. That is, they have been cleansed from their sin by the blood of Jesus. They were wearing golden crowns. It is not the Greek word for royal diadems like a king wears, but the word for crown like the reward that a victor would get in the athletic games of that day. Each elder wore one of those. Who are these 24 elders? There are at least 13 different explanations for who they are. Sometimes symbols are hard to interpret (especially here!), but it appears that the majority opinion from the scholars is that these elders represent the redeemed of all ages. Some would say from just the Old Testament; some would say from just the New Testament. I think they are representative symbols of the redeemed of all ages, both Old Testament and New Testament. These 24 elders have the privilege of sitting around the throne.

Again, a Jew reading this would have read 24 and would immediately have thought of the division of the priesthood in the Old Testament, where 24 priests served on a rotating basis. It was always 24, but each for a short time followed by another group of 24. So, it is possible that these 24 elders in heaven sit there on a rotating basis. We are not told, but as representatives of the redeemed they have the opportunity to be there surrounding the throne of God. Around the throne there was also a rainbow. He says it was *like* (there's that word again) an emerald in appearance. Again, there is speculation about what the rainbow symbolizes there. We know what a rainbow is in the book of Genesis: it's a promise that God will never again flood the whole earth. Perhaps it is there as a reminder that when God judges He is also merciful. It also shows God's glory.

If you take all of these colors together, John must have been overwhelmed. We know that what will happen in the rest of The Revelation is a massive storm of judgment. It is interesting that here the rainbow appears *before* the storm! We normally see a rainbow after a storm.

What else did he see around the throne? There were four creatures or living beings. (Some translations say beasts—a bad translation for the living beings.) He says they have eyes in the front and behind. (Sounds kind of like what mothers need, right?) They have eyes literally in front and behind—a symbol that they see all. The first is a lion. We're not sure about the second one: some translations say calf; some translations say bull. The third has a face like a man, and the fourth a flying eagle. Some scholars have suggested that these are the same creatures that Ezekiel saw in Chapter 10. We should compare those because indeed there are four living creatures in each vision. In Ezekiel 10 they are named cherubim, but there are differences. Ezekiel's four creatures had four wings; those here in Revelation 4 have six wings. Ezekiel's creatures had four faces; these have eyes in front and back. I must conclude that the number four is not enough to say they are the same; there are too many differences.

What we can say with a great deal of confidence is that these are angelic beings and they represent the most important characteristics of the Triune God. What do we mean by that? The lion is a symbol of God's Divine majesty. What do we call the king of the jungle? The skunk, the turtle? No! The lion—same symbol here. The second is a calf. Some scholars would tell us it is a servant animal, a symbol of Christ on earth, who came as a suffering servant. The man, third living being, represents the intelligence and purpose of the Lord God Almighty. He is not an impersonal "Force" like in the *Star Wars* movies. And the eagle represents God's swiftness in detecting evil and judging it. There is an old rabbinic saying which goes all the way back to the year 300 A.D., or possibly before that. It simply says this, "The mightiest among the birds is the eagle, the mightiest among the domestic animals is the bull, the mightiest among the wild beasts is the lion, and the mightiest among all is man."[34] One commentator says: "The four forms suggest whatever is noblest, strongest, wisest, and swiftest in animate nature."[35] Thus nature, including man, is represented before the throne, taking its part in the fulfillment of the Divine will, and the worship of the Divine Majesty. Other scholars see here (this also makes sense) four pictures of Jesus in the Gospels. Matthew presents Jesus the King—the lion. Mark presents the suffering servant. Luke presents the Son of man, and John presents the one who is Deity, God incarnate.

We cannot say for certain, but all those explanations have validity. Certainly all creation glorifying God is contained in these four creatures, and they do present a picture of who God is. It is certain that awe and reverence are the proper response to everything that John saw. That's why we come to worship each Sunday. As imperfect as our worship is in our fallen world, we should gather each week for worship with awe and reverence. That was *around the throne.*

From the throne

What came from the throne? According to 4:5, flashes of lightning and peals of thunder. Clearly it is a sign of judgment. That is what we will see for the next 17 chapters— judgment of the world. But before we get there we see the One who is qualified to judge the earth. We have seen Him in His glory, and this vision reminds us that He is the only One with the right to judge. He can and He will. As we noted in v. 1 He *must* judge.

Toward the throne

There was what toward the throne? There was worship. The four living creatures cry out, **"Holy, Holy, Holy, is the Lord God, the Almighty, who was and who is and who is to come"** (4:8). If you compare that to 1:8, you will find the same wording: **who was and is and who is to come.** Notice that it starts with *holy.* Worship starts with the holiness of God. The central attribute, the foundational attribute of God, is His Holiness. If He is love, it is a holy love; if He is just, it is a holy justice. If God is all-powerful, it is a holy power. If God gets angry (and sometimes we are told in Scripture that He does), it is a holy anger. If God is good, it is a holy goodness. If God is merciful, and He is, it is a holy mercy. And if He is gracious, and oh He is, it is a holy grace. If God is wise, it is a holy wisdom. And if He is glorious, it is a holy glory. It is the foundational attribute of who God is: His holiness. Worship also comes from the 24 elders who cast those victor crowns before the throne, because they recognize that the victory they have, the redeemed status that they have as children of the King, comes not through their own effort, not through their own training, not through making themselves better and better, but solely by the mercy and grace of the Lord Jesus Christ. So, they cast those victor crowns before the throne and they cry out, **"Worthy are You, our Lord and our God, to receive glory and honor and power; for You created all things, and because of Your will they existed, and were created"** (4:11).

Warren Wiersbe says about this kind of attitude toward the Creator, "Acknowledging the Creator in worship is the first step toward trusting the Redeemer."[36] You must understand that's why the evolutionist has to come up with a different explanation for how we got here. To admit that we couldn't exist by chance, that we couldn't just make ourselves better and better until that one-celled amoeba gradually by random selection became us, there must be an external force, and that external force is God. Once they acknowledge God as the Creator, then they are obligated to Him as Judge. And once they are obligated to Him as Judge, they know they stand guilty before Him. Then they need a redeemer (only the Lord Jesus Christ qualifies), and they don't want someone else running their lives. So, they make up this whole myth about how we all got here, and they have all these pleasant-sounding "scientific" gobbledygook theories. What they are doing in the end with their theories of evolution is worshiping the creation rather than worshipping the Creator. Acknowledging the Creator is the first step toward trusting the Redeemer.

Chapter 5

So, we have looked at on the throne, before the throne, around the throne, from the throne, and toward the throne. That takes us into the next chapter (Chapter 5), where we see what is owned by the throne. Chapter 5 starts with the word *and* connecting it directly with Chapter 4; this is all part of the same experience for John. He says, **"I saw...a book"** (5:1). A book in that day would have been a scroll. He says it was written on both sides. It was somewhat unusual for a scroll to be written on the front *and back* on the papyrus. It was sealed with seven seals. It was likely written, rolled, sealed, more written, then sealed again, then written and sealed again, so that it unrolled gradually as each seal was removed. Anyone in the Roman Empire would immediately have understood what that meant. Roman wills were sealed seven times. Do you know who could open a will? Only the appointed heir had the legal right to open the seven seals on a Roman will. This particular scroll is the title deed to the world and its judgment.

A cry goes out, **"Who is worthy to open the book...?"** (5:2) *Who is worthy to gradually remove those seven seals?* Well, let's conduct a search. Let's see if there is a person who has ever lived who is worthy to open the seals. Harry Ironside says this:

> *Adam, what about you? Wasn't that world given to you? Can't you open the deed to the world? When God created you and placed you in the Garden of Eden, did He not say that all of this was yours? Why do you not come forward, take this title deed and claim your property? Adam says, "I forfeited my inheritance because of sin, it was mine, but I sinned it away. The devil cheated me out of it, and I have no longer any title to it."*[37]

So it is with everyone descended from Adam. No one is found who is worthy to open the scroll. John weeps because he wants desperately to know what things *must* take place "after these things," and he knows that this scroll is going to tell him. But then he hears a voice, *Don't weep, look.* He describes the Lion from the tribe of Judah, the root of David. (It is not descendant of David. Yes, He is that, but He is also the root of David. He is the One who is eternal. Jesus had a debate with the Pharisees once. He asked them whose son the Messiah is: *Messiah is the descendant of David* they answered. He said, **"Then how does David in the Spirit call him 'Lord...?'"** (Matthew 22:43) if He is David's descendant. [David wrote in Psalm 110, **"The Lord said to my Lord, 'sit at My right hand.'**) Only because this Descendant of David is eternal is He the root of David as well as the offspring of David. John is told He has overcome, He has defeated death, He has lived a sinless life, so He is worthy.

Then John says, **I saw...a Lamb standing as if slain** (6:6). Now there's an oxymoron. If you have been at the bedside of someone in his or her last moments before a promotion to glory, you know that when that person passes on, the body isn't standing up. The body is prone. But John sees a lamb as if slain, *standing.* You get it, right? This can only mean that the Lamb who was slain and still bore the marks of Calvary is alive. Besides, if He's dead He can't open the scroll! He has overcome (death). He has seven horns which represent perfect strength (omnipotence), He has seven eyes which represent perfect knowledge (omniscience), and the eyes also are the seven spirits of God (Holy Spirit) going out into the whole earth to see all (omnipresence). Harry Ironside says:

> *The lamb that speaks of innocence, meekness, gentleness, and sacrifice is the One who is to go forth as the mighty conqueror and claim this world as His own. What right had He thus to act? Because He went to the cross and in infinite grace to pay the great debt of sin, thus to redeem this forfeited inheritance and free it from Satan's domination. The Lamb has title to the book! The Lamb can claim the title deed to this world because when He died on Calvary's Cross He purchased the entire world to be His own— in which the glory of God is to be displayed...It was His because He created it. He gave it to man, but man forfeited it through sin. And the Lord Jesus Christ bought it all back when He hung on Golgotha's tree.*[38]

He is worthy. Once He starts to open the seals on that scroll, we will gradually move toward the glorious affirmation that we're going to read in Revelation Chapter 11: **The Kingdom of this world is become the Kingdom of our Lord and of His Christ, and He shall reign forever and forever, Amen** (11: 15). Sadly, that's where we must leave this lesson. He took the scroll. He will start to open it in our next lesson.

The Rapture

However, before we conclude we need to look at one more thing. It has to do with these two verses in I Thessalonians 4:16-17. **The Lord himself will descend from heaven with a shout, with the voice of the archan-**

gel, and with the trumpet of God; and the dead in Christ shall rise first. Then we who are alive and remain shall be caught up together with them in the clouds to meet the Lord in the air, and thus we shall always be with the Lord. This "catching up" is what we call the rapture. Where does it fit into the book of The Revelation? When does this catching up (the rapture) happen, *because these words from I Thessalonians are not repeated in the book of The Revelation?* There are three different views that scholars take about when the catching up or rapture takes place. One is that it takes place here at the beginning of Chapter 4 before the tribulation, the seven years that we are going to study. That view is called a pre-tribulation rapture. A second view is that the rapture happens at the midpoint after three and a half years of the tribulation (or close to the midpoint); it's called a mid-tribulation viewpoint. Then there is a viewpoint that the rapture comes at the end of the tribulation, a post-tribulation view.

We will look at these three different viewpoints when we come to them. Today I want to look at the argument for a pre-tribulation rapture. In this view the rapture happens here between Chapter 3 and Chapter 4. The arguments go like this.

First is the outline of the book itself. We passed the Church age when we arrived at Chapter 4. After Chapter 3 the Church is not mentioned again until Revelation 19, which would seem to be some evidence that the rapture happens here. Do you remember the phrase, **He who has an ear hear what the spirit says to the churches** (2:7, 11, etc.)? Remember that at the end of each letter? The phrase **If anyone has an ear** is used again in Chapter 13:9, but it simply says. **If anyone has an ear, let him hear.** It doesn't say anything about the Church or the Holy Spirit. Why not? Because the Holy Spirit is no longer present in the hearts and lives of the Church because the Church isn't on earth. I Thessalonians is another place that describes the Restrainer (Holy Spirit) being taken out of the way, and then judgment is going to come. Without God's supernatural intervention, if there were no restraining force against evil on earth, all hell would break loose tomorrow.

Second, thunder and lightning coming from the throne would indicate the day of grace is over. The era in which we live, the Church age, is the age of grace. Some would even argue that the rainbow shows no judgment on the Church because the Church will be taken away (raptured).

Third, Revelation 3:10 speaks of those who have kept the word of Jesus being kept from the hour of testing, which is the Tribulation that is to come upon the whole world.

Finally, people with this view tell us that John represents the Church; so when John saw an open door in heaven and a voice saying **come up here** (4:1), it is symbolic of the Church being told to come on up.

That summarizes the arguments for a pre-tribulation rapture. When we get to the midpoint of the tribulation, we will look at arguments for a mid-tribulation rapture, and when we get to the end of tribulation, we will look at arguments for a post-tribulation rapture.

Keith, you're not going to tell me what to believe? No. I'll tell you why. I had lunch with four other people after church recently. We were talking about my sermon series in The Revelation, and the tribulation, and this subject of the rapture came up. I asked them what they believe about the rapture. Of the four one said pre-tribulation, one said mid-tribulation, one said post-tribulation, and one wasn't sure. So, I will not tell you that you have to believe a certain way about the rapture. Great scholars who have studied this doctrine have not united around one particular view. This debate has continued for quite some time, most recently the last two centuries. We saw in our last lesson that scholarship about the second coming was neglected for a very long time. You mean I can believe whatever I want? No, you must believe in the return of Christ. I will tell you what my church believes about the second coming of Christ:

> *We believe in the personal, bodily return of our Lord Jesus Christ at a time known only to God. We believe in the final judgment of all people: those who do not know Christ will be condemned to eternal separation from God, and those who do know Christ will enjoy the glory of God with Christ in His kingdom forever.*[39]

If you are a pre-tribulation person, does that fit? Yes. If you are a mid-tribulation person, does that fit? Yes. If you are post-tribulation, does that fit? Yes. What's the point of unity? Jesus is coming again! We can't get so narrow that we say, *Our pastor told us that we have to believe a certain way, and our pastor is never wrong, so if you don't agree with him, you have to come to my church because he'll straighten you out!* Please understand how narrow that is. Scholars who have far more education than almost all of us and have studied this more thoroughly than any of us, me included, can't agree. So, I will present their arguments as we come to each particular place where this could happen. The point of unity is *Jesus is coming again.*

The Trinity

Finally, did you notice the Trinity? God the Father on the throne. God the Son: the Lamb who is the Lion. God the Holy Spirit: seven lamps of fire; seven eyes on the Lamb. The acknowledgement of 3x holy: Holy, Ho-

49

ly, Holy. You cannot read the book of Revelation with an open mind and not see the Trinity everywhere—the Triune God: Father, Son and Holy Spirit.

ATM (Apply to Me)

1. I must cry out with the living beings: *Holy, Holy, Holy is the Lord God Almighty who was and who is and who is to come.* The things that will happen in judgment must happen. I must fall before Him and acknowledge Him as the One who is worthy to judge.

2. About worship Charles Swindoll says: "It has become too commonplace for Christians to surrender everything for their work but sacrifice nothing in worshiping the One who gave His life to save ours."[40] If that is in any way true of any of us, let us allow God to search our hearts and ask if we are sacrificing more for work than for worship of the Creator.

3. Warren Wiersbe has a great application for us: "We do not worship a babe in a manger or a corpse on a cross. We worship the living, reigning Lamb of God who is in the midst of all in heaven."[41] So here are individual questions for each one of us. Do you personally know the Lamb who died to save us? Do you know Him as your Savior? Have you personally?

surrendered Him? Can you name a moment in time (you might not remember exactly when it was), when you said, *Yes, Jesus I'm a sinner, I need salvation. I need you to be my Lord and Savior.* You do not want the tribulation time to come without having answered that question in the affirmative. I am compelled by Scripture to sound that warning.

4. Never forget this: God is still on the throne of the universe. It might be a virus in China and a stock market that goes up and down, marches and protests everywhere, or wars. God is still on the throne. No one else is ever going to sit on the throne. Buddha is never going to sit on the throne—he's dead! The One on the throne is the One who was and is and is to come.

5. Finally I must cry out with the elders, **"Worthy are You our Lord and our God, to receive glory and honor and power; for You created all things, and because of Your will they existed, and were created"** (4:11).

Lesson 6

Read 5:8 – 6:8

24 Elders and 4 horses

You will recall from our last lesson that the One who was sitting on the throne held a scroll or a book (in those days it would have been a scroll). It was a title deed to the earth and to its judgments. The question was asked, **"Who is worthy to open the book?"** (5:2) They searched all of heaven and all of earth and they were told that no one was found worthy. John cried because he wanted to know what was in the scroll; he wanted to know the future. Then he was told not to weep because the Lamb is worthy. He saw a lamb standing, looking as if it had been slain. This is clearly a reference to the resurrected Lord Jesus Christ. In our last lesson we saw that the Lamb came and took the scroll out of the right hand of Him who sat on the throne.

Before he begins to open the seals of that scroll there is more worship. The 4 living creatures and the 24 elders (which we said probably represent all believers of all ages) sang a *new* song about why the lamb is worthy to break the seals. What is the meaning of *new* song? The worship in Chapter 4 was worship to the Creator for the glory of **creation**. Now we have a song to the Lamb, the new song of **redemption** in 5:9-10:

> **"Worthy are You to take the book, and to break its seals, for You were slain and, You purchased for God with Your blood men from every tribe and tongue and people and nation. And you have made them to be a kingdom and priests to our God; and they will reign upon the earth."**

The song of redemption. Notice also that the 24 elders have golden bowls of incense. We are told what they represent, which is the prayers of the saints. Isn't that wonderful? Leon Morris in his commentary on The Revelation says, "On the earth the saints are despised and accounted as of no importance. In heaven their prayers are precious, being brought into the very presence of God Himself."[42] Never forget that when you pray. Those prayers are brought into the throne room of God Himself.

We're told that John also sees many angels: myriads and myriads and thousands of thousands. We know that thousands of thousands are a million. He said myriads of myriads and thousands of thousands of angels. He's telling us there are so many they could never be counted. Lest you think there are maybe ten or twenty or a hundred angels running around heaven and/or working as ministering servants on earth, that's not the case.

51

Myriads of angels serve at the pleasure of the King of the universe. And they sang, **"Worthy is the Lamb that was slain to receive power and riches and wisdom and might and honor and glory and blessing"** (5:12). Then we're told that all of creation joined in; the four living creatures said, "Amen"; the 24 elders fell down and worshiped.

When we come to Chapter 6, however, we have crossed the great divide. Chapters 4 and 5 were worship. Why are they there? First John saw the resurrected, glorified Christ, then we read the letters to the churches, and now we want to be told the things which shall take place *after those things*. John is transported to heaven and for two chapters he sees worship. Why is that? Because we are to understand that the One who is going to pass judgment on the earth is the One who is worthy of worship: God the Father and His Son the Lord Jesus Christ. Therefore, they are worthy of worship as Creator and as Redeemer. They alone have the authority to judge the earth.

So, we have had worship, and now in Chapter 6 starts *wrath*. I must tell you this is where it gets really, really challenging. We're going to do our best to understand what God has given to us, for God did not give us His word to confuse us. He gave us His word so that we could be instructed, and in order to be instructed we have to understand it. *He gave it to be understood.*

Now you might say why wrath? Can't God find a better way than what is about to be described on earth. Do you have a better way? Do I have a better way? If we do, we need to call Jesus aside and say, *Hey, You know we don't need all that wrath stuff. I've got a better answer for You. How about this? Why don't You just come back to earth and go to some of the rulers on earth and ask them turn over their authority to You?* How do you think that would be received in the Kremlin? Do you think Putin would say, *Why sure, here are the levers of power?* How about in China, you think they'd say that? How about the nominating conventions every four years in this country for the Republican Convention, the Democratic Convention? Jesus shows up there and says, *Why don't you just make Me president?* Do you think either political party is going to give up its power? No one on earth is interested in submitting their authority and their power that they have (in a limited way for a limited time) to the Lord Jesus Christ. There needs to be judgment because there needs to be justice and righteousness.

So, it begins to happen in 6:1-8. The first four seals on this scroll are broken. As each scroll is broken, another horseman is sent. The first horse was white and had a rider with a bow and a crown, the second horse was red with a rider who removes peace, the third horse was black and had a rider with a pair of scales, and the fourth horse was pale. It had a rider who is named: his name is Death, and he was followed by Hades.

Why horses? We use horses for racing and for work and for riding enjoyment, but to the Jewish mind this would have made perfect sense. The horse was a symbol of a battle, and a horse was a symbol of victory. A horse was the one who was never afraid. When God was rebuking Job (Job 39:19-25), He said this about the horse:

> **"Do you give the horse his might? Do you clothe his neck with a mane? Do you make him leap like the locust? His majestic snorting is terrible. His paws in the valley, and rejoices in his strength; he goes out to meet the weapons. He laughs at fear and is not dismayed; and he does not turn back from the sword. The quiver rattles against him, the flashing spear and javelin. With shaking and rage he races over the ground; and he does not stand still at the voice of the trumpet. As often as the trumpet sounds he says, 'Aha!' and he scents the battle from afar, and thunder of the captains, and the war cry."**

The Jews would have understood very clearly. The horse goes out at the sound of the trumpet and does not fear the battle.

Seal 1

So, let's look at these first four seals, these four horses. The first horse comes when one of the four living creatures speaks with a voice of thunder. He says *Come*. He means come and go and do your work. Thunder is a symbol of judgment. The horse is a white horse, but who is sitting on the white horse? There are some who believe that the one sitting on the white horse is Jesus, because near the end of The Revelation we see Jesus sitting on a white horse:

> **I saw heaven opened; and behold, a white horse, and He who sat upon it is called Faithful and True; in righteousness He judges and wages war.... His name is called The Word of God** (19:11,13).

Clearly in Revelation 19 the One sitting on the white horse is the Lord Jesus Christ. But who is this rider in Chapter 6? If this is Jesus, it must represent His ministry after He ascended, which is the gospel being spread. So, as some have speculated, the rider represents the spread of the gospel.

I disagree fairly strongly, because in Revelation 6 and Revelation 19 *white* is the only thing that's the same—the color of the horse. Note the differences. In Revelation 19 Christ has a sword. In Revelation 6 the rider has a bow. In Revelation 19 Christ wears a diadem. It is the crown of Kingship, of Majesty, the crown which only He is qualified to wear. In Revelation 6 the rider wears a victor's crown: the type of crown given to someone who competed in the athletic games of those days. In Revelation Chapter 19

Christ comes at the *end* of the judgment, the judgment is over, and He comes to establish His kingdom, the Eternal Kingdom. Here in Revelation 6 this rider on the white horse is going out at the *beginning* of the judgment. So to say that this rider is Jesus just because the horses are the same color is not a good interpretation. In addition, note that the other three horses here in Chapter 6 are clearly symbolic of horror, terror, and destruction. We should see these four horses and their riders (often called the Four Horsemen of the Apocalypse) as similar.

Also remember our book outline. The things starting in Chapter 4 are the things *after* the church age. If this rider is Jesus and He is going out to conquer by the spread of the gospel, there is a problem. The spread of the gospel comes at the *beginning* of the church age, not the *end* of the church age. And remember what I said about the voice of thunder. It signals the start of judgment, not salvation and the spread of the gospel.

Who then is the rider on the white horse? In order to understand what is happening, we must at this point go back to the book of Daniel, because Daniel and The Revelation exist together in prophesying key things about the end times. In Daniel 9:27 Daniel says this: **He** [referring to Antichrist] **will make a firm covenant with the many** [that is with the Jewish nation] **for one week.** One week here is not 7 days but 7 years. But in the middle of the week, (that's after three and a half years) **he will put a stop to sacrifice and grain offering; and on the wing of abominations will come one who makes desolate, even until a complete destruction, one that is decreed, is poured out on the one who makes desolate.** Here's what will happen, according to this prophecy from Daniel: Antichrist will confirm a covenant with the many (with the Jewish nation) for a final seven-year period. This accord will allow for the rebuilding of the temple in Jerusalem, and animal sacrifices will be restored for the first time since 70 A.D. When that happens, we will know that the 7 years of tribulation (the one week) have begun. Now if the pre-tribulation view of the rapture is accurate, then the rapture will precede the rise of this world leader, and the signal that the 7 years of tribulation are about to begin will have already been as clear as anything has ever been. But either way (with or without the rapture), when you see this prophesied peace agreement, you can know that the *final seven years* leading to the second coming of Jesus Christ have begun.

The world government under the control of Antichrist will be the culmination of years of planning that are already in progress today. Many people today are already dreaming of two ways to make this happen:

1) Do away with nation-states and force everyone on earth to pledge allegiance to one single, ultimate political authority—a world govern-

ment. Have you heard people talk about that great "utopia"? Oh yes, you have.

2) Abolish the doctrinal differences between all religious organizations and coerce all leaders to sign declarations of unity with a single, all-inclusive religious authority—one world religion. Haven't you heard people talk about that as well?

So, I would submit to you that the rider on this horse is not Christ but Antichrist, who comes to power at the beginning of the seven years. Anti means against but it also means antithesis—an imitation of Christ with his own white horse, but his motives are evil.

He carries a bow; but there is no mention made of arrows. Some scholars have said that means he will conquer through peace. But it's also possible that the arrows are implied by the fact that he has a bow. Either way he will not initially be a warrior. He will be hailed as a peacemaker, and he will pretend to be a peaceful unifier. When it says he goes out to conquer, it means he wants to have everyone under his authority: one world government with him at the head; one world religion which ultimately will become worship of him. Initially (and very briefly) the world will be happy there is peace. *Yahoo, world peace!* All those beauty pageant contestants, what do they want? World peace! Paul warned about it, however, in I Thessalonians 5:3. **While they are saying, "peace and safety!" then destruction will come upon them suddenly like birth pangs upon a woman with child; and they shall not escape.**

Seal 2

The second horse goes forth. He is red, symbolizing blood, and we are told that he takes away peace from the earth. The second horseman is easy to identify; he is war. We're told that man on earth will kill one another. We're good at that; we're really good at that. Do you want to know how good? (Somebody counted, I really admire this.) In recorded history there have been 14,550 wars. Yes, we're good at it. Do you know how many lives were lost in World War I? 10 million lives. That was "the war to end all wars"! Twenty years later we had World War II, and 32 million lives were lost. Since World War II there have been at least 73 wars on earth. Yes, we're good at it. And when peace is taken away by this horseman, anything that happens will be far worse than the 42 million dead in the two world wars and the 14,500 plus wars in history. In II Thessalonians 2:3-7 Paul warned the church: **The man of lawlessness [will be] revealed,** [that is Antichrist]: **the son of destruction, who opposes and exalts himself above every so-called god or object of worship, so that he takes his seat in the temple of God.** That will happen later in The Revelation; we will see him, displaying himself as being God. **Do you not remember that while I was still with you, I was telling you these things?** Now listen to this: **And you know what** *restrains* **him now, so that in his time he may be revealed. For the mystery of lawlessness is already at work;** *only he who now restrains will do so until he is taken out of the* *way."* (my italics)

Who is the restrainer in the world who restrains the forces of evil? I believe it's the Holy Spirit, present specifically in the hearts and lives of believers but also generally as a global restraining force so that we don't annihilate each other completely. When the Holy Spirit is removed and His restraining influence is taken out of the way, this horseman will be able to remove peace from the earth. There will be war like we have never seen on earth. We now have nuclear weapons 1,000 times more powerful than the bomb that was dropped at Hiroshima. What if the nations resorted to using those weapons? Thousands of them are possessed by nations in this world. Even without those, what are the "conventional" kinds of weapons that could be used? What destruction would follow? Ten million, thirty-two million would be nothing compared to what man is capable of doing. When the second seal is opened and peace is removed from the earth, there is war and it is literally hell on earth.

Seal 3

The third horse is told to come. The horse is black; the rider carries scales and he uses the scales to measure out the price of food. He is told this: **a quart of wheat for a denarius** (6:6). Let me explain what that means. A quart of wheat was recognized as the amount of wheat that was needed for one person to sustain himself for one day, and a *denarius* was the wage for a common laborer for one day. Put those together. If you have to work one day for a denarius and with that denarius you can buy just enough food for yourself to sustain your life, what does this horse represent? Clearly he represents famine. If you have a family of four, and one of the four is working, how are the other three going to be fed? There will be worldwide famine. Then there's a curious statement about which scholars disagree: **Do not harm the oil and the wine** (6:6). Some think it means that just as poverty and famine always hit the poorest the hardest, the rich will have enough to sustain their higher standard of living. That includes oil and wine because the rich will be able to avoid being touched by this famine. Other scholars believe he's saying there will be no oil and wine—not even the rich will escape. So they don't agree on the interpretation of this verse. We won't start a separate denomination over that one either. It means one of those two things, I am certain, but the point here is famine follows war. Of course it does.

56

Seal 4

That brings us to the fourth horse. This horse is pale, and this time the rider is named. We don't have to figure it out; it's Death with Hades following behind. Death kills the body; Hades kills the soul. We are told that he has authority to use the sword (that's war), famine (we just saw that), pestilence, and wild beasts. As I write this, we're in the middle of a global coronavirus outbreak. All of the efforts that countries made to try to stop this thing from spreading have been in vain. We are too interconnected globally for that to be possible. It's going to spread. It's going to keep on spreading. Thankfully, most of the people who get the coronavirus will recover, but what if this were pestilence from which no one recovered? Some have speculated that it could even be biological warfare, in addition to other kinds of weapons of warfare. Then think about wild beasts. If the earth suddenly becomes a complete war zone, and wild beasts are not able to get their usual food, even those who are normally vegetarians, what will happen? They will get food wherever they can and they will devour as well. We're told that 1/4 of all the people on earth will die.

Now we do not know if this will be distributed evenly around the world or if "civilized" nations (the ones with the most weapons!) will suffer the most because they'll be the ones that will be attacked. But overall on this earth 1/4 of all people will die. You might say, "we are already seeing war, we are seeing famine, we are seeing disease, and we are seeing much death. How do we know when we get into this period of the horseman?" Again, the first horseman (worldwide government) is the signal that we have entered the seven last years on earth. David Jeremiah says: "What we see now of these horrible things is a shadow or foretaste of these darknesses to come."[43] Vernon McGee calls present events the setting of the stage.[44] Remember that Jesus warned of wars and rumors of wars, but that wouldn't yet be the end. When we arrive at Revelation 6 we are at the last seven years.

Summary

What shall we conclude from all of this? *Keith, this is not right; I thought God was loving?* He is loving, He is very loving. He is also holy, and He is just, and He is righteous, and if He does not judge sin, He is not loving because He is allowing sin to go unpunished, and that's not love. This is all part of His love; it all works together.

Have you ever heard someone say this, *Why doesn't God do something about sin and suffering on earth?* He did. He did it two thousand years ago. He is doing something today every time a person comes to Jesus Christ and surrenders his or her whole life. The angels in heaven rejoice because that life has been turned from an eternity of death to an eternity of life with the Lord Jesus Christ, a life that can be transformed from within by the renewing of the mind. And finally at the end of time He will put an end to all sin and suffering on earth.

So here we go, we crossed the great divide in this lesson, didn't we? We will be on this side of the judgment chapters for quite a few lessons, as we work our way through the entire book of The Revelation. Some of it isn't fun to read about but remember Chapters 4 and 5. Remember Who is in heaven, remember Who sits on the throne, and remember that He is worthy of worship, and He is worthy to judge.

ATM (Apply to Me)

1. There are some terrible times coming on earth. We must understand that the world is not going to change because man is going to get better and better and better, and then we're going to become perfect with world peace. It's not going to happen. There are some terrible times coming on earth.

2. Are you ready? If the pre-tribulation view of the rapture is correct, are you ready for that? When all believers are taken out of this world (if that happens before the tribulation), are you sure you'll be taken up? If the rapture doesn't occur until the middle or after the tribulation, are you ready? Are you ready because you know that no matter what happens on earth you have an eternal destiny with the Lord Jesus Christ? If you've never surrendered your life to Him, this isn't fairytale—this is real. These are not the writings of a lunatic; these are writings that God gave to John to give to us so that we can *understand* them. Oh, don't move on to the next lesson if you haven't made that decision to be sure you are ready.

3. The Triune God—Father, Son, Holy Spirit—is worthy of our worship for time and for eternity. When we gather each week for worship, it's a rehearsal. It's worship now, but it's also a rehearsal for eternity. He alone is worthy of our worship.

Postscript

Finally, as we continue this study, we will not be certain of the meaning of every last symbol in The Revelation. Brilliant scholars have studied this book for a very long time, and they do not all agree. Only one can be right, and all the rest must be wrong. So, we don't want to get too dogmatic. But the things that are clear I will teach with confidence. We shall remain humble about the things over which there is disagreement. And we shall never say, *Keith said it, so it has to be this way. Everyone else is a heretic.* No, No. We must all approach this book with humility. Where there is disagreement about the finer points, we must sometimes agree to disagree, and we must affirm together the great truth that Jesus is coming again.

Lesson 7

Read 6:9 – 17

Martyrs in Heaven and Judgment on Earth

When I first preached this message, the world was in the midst of a pandemic. At the time, 1 out of 1,052 people had been infected worldwide. In the United States 1 out of 165 people had been infected. Worldwide 1 out of 18,682 people had died. In the United States 1 out of 2,930 had died. At the opening of the fourth seal, which we studied in our last lesson, Revelation Chapter 6:8 talks about 1 out of 4 people being dead. Now, I do not want to say that the pandemic was nothing or minimize it, because every one of those dead persons represents a soul slipping into eternity, some (perhaps many) without the saving knowledge of Jesus Christ. That is extremely serious, and it should never to be minimized. But I do want to say that what will happen with the opening of Seal 4 when these prophecies are fulfilled is exponentially worse than the coronavirus pandemic.

I think of how quickly our lives changed during the pandemic. Imagine what the world would be like if one out of four people died (Seal 4). Think about that. What it would do to business, to the government, to families? We ask, *How could people possibly want to have one world ruler ruling over them?* Well, some charismatic figure who had already shown himself to be a great political leader and who says, *I have the solution, I will take care of all of you* will be able to do it. Oh, I think people would be very quick to surrender all of their freedoms to that person. And I think this has been a lesson learned during the pandemic. We surrendered our freedoms very quickly.

Before we get to our passage for this lesson, I want to remind you that differences in interpretation for the book of The Revelation are very important. Do we interpret it chronologically? Starting with Chapter 6, is there just one long chronological sequence all the way to the new heaven and the new earth at the end of the book? Or is it a thematic book? We have this theme and that theme, and some of these themes are repeated and some of them overlap, and the book teaches general truths about the second coming of Christ. Or is it a mixture of chronological and thematic? How you answer that question greatly affects your interpretation. Scholars have not agreed for 2,000 years, and that's why we must continue to approach this book with humility.

There is also the question of what is literal and what is symbolic. That will impact some of what we're looking at in this lesson. We know that some of these things are very clearly symbolic. The question really is how much of it is literal. Some people say most of it. Some people say very, very little or none.

It's also very important to keep our eye on the geography. What I mean by that is that there are things John sees in heaven, and there are things John sees on earth. We must pay attention to where he is geographically in order to understand what he is describing. That also will be very important in this lesson.

Seal 5

That brings us to our passage for this lesson. We are continuing to talk about the scroll and the seven seals; this lesson involves Seals 5 and 6. When Seal 5 is opened, John says he saw martyred souls under the altar. Now we should not think that John peeked under the altar and he saw the eyes of these souls peeking back at him. This is symbolic; the altar in heaven represents the one necessary and sufficient sacrifice of the shed blood of Jesus Christ. Those who are under the altar are under the blood of Christ, which means they are forever saved from the judgment of God. And we are told they are there because of the Word of God and because of their testimony. First, they stand on the Word of God. Do you remember the old Sunday school song? *The B-I-B-L-E. I Stand Alone on the Word of God...* They would not deny that the 66 books of the Bible are all God's word. And their testimony: they have surrendered their lives to Jesus Christ. It's the testimony that we ask people to make when they are baptized, putting a flag in the ground and saying, *I belong to Jesus now and for the rest of my life and for all the time and for all of eternity. That is my testimony. He is my Lord and Savior.* They would not deny the Word of God and they would not deny their testimony. Because of those two things they were martyred.

John himself was on the Isle of Patmos in exile. It was a penal work colony for those who had crossed Rome. Back in 1:9 John says, **"I...was on the island called Patmos, because of the word of God and the testimony of Jesus."** For the same things John was exiled; these were martyred, and they cry out to the Lord. In the Greek it is not the normal word for Lord. We say the Lord Jesus Christ, and *Kyrios* is the normal word for Lord: Eternal God—the Lord. But the word they use here when they cry out is *despotes*. You will recognize that we get our word despot from that root word. What they are saying is, *You who are all-powerful in government and in judgment (the despot), the righteous.* We normally think of despot negatively, but this is a righteous despot, all-powerful. The One who has all authority to judge and the One who is holy and true: in other words, a good, righteous despot. And they say, **"How long...will you *refrain* from judging and avenging our [blood as martyrs]?"** 6:10 (my italic). They don't say *Will* *you do it?* They know He will do it. They simply ask how long they will be kept waiting until their blood as martyrs is avenged. And they ask when that judging will fall on those who dwell (present tense) on earth. That probably gives us insight into when these people were martyred. They were martyred right then at that time, because their persecutors are still dwelling on earth. I admit the possibility of them being symbolic of all who have ever dwelt on earth. It certainly is possible that these are martyrs of all time. If that is not true literally, they at least *represent* martyrs of all time. But these specific martyrs seem to be talking about people who dwell on earth *at that time* who have killed them.

Now come with me on a little journey. If one accepts the pre-tribulation rapture view, the Church (all the true believers) are caught up as Paul described in I Thessalonians before the tribulation begins. That means when the tribulation starts there are no believers, and in turn that means that these martyrs must have turned to Jesus Christ during the time of the tribulation. Some people might say that sounds like a second chance. Well, they're still alive; they aren't getting a second chance after death. No such chance exists. But the only conclusion you can reach if you say the Church has all been raptured is that these people came to faith after that event. These people must have opposed the one world government that arises because of the four horsemen of the apocalypse and all of the death. If the Church is still on earth during this time (no rapture yet), then these are people who have walked with the Lord for years or decades and they have said, *I will not change my stance; I stand for the Word of God and I stand for my testimony of Jesus Christ.*

In any event, after being given white robes, which are symbolic of being worthy of a future reward, they are told to rest **for a little while longer** (6:11). And they are told there are more martyrs who are still to come. In other words, things are going to get even worse. There will be more martyrs. What is implied is: don't worry; God will have the last word. It is as certain as the question about when (not if) judgment would fall on the persecutors. God *will* have the last word. That is Seal 5, the martyrs under the altar.

Seal 6

Then Seal 6 is opened. Notice that we are not in heaven now. The geography has changed; we're back here on earth. We are told there is a great earthquake. There is an episode of the original *Star Trek* series where the crew of the Enterprise is exploring a planet, and there is a man there who claims to be a god. This "god" demands their allegiance and their worship. He has great power, power that emanates from a source on the planet such that he is able to apply pressure to the whole Spaceship Enterprise while Captain Kirk and several others are on the planet. If he (the "god") wishes, he could crush the Enterprise completely, and to demonstrate his power he gives them a visual aid of a massive hand holding the Enterprise. He didn't really have a hand that big; it was just a picture that he used to show them what he could do with his power. Unless they relent, he will close his "hand" and crush the Enterprise. They must temporarily relent until they can find a way to destroy his source of power.

Now what if God took His hand (I know God is Spirit, but symbolically) and took the whole earth and shook it? People talk about the Big One that's coming in California. The earthquake here in Chapter 6 would be *the* big one. We're told that the sun became black as sackcloth made of hair, the moon became like blood, and the stars of the sky fell to the earth like a fig tree yielding up its fruit. The sky split apart like a scroll, every island and mountain were moved. A "wow" moment: *the big one!*

Literal or symbolic? The scholars don't agree here. Charles Swindoll describes very graphically what this would mean literally:

> ***An earthquake shakes the entire globe, and volcanic eruptions spew ash and gases into the atmosphere, veiling the sun like a dark, rough burlap cloth. Putrid ash distorts the color of the moon, and the heavens rain down meteorites. When people head for the mountains, they discover that their hiding places have collapsed. When they head for the islands to escape the mass hysteria, they quickly realize the islands have been submerged.***[45]

That would be a literal interpretation of what John is saying he saw when the Seal 6 was opened.

Harry Ironside completely disagrees. He says this is symbolic of the destruction of the current order—political, social, and ecclesiastical order reduced to chaos, the breaking down of all authority, and the breaking up of all established and apparently permanent institutions.[46]

Who is right? How do we know? Is this to be taken literally, a physical earthquake (the real big one), or is this symbolic of an upheaval of all earthly authority? I come down on the literal side, and I believe that the answer is found where Joel (Joel 2:1-2) describes this event:

> **Blow trumpet in Zion and sound an alarm in My holy mountain! Let all the inhabitants of the land tremble, for the day of the Lord is coming; surely it is near, a day of darkness and gloom, a day of clouds and thick darkness. As the dawn is spread over the mountains…. There has never been anything like it, nor will there be again.**

I think what Joel is describing is literal and physical, and I think that tips the scale toward a literal interpretation here in The Revelation. (Again we won't start a separate denomination over it.)

John then identifies seven groups of people who will be affected by this great earthquake; he mentions kings, great men, commanders, rich, strong, slave, and free. You can see that they are symbolic all the way down to the lowly slave in Roman times, but the *emphasis* is on the powerful. It won't matter how much power, or money, or prestige one has; all will be affected by this event. They will seek out places to hide in caves and mountains, and what do they do? They will beg the mountains to hide them **from the presence of Him who sits on the throne, and from the wrath of the Lamb** (6:16). They know this is true judgment.

That's an odd phrase we find: to be hidden from the *wrath* of the *Lamb*. Have you ever been out walking or driving somewhere, or you go to a junkyard or some other business, and you see one of these signs: **"Beware of the Dog"**? Some people have them on their fences at home. But have you ever seen a sign that says, **"Beware of the Lamb"**? We would almost laugh, wouldn't we? But in this case it's true; the Lamb of God who takes away the sin of the world is now the Lamb who is judging the world and all those who rejected Him. Charles Swindoll again says, "The absolute panic experienced by these wicked people doesn't grip them because God is unjust, but because they know He will give them exactly what they deserve."[47] The wrath of the Lamb: beware of the Lamb. Now, wouldn't you think that instead of begging to be hidden **from the presence of Him who sits on the throne, and from the wrath of the Lamb** (6:16), they might seek an alternative? What would that be? It starts with an R: repent. *Who can stand against their wrath?* How about the one who repents? That would be the answer. So why doesn't that happen? David Jeremiah offers an explanation: "Sin so hardens the heart that even when confronted by God, people would rather die than repent and be forgiven."[48]

I think Seal 6, a seal of judgment, is an answer to the question of Seal 5. How long will you refrain from judging those on earth? When the time comes here's the way it will be. The earth is shaken. The greatest mansion isn't going to help you; a cave would be the most valuable piece of land to own.

ATM (Apply to Me)

1. Will I be spared from the wrath of the Lamb? Will you be spared from the wrath of the Lamb? If you have come to a saving knowledge of Jesus Christ, if you have surrendered your life to Him, you do not

have to fear the wrath of the Lamb. If you have put your faith and trust in Jesus Christ as your Lord and Savior, you are forgiven; you can be confident of a future that does not include these judgments. But if you have not, oh I plead with you. Scripture compels me to warn you that the gospel is love and grace and the perfect sacrifice of Jesus Christ, but the gospel is also this: if you reject the one way of salvation, there is judgment. Warren Wiersbe says, "If men and women will not yield to the love of God and be changed by the grace of God, there is no way for them to escape the wrath of God."[49] It's one or the other, the grace of God or the wrath of God.

2. The gradual increase in severity of judgments as we have progressed through these seals shows God's great patience. Even in these last years of the earth itself, God is being patient and He is giving men and women a chance to repent—a final chance.

3. Remember this quote, again from Warren Wiersbe: "We do not worship a babe in a manger or a corpse on a cross. We worship the living, reigning Lamb of God who is in the midst of all in heaven."[50] You and I are on the winning side. We don't have a dead savior—we have a risen Savior who gave His life as the one all sufficient sacrifice for our sins.

4. God is still on the throne of the universe, and the judgment of humanity is completely under His control. He has never been knocked off the throne and He never will be knocked off the throne. He is in control of all of it from start to finish. He is the King of the universe.

5. Finally, for Americans, we are privileged to live in a country where people do not lose their lives for their faith. And I must tell you that is the very, very small minority throughout history. We accept it as the norm because it is where most of us were born and how we grew up. What if that changed? Who would take a stand for their testimony and for the Word of God? We probably won't face martyrdom, but let's determine that no matter what, like the saints of old who did give their lives and the saints in the future who will give their lives for their testimony and for the word of God, we're going to live for Jesus Christ.

Lesson 8

Read 7:1 – 17

144K Plus a Great Multitude

(An Interlude of Mercy)

Keep your eye on the geography again; that is very important in this lesson. John sees some events on earth and some events in heaven, and they are different: two scenes, two different groups of people. In vs. 1-8 there is a scene on earth with 144,000 people. Verses 9-17 are a scene in heaven, and there is a great multitude. The two sections are introduced with **After this...** (7:1) and **After these things...** (7:9). That tells us John sees these two visions successively *after* he saw the events caused by the opening of the first six seals of the scroll.

But how many seals are there on the scroll that the Lamb of God is opening? Seven. So we would expect that this lesson would be the opening of Seal 7. Or not. I found something in my study of this passage that really excited me: all the scholars I read agreed on something! Noting that this isn't Seal 7, they all said this is an interlude. Finding even two scholars to agree on anything in The Revelation is a near miracle! But here they all agree—this is an interlude.

We have had wrath and despair and pain as God's judgments have fallen on the earth. But right here, when things seem to be almost at their worst (certainly the worst so far), there is this wonderful interlude between the opening of Seals 6 and 7. It is an interlude of mercy in the midst of judgment, it is an interlude of hope in the midst of despair, and it is an interlude of glory in the midst of pain.

As I said, there are two groups: a group of people on earth and a group of people in heaven. Let's look at those individually. Let's see who they are, and then let's see what they mean in terms of God's eternal plan for mankind.

144,000 on Earth

For group 1 the scene, as I said at the beginning, is on earth. Four angels are standing north, south, east, and west: that's what four corners of the earth means. (It does not mean that John was a member of the flat earth society!) The angels are holding back the four winds, which are symbolic of the winds of judgment which have been blowing across the earth. Between Seals 6 and 7, during this interlude, the winds of judgment are held back.

Then a fifth angel (some believe it to be Jesus Himself) comes from the east (from the rising of the sun) and he gives a command to the four other angels: **"Do not harm the earth or the sea or the trees, until we have sealed the bond-servants of our God on their foreheads"** (7:3). Why is that important? If we were to skip ahead to Chapter 8, when we read of the trumpet judgments, we would see that the first things harmed are the earth, trees, and the sea. So, before those judgments fall, the winds of judgment in this interlude are temporarily *stopped.* This fifth angel puts up a sign that says *HALT! Road Closed!* Have you ever come across one those when you're driving? Not so much fun, is it, especially when you didn't know about it? But this is a good halt. The road of judgment is temporarily closed for a specific reason.

John is telling us that the bond-servants of God have to be sealed with the seal of the living God. What is the seal? We can't get the scholars to agree on that one, but it is something that is placed on the forehead of these bond-servants of God. That means it is visible; it's not hidden on the back or the bottom of the foot. It is placed right on the forehead, where it can be seen. Now, who are the people who receive this seal of the living God? Verse 4 says they are 144,000 Jews: a specific number and a specific race of people.

Why Jews and why 144,000? To help answer that question, we first need to ask the question of who are they *not.* They are not 144,000 converts to a sect or a cult. You might have heard some teachings from different religious cults or sects who say, *We are the 144,000.* Some of them started that way and then when they grew past 144,000 they had a real problem, and they didn't know what to do. They thought they'd only grow to 144,000 and then the Lord would return. They also have a problem in that this text says very clearly and specifically that these 144,000 are Jews. The religious groups I'm talking about were/are not exclusively Jewish.

They also are not the Church. They are 144,000 specific Jews. And they are not all the Jews on earth. In John's day, as in our own, the number of Jews was/is in the millions. They are a select 144,000. Now before we answer the questions of why them and how they were chosen, we need to answer some interesting questions about their tribal identities. There are 12,000 from each Jewish tribe, and the tribes are listed in this order:

Judah
Reuben
Gad
Asher

Naphtali
Manasseh
Simeon
Levi
Issachar
Zebulun
Joseph
Benjamin

Did you know that in the Old Testament there are 20 lists of the twelve tribes of Israel, and they appear in 18 different orders? That should make you scratch your head, because order is virtually always important in Scripture. Here we have something unique because neither birth order nor geography (where in Canaan the tribes settled) is used. But it should be obvious to every believer in Jesus Christ why Judah is listed first. Who is the central character of the book of The Revelation? It is Jesus; if we miss Him, if all we are concerned about is what country this or that represents today (etc.), then we have missed the main Character of the book: Jesus, who of course is from the tribe of Judah.

You might also notice that there is a missing tribe; Dan is not listed. There has been a great deal of speculation about why there are not 12,000 from the tribe of Dan. Here are some things we know. In the nation of Israel, Dan was the first tribe to fall into idolatry; they were the most susceptible to the temptation to worship idols. If that has continued through the centuries, then there would possibly be no one left from the tribe of Dan. Compromise with the world would ultimately dilute their lineage until no one was left. We also know that when Jacob was giving his final blessings to his 12 sons, he called Dan a serpent. Some have suggested that Antichrist therefore would come from the tribe of Dan, so that is why they are not listed. About these things we can only speculate, but we do see clearly that Dan is not listed.

In most of the lists in the Old Testament Levi is left out. If you know your Old Testament history and theology, you know that was because most of the lists deal with the allotment of the land in Canaan, and the Tribe of Levi was not given any land. Levi, as the priestly tribe, lived in cities in the land of all the other tribes so they could teach others how to live for God, how to obey God, and how to serve God. Since they had no land of their own to grow food, they were to be provided for by the tithes of the other 12 tribes. Of course if each of the other 12 tribes gives 10%, there would be more than enough to provide for the thirteenth tribe (Levi). Here, however, Levi is included in the list and, as we noted, Dan is left out.

Here is the most curious thing in the list. Manasseh is listed, and Joseph is listed. You do not see that anywhere else in Scripture. Why? Let's review our history of Jacob's 12 sons. Joseph was one of the 12, and not just any one, but his favorite son. A symbol of that favoritism was the coat of many colors given to Joseph by his daddy. The story has been immortalized on stage in *Joseph and the Amazing Technicolor Dreamcoat*. Joseph, the favorite son, had two sons, Ephraim and Manasseh. Because Joseph was Jacob's favorite son, Jacob told Joseph that he was giving him a double inheritance, so that there would not be a Tribe of Joseph, but rather there would be the Tribe of Ephraim *and* the Tribe of Manasseh. Each of Joseph's sons was to receive as much as Jacob's 11 other sons. What does that do the number of tribes? It makes the total 13, so if you're going to list *12* tribes of Israel, you can't list Ephraim and Manasseh separately without omitting a tribe.

So, with one tribe omitted (Dan), it should be Manasseh and Ephraim, right? Instead, we see Manasseh and Joseph. Another head scratcher! If Joseph is listed, why list Manasseh separately? And if Manasseh is listed, shouldn't the complement to that be Ephraim?

There is a theory that explains all of this. Follow this closely: Dan was actually on the original list, but over the centuries of manual copying of Scripture, Dan accidentally became Man, an abbreviation for Manasseh, and it eventually was spelled out to become Manasseh. If that be true, then you have the following list, which includes Dan, and then Joseph encompasses both Ephraim and Manasseh:

Judah
Reuben
Gad
Asher
Naphtali
~~*Manasseh*~~ *Dan*
Simeon
Levi
Issachar
Zebulun
Joseph
Benjamin

Note that this has nothing to do with the inerrancy of Scripture. Christians believe that all of the Bible, as given by God, is perfect and without error. The error here would be a copyist's error, not an error in the giving of Scripture. Looking at this theory, we are tempted to say *Wow, this is great; it ties everything into a neat little bow!* We have the Tribe of Dan back, we understand why Joseph is listed—it's the original 12 sons of Jacob—so problem solved. The difficulty with this solution is there is no historical or textual or manuscript evidence whatsoever to support this theory. It's a tidy theory that explains everything, but that's all it is. It is without objective support.

So we are back to where we started. We know why Judah is listed first, we understand reasons Dan might have been left out, but the question of Manasseh and Joseph remains a mystery. I must confess I have no idea, and I am not alone in saying that. Apart from the unsupported theory I have presented, no one has an answer. It is one of those mysteries that will remain unsolved this side of heaven. I have probably devoted more words to this question than I should have, but I did not want to just gloss over this question without discussing it.

There is one more question we must answer, and this is much more significant. How do we know what tribe these people are from? If you know someone who is Jewish, can you ask what tribe he or she is from? If you do, you'll receive an *I don't know* answer. When Assyria overran the northern kingdom of Israel in the eighth century B.C., those records of the 10 tribes were all lost. When Rome sacked Jerusalem in 70 A.D., any remaining records were lost. There are no longer any tribal records, so how would we know? Who knows? God knows! God can trace the lineage of everyone of us all the way back to Noah. He knows exactly which tribe every Jew is from. That is how He can be so specific and say 12,000 from each tribe.

But most importantly is the question of why the 144,000 are sealed. *Why* is more important than *who*. First, they are sealed for protection. The judgments that have been coming on earth will only get worse after this interlude of Chapter 7, and these who are sealed will not be harmed. Can God do that, protect these who are sealed from the winds of judgment? Do you remember Passover in Exodus? The death angel was going through the land of Egypt in judgment to kill the first-born male in every household. But the Jews were told that each household was to kill a lamb and put the blood around the door of the house. God said, *When I see the blood, I will pass over that house. Your first-born will be safe.* It is the same idea here. *When I see the seals on their foreheads, they will be protected.* Sealed for protection.

Second, they are sealed for power. Remember that in v. 3 they were called bond-**servants**. If they are bond-servants, they must have a *service*. The near-unanimous opinion among scholars is that their service during this time on earth is evangelism. They will be heralds to carry the news, specifically (though not exclusively) to their fellow Jews, that Jesus, who is coming again almost immediately, is the Messiah most of the Jews missed when He came the first time. These 144,000 will spread the word that Jesus is the Promised One. Imagine, if you can, 144,000 Billy Grahams or Billy Sundays or D. L. Moodys or John Wesleys or George Whitefields. Imagine

144,000 evangelists like that, empowered by the seal of God, to preach the gospel specifically to Jews, evangelists who understand the Old Testament Scriptures: Isaiah 53, Psalm 22, and all of the prophecies that predicted a suffering Messiah, and then also a risen, glorified, reigning Messiah. Imagine them proclaiming with power throughout the whole earth that Jesus is the long-ago prophesied Messiah of the Jews. What kind of impact would that have on the Jewish people worldwide? We would see what Paul described in the Book of Romans as a great awakening of the Jews, as hundreds of thousands or probably millions turn to Jesus Christ, recognizing Him as their Messiah and Savior. 144,000 Jewish evangelists. Wow, what an impact that would have!

That is scene 1 in this chapter. It is a scene on earth of 144,000. We can't fully understand the list of the tribes, but we understand what God is doing. The winds of judgment are held back, there is an interlude, and the gospel is proclaimed through these evangelists.

A Great Multitude in Heaven

The second scene for John, beginning with v. 9, **after these things I looked...**, (my italic) is a group of people in heaven. How do we know that? These people are described as being before the *throne*. They are a multi-racial group; we are told that they come from every nation and tribe and peoples and tongues. They are uncountable; it's a multitude so massive that no one would attempt to count them.

After their worship is described (which we will discuss momentarily), an elder asks John who they are. John says, *Beats me.* That's my paraphrase, but that is the meaning behind his words **"You know"** (7:14), which is his way of saying *I don't have a clue; why don't you tell me?* He is told they are the ones who have come out of The Great Tribulation. That itself is worthy of discussion: who are they, and who are they not? What has been going on in Chapters 5 and 6? It is the opening of the seals of judgment, and from them has come great death. With the fourth seal alone 1/4 of the world's population died. That would be billions of people, and here are the believers from that group. (We know that they are believers because they stand before the throne and they worship God and Jesus Christ. They are clothed in white robes, a symbol of purity that comes only from the blood of Christ.) The text does *not* say that they are martyrs. (We met some martyrs at the opening of Seal 5.) It simply says they died during The Great Tribulation. If you hold a pre-tribulation view of the rapture, that it comes at the beginning of Chapter 4 and all of the Church is taken up to heaven, you must conclude that these are people who come to faith during the judgments of the first six seals. They died because of the judgments and are now in heaven before the throne. If you believe that the rapture has not taken place yet, then these would be believers living on earth when the tribulation begins plus new believers from the tribulation time; again they have died during the events of Chapters 5 and 6. Those who argue for a pre-tribulation rapture have a strong case here because I Thessalonians 5:9 says that **God has not destined us [believers] for wrath**, and the end of Chapter 6 specifically mentions the *wrath* of the Lamb. (But remember that scholars hold different views about the rapture.)

There is more evidence that they died during the first part of the tribulation period. They are told that they will hunger no more. Think about all the events of Chapters 5 and 6. Don't you think there would be massive *hunger* on earth? Imagine 1/4 of the world's population dead. What would that do to the global food chain? There would be widespread hunger. There would also be widespread thirst, and they are told they will not thirst any more. The geological changes on earth (earthquakes, etc.) would probably lead to intense heat of the sun, and these people are told they won't experience that any longer. There would certainly be many tears, and we're told that God will wipe away their tears. All of that is clear evidence that these are people who died because of the events of the tribulation. The good news for them is in v. 17: **the Lamb in the center of the throne shall be their Shepherd, and shall guide them to springs of the water of life**.

Did you also notice the paradox about their robes (v. 14)? They have washed their robes and made them white in the blood of the Lamb. Have you ever gotten blood on a garment, especially a white one, and then tried to clean it so no evidence of the blood remained? Hard to do, right? But that's physically speaking. Spiritually speaking, the blood of the Lamb is the one and only one thing that makes us pure and gives us the right to wear a white robe, symbolizing forgiveness and purity.

Palm branches are in their hands, which are a sign of victory. When Jesus rode into Jerusalem and people waved palm branches, they were thinking the wrong kind of victory. They were thinking victory over Rome, victory over oppressors. They thought that was why the Messiah was coming. But these here in heaven understand it is victory over sin, victory over death.

What do they cry out? **"Salvation to our God who sits on the throne, and to the Lamb"** (7:10). Does salvation *to* our God mean that God needs to be saved? Of course not. It means that salvation was planned in the mind of God before the foundation of the world. It was all His plan, the coming of His Son Jesus Christ, who died and rose again that we might have eternal life. It was all God; we ascribe salvation to Him and to Him alone. It is not something that mankind invented. Contrast that with every religion of the world that is not based on faith in Jesus Christ. All are manmade, and all are dependent on working hard enough to make yourself good enough to be accepted by God. That is why none of them are worth anything. Salvation comes from God; salvation is by grace through faith in Jesus Christ. Salvation to our God who sits on the throne, and to the Lamb, who made it possible through His death and resurrection.

Then they are joined in worship by elders and angels and four living creatures we met back in Chapter 4. This is yet another way we know this scene is in heaven. They join in the chorus of praise: **"Amen! Blessing and power and glory and wisdom and thanksgiving and honor and power and might be to our God forever and ever. Amen!"** (7:12). Notice that their praise to God is for His attributes. Angels do not praise God for salvation because angels do not have the opportunity for salvation. Fallen angels have only one future: judgment. But by His mercy, God has provided a way of salvation for human beings: salvation to God. The praise of the angels is for God's attributes. They are angels who were there when God spoke worlds and galaxies and the universe into existence.

So, there it is. Two groups: 144,000 Jews on earth and an unnumbered multi-racial multitude in heaven before the throne in this interlude between Seal 6 and Seal 7. An interlude of mercy: what a wonderful and powerful passage of Scripture. In our next lesson we will return to the scroll and Seal 7.

ATM (Apply to Me)

1. I must cry out with the angels and the elders and the four living creatures, **Blessing and power and glory and wisdom and thanksgiving and honor and power and might be to our God forever and ever** (7:12). If I have not learned the worship of God, my Christian life is sorely lacking. I must be a person who delights to come before Him in worship and give Him glory for all that He is and for all that He has done.

2. Let's not wait for the 144,000 for there to be evangelism. We can do that right now. We might not have a seal on our foreheads, but we have the seal and the power of the Holy Spirit living in us. Let's not be timid. We have the greatest news ever. We know the one and only one way to salvation. Let's use our knowledge and our brains and our tongues to share the gospel with everyone we can.

3. In this interlude we see that God's wrath is not without mercy. When God judged the earth with a flood, there was mercy for Noah and for his family. When God judged Sodom and Gomorrah, there was mercy for Lot and for his family. When God judged Jericho, there was

mercy for Rahab and for her family. And here, where God is judging the whole earth, there is mercy. God's arms are always open to the end. He is not willing that any should perish, but that all should come to repentance.

4. Salvation is all God's work. Do we fully grasp that? Do we ever think, "Jesus died for my sins, and I have accepted Him, and now I have to earn my way into heaven? Jesus' death was only enough for me to be 95% or 98% or 99% forgiven, and the other 1 or 2 or 5% I have to earn myself?" That is a heresy from the pit of hell; do you understand that? It is all God's work, and when we are saved, we are saved *completely*—100%. Salvation is a complete work of God. When we pass from this earth, we do not have to pay for sins in purgatory: Jesus paid it *all*. It is all God's work, it is a perfect work, and it is complete. If you have never surrendered your life to Jesus Christ, do it today. It is a free gift, the greatest gift, the greatest news ever: surrender to Him.

Lesson 9

Read 8:1 – 13

The Drama of Music: Silence and Trumpets

Will you take a trip back we me in time to July 2, 1776? Representatives of the 13 U.S. colonies were preparing to vote on the Lee Resolution; it simply stated that the 13 colonies were now independent from the rule of Great Britain. Each colony was to have one vote. There had been a test vote the previous day, and there was a problem. The 3-member delegation from Delaware was missing one of their delegates, and they were deadlocked with one vote for independence and one vote against. From Pennsylvania two of their five delegates were for independence, but the other three were not. South Carolina was reluctant to vote in favor of independence if the vote was not unanimous.

But then something amazing happened between July 1 and July 2. One of the unsung heroes of the American Revolution is Cesar Rodney from Delaware. He was ill with cancer that would ultimately take his life. He had been present for some of the debate, but he had returned home because he was in such poor health. So, he was not there for the test vote. But Cesar Rodney, a profile in courage, rode all night on his horse to be there on July 2 to break the tie for the colony of Delaware, so the vote would be 2 to 1 in favor of independence. Two patriots from Pennsylvania, John Dickinson and Robert Morris, were persuaded that the unity of the colonies was more important than their personal opinions against independence, and they agreed to stay away from the Pennsylvania State House that day, so that the Pennsylvania vote would be 2 to 1 in favor of independence instead of 2 to 3 against. Then the South Carolina delegation, confident that the vote would be unanimous, changed their vote and said they also would vote in favor of independence.

So, the stage was set on July 2, and—one colony at a time—the role was called. (New York abstained because they did not yet have instructions from back home, but a week later they would change their vote to affirmative.) As the role was called, one by one the colonies cast their votes for independence. *Aye, aye, aye*.... As the last *aye* vote echoed through the Pennsylvania State House, a building that today we know as Independence Hall, historians tell us that there was silence in the hall; no one spoke a word as the gravity of what they had just done fell upon them.

Why silence? They looked forward through the corridor of time, and they could see 13 colonies still bitterly divided over the issue of slavery. (It would take more than 100 years and the loss of over a half million lives until we finally got rid of the evil of slavery.) Beyond that there were immediate concerns. There was an army that was ill-equipped against the much better trained British army. There was a need to put together a form of government; that would be established in the Articles of Confederation. Those articles would only last 11 years until they were replaced by the constitutional republic that we have today. War was certain to bring about destruction in many places and, even if there was victory, there would be a massive amount of rebuilding needed. A fledgling economy was on shaky ground. And those were all the things they had to look forward to if they *won*. If they lost, they would all be rounded up and hanged as traitors against the Crown. Yet, in spite of all that, John Adams, second president of the United States, who was a major advocate for independence, wrote to his wife some very famous words following the vote:

The Second Day of July 1776, will be the most memorable epoch in the history of America. I am apt to believe that it will be celebrated by succeeding generations, as the great anniversary festival. It ought to be commemorated as the day of deliverance by solemn acts of devotion to God Almighty. It ought to be solemnized with pomp and parade, with shows, games, sports, guns, bells, bonfires and illuminations from one end of this continent to the other from this time forward forever more.[51]

John Adams had most of it right, because that is indeed how we celebrate Independence Day. He just had the date wrong. He was counting on the celebration day to be the day the colonies voted to be independent. The actual Declaration of Independence was still in draft form, and the final document was not ready for a vote until two days later on July 4. That document says:

4 July, 1776 In Congress

When in the course of human events, etc., etc.,…life, liberty, and the pursuit of happiness, etc., etc.,…we mutually pledge to each other our lives, our fortunes, and our sacred honor.[52]

So July 4 became the day we celebrate. But it was on July 2 that the key vote took place, and when it was over, there was *silence* in the Pennsylvania State House.

As we come to Chapter 8 of The Revelation and the opening of Seal 7, we are told in v. 1: **"When He broke the seventh seal, there was *silence* in heaven for about half an hour."** We know that there is no time in eternity, but apparently in John's great vision of the future, time was something that he could still measure. Just as in the Pennsylvania State House, he says there was silence in heaven—dramatic silence.

Now this is stunning. Have you been paying attention as we have worked our way through the first seven chapters and the visions of heaven? Whenever we have had a vision of heaven, there has been worship from everywhere: 24 elders, 4 living creatures, uncounted multitudes of angels singing the praise of the triune God, ascribing salvation to Jesus the King, worshiping the Creator of the universe. And in stark contrast to that there is silence for 30 minutes, just like in the Pennsylvania State House. *It is a solemn silence, a silence of awe, expectancy, and foreboding.*

I have titled this lesson *The Drama of Music: Silence and Trumpets.* Great music is made up of sound we call notes and silence we call rests. The contrast between those two things is the same kind of contrast that we see here because we have silence for half an hour, and then we have seven angels who are given seven trumpets in v. 2. But between the silence and the sounding of the trumpets, we first see another angel. This would be an eighth angel (v. 3), and he has a censor. It is described as a *golden* censor—gold representing how precious it is. We are told that incense (a censor is used to burn incense) from the censor was added to the prayers of the saints. (Remember that in Scripture saints always means believers: anyone who is a believer in Jesus Christ is a saint.) As the incense from that golden, precious censor makes its way to the heart of God, it is mixed with the prayers of believers. What a wonderful promise. Leon Morris says:

> *Prayer is not the lonely venture it so often feels; there is heavenly assistance, and our prayers do reach God. The prayers of God's people play a necessary part in ushering in the judgments of God.*[53]

We are told that, mingled together, the prayers and the incense ascend to God. What prayers? Many scholars tell us these are the prayers of the saints we saw under the altar when the fifth seal was opened, those who had been martyred for the Word of God and for their testimony. They asked God how long it would be until He avenged their deaths. I certainly believe that is part of the prayers that are being talked about here, but I believe there is more to it. I believe that every person who has prayed over the last 2,000 years, **"Thy Kingdom come, Thy will be done on earth as it is in heaven"** (Matthew 6:10), those prayers are included here. Additionally, I believe that every person who has ever prayed *O, come Lord Jesus*, has those prayers included here, as we pray for the consummation of all of creation and all that God has planned. Thomas Torrance says:

More potent, more powerful than all the dark and mighty powers let loose in the world, more powerful than anything else, is the power of prayer set ablaze by the fire of God and cast upon the earth.[54]

So these prayers ascend to God.

Then we are told that the *golden* censor is filled with fire from the *golden* (there's that word again) altar and thrown to earth. What does the altar in heaven represent? It represents the shed blood of Jesus Christ, the one perfect, necessary, and sufficient sacrifice to pay the penalty for all my sin, for all your sin—one sacrifice for all time. From that golden altar, representing that perfect sacrifice, the golden censor is filled with fire. Why fire? Because individuals have a choice. They can accept the perfect sacrifice of Jesus Christ and His blood, or they can reject that sacrifice and pay the penalty themselves for their own sin. This fire represents the fire of judgment from the golden altar, and it is thrown down to earth. There is thunder and lightening and an earthquake, which shows us that severe judgments are coming.

Now just before we get to the sounding of the trumpets, I want to mention that there are different interpretations about the seals, the trumpets, and the bowls (seven of each). Some people will tell us that the seals, the trumpets, and the bowls are the same judgments; they are simply looked at from different perspectives, describing *one* series of seven judgments. Therefore, when looked at from different perspectives, we get different descriptions. I think it's important to look at that theory and see if it lines up with what the Scripture tells. We will look at the seals and the trumpets side by side.

<u>Seals</u>	<u>Trumpets</u>
1. White horse: conquering	1. Hail, fire, blood
2. Red horse: war	2. Seas turned to blood
3. Black horse: famine	3. Rivers contaminated
4. Pale horse: death	4. Sun, moon, stars are affected
5. Souls under the altar	5. Stinging locusts
6. Great earthquake	6. Army of 200,000,000 with smoke, fire, brimstone
7. Silence, then 7 trumpets	7. Christ's Kingdom

Comparing these lists, I must reject the interpretation that these are simply different viewpoints of the same thing. I know there are sincere scholars who believe that theory, but I don't believe it is consistent with the text of Scripture. What I believe is accurate would be a diagram like this:

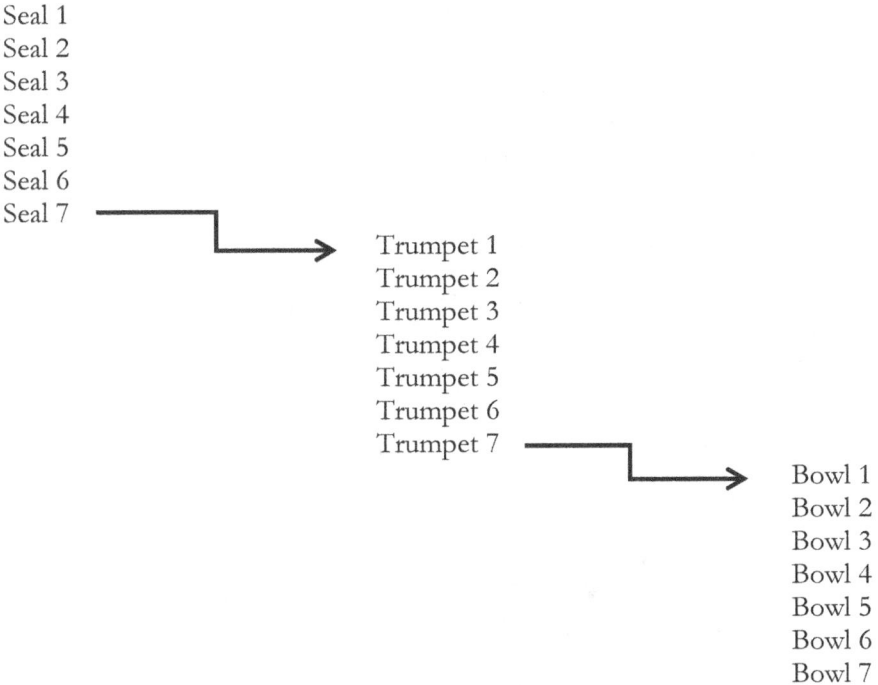

Seal 1
Seal 2
Seal 3
Seal 4
Seal 5
Seal 6
Seal 7

Trumpet 1
Trumpet 2
Trumpet 3
Trumpet 4
Trumpet 5
Trumpet 6
Trumpet 7

Bowl 1
Bowl 2
Bowl 3
Bowl 4
Bowl 5
Bowl 6
Bowl 7

The 7 trumpets come *out of* the seventh seal, and the 7 bowls come *out of* the seventh trumpet. The bowls are the final judgments of God. I believe this interpretation, with increasingly severe judgments, fits the text. That means the 7 seals, trumpets, and bowls are not *concurrent*, but rather are *consecutive*: first the seals, then the trumpets, then the bowls.

The trumpets themselves are literally war horns—the sound that was used to prepare for battle. In this lesson we will look at Trumpets 1 through 4. They are much more severe than what we saw in Seals 1 through 6 (remember that the seventh seal *is* the 7 trumpets). Do you remember that when we first saw the scroll, it was written on both sides? Now that it has been opened, it can be read on the inside *and* the outside. We also said that it represents the title deed to the planet Earth, and only the Lamb of God who takes away the sin of the world has the right to open that title deed. Since it is now open completely, it means that the judgments will fall with ever increasing severity, which is what is written on the scroll.

We are also told that the angels prepared to *sound* the trumpets. I love this. These seven angels raise their trumpets, and they look to the Composer and Conductor of the universe, the Lord Jesus Christ Himself, and they wait for their cues to sound their trumpets one at a time.

Trumpet 1

The first trumpet sounds, and there is hail, fire, and blood. Now, we know what hail is. Have you ever been caught in a hailstorm? You've been out in your car with golf ball size hail falling? You're thinking, *Oh, that's going to be an insurance claim!* Maybe you've had hail damage to the roof of your house. You know how dangerous hail can be. But we don't know about hail like this. The Lord spoke to Job (Job 38:22-23):

"Have you entered the storehouses of the snow, or have you seen the storehouses of the *hail,* which I have reserved for the time of distress, for the day of war and battle?"

This is hail like we have never seen on earth. It has been stored up for the day of distress.

We're also told there is fire. That probably means lightning. We know how lightning can cause fire when it strikes objects on earth. But maybe fire means fire! Why do I say that? Because a third of the trees and a third of the grass are burned up (all the grass means all the grass in 1/3 of the Earth). And then blood? Yes, that's what the Word of God says will happen: hail and fire and blood are *thrown* to earth. This is clearly a supernatural storm from the hand of God. The most severe thunderstorm you have ever seen is small stuff compared to this. This is God responding to Trumpet 1 and sending a supernatural storm to Earth that even includes blood.

Trumpet 2

The second angel sounds, and John describes something *like* a great mountain. He doesn't say it *was* a great mountain; the text says *as it were.* That is an idiom for *I don't know what it was, but my description is that it was something that looked like a great mountain. It was something I've never seen before.* It looked to John like a great mountain, and it was thrown into the sea. A third of the sea life died, and a third of the ships were destroyed. Can you imagine what this would do to the oceans if a third of the sea life were to die and a third of the tens of thousands of registered ocean-going ships were to sink? What kind of cargo might they be carrying? Some of them will be oil tankers, no doubt. Imagine the pollution from dead fish and wrecked ships. The seas would be a mess.

I want to interject something here. Do you remember that between Seal 6 and Seal 7 there was an interlude of mercy? (We saw that in our last lesson.) Do you remember that four angels who stood at the four corners of the Earth (i.e., the four directions: north, south, east, west) were told to temporarily withhold the winds of judgment? They did, and 144,000 Jewish servants were marked with the seal of God. They were told not to harm—notice this—earth and seas and trees. They obeyed that command while 144,000 were sealed. But now in this chapter the winds of judgment are no longer being withheld. When we come to the trumpet judgments, what are the first things that are harmed? The earth, the seas, and the trees. *The interlude is over.*

Trumpet 3

A great star falls from heaven; it is probably a meteor/meteorite. The rivers and streams are affected. The star is called wormwood, meaning bitter. Many people die. There are many types of wormwood, and none of them are known to be poisonous. So, do they die from some type of wormwood we don't know about that is poisonous? Possibly. More likely they die from thirst because the water is so bitter they can't drink it. Drinking it only made people thirstier. If you're ever stranded at sea and you're thirsty, don't drink the sea water. It will only make you thirstier. I'm reminded of Exodus 15:22-23:

> **Moses led Israel from the Red Sea, and they went out into the wilderness of Shur; and they went three days in the wilderness and found not water. And when they came to Marah, they could not drink the waters of March, for they were bitter; therefore it was named Marah [meaning bitter].**

So, we've seen destruction of the earth, the trees, the grass, and the seas, and the fresh water.

Trumpet 4

The judgment is on the sun, the moon, and the stars. John talks again about 1/3, and it is not entirely clear what he means. Scholars disagree. Does he mean that 1/3 of each failed, i.e. the sun, moon, and stars became 1/3 less bright and powerful? Or does it mean that 1/3 of the time there was no light all? A certain conclusion is difficult. Here is what we know without question: the Earth depends on the sun to support all its life systems and, as this judgment falls on sun, moon, and stars, we have reached a point where there will be complete chaos on Earth. Jesus talked about this particular trumpet, saying,

"There will be signs in sun and moon and stars, and upon the earth dismay among the nations, in perplexity at the roaring of the sea and the waves, men fainting from fear and the expectation of the things which are coming upon the world; for the powers of the heavens will be shaken" (Luke 21:25-26).

Summary

To summarize these first four trumpets, the entire ecosystem will be affected. Things will be in complete disarray. From storms and from everything else, the air of the atmosphere will be difficult to breathe. Food and water supplies will be greatly affected and living conditions on Earth will be drastically changed. The changes brought on by the coronavirus pandemic that we are experiencing as I write these words are nowhere near the drastic changes that the trumpets will bring. Charles Swindoll describes it this way:

Places in the area hit hardest by these plagues will have already lost power and deteriorated into desperation and despair. Add natural darkness to this situation, and the result would be anarchy and chaos. Rioting, looting, and crime would exacerbate the horrors experienced around the globe. The judgments described in Revelation 8 will be so dreadful that no amount of government aid, relief efforts, or advanced preparation will be able to bring recovery.[55]

Did you notice that even as these judgments have gotten more severe, there was an overall emphasis on 1/3? Why not just get it over with all at once? Why 1/3? Why this gradual progression? Because God is always merciful, waiting and wanting people to come to repentance. During this time, those who survive who don't know the Lord Jesus Christ will still have the opportunity to be saved. 1/3 is billions of people, but 2/3 is still a huge number. People will yet have the opportunity, if they will listen to the voice of God—to turn to Him.

One More Verse

What about v. 13? An eagle (some translations say angel, but the best scholarship tells us the word means eagle) is flying in heaven. Before we discuss what the eagle says, let me ask you if you have ever been in the following situation. *I was discouraged about many things. People said, "Cheer up, things could be worse." So I cheered up, and sure enough, things got worse!* That is the situation here. This eagle cries out, **"Woe, woe, woe [3 woes] to those who dwell on the earth, because of the remaining blasts of the trumpet of the three angels who are about to sound"** (8:13). One woe for each trumpet. The phrase **those who dwell on the earth** (the inhabitants of the

82

earth in some translations) is used 11 times in Revelation, and it describes generally not those who are living on the planet, but it means those who have rejected God, who have gone their own way, who have bought in to the world's system, who have been conformed to culture, whose pursuit has been riches and fame: the inhabitants of the earth. In other words, the eagle is telling us that *the worst is yet to come.*

ATM (Apply to Me)

1. Even in these harsher judgments (which, be warned, will get even worse), there is still restraint: 1/3, 1/3, 1/3, 1/3. God is merciful, even in judgments.

2. In The Revelation we see God having the last word: His plan for time and eternity will be accomplished. There *will* be justice. There *will* be judgments.

3. If you don't know Christ personally, don't wait any longer. Surrender your life to Him; accept His provision for sin; make Him your Lord and Savior. Do *not* delay any longer.

4. Some of you reading this might be thinking, *Can't you just teach about nice stuff like love, etc?* These judgments are offensive. Hear the words of David Jeremiah: "If we are offended by the terrible things to come upon the earth, think how much man's sin is an offense to a holy God."[56] Think about that. *God judges sin.*

In these judgments, before which there is silence in heaven, the music of the trumpets tells us that God will have the last word. And, believers in Jesus Christ, thank Him for His mercy because you have a glorious future ahead, not dreadful punishment.

Lesson 10

Read 8:13 – 9:21

Woe!

The last verse we read in our last lesson is the first verse we read in this lesson, and that is about an eagle flying in heaven. He says, **"Woe! Woe! Woe because of Trumpets 5 through 7, which are about to sound"** (8:13). Trumpet 5 is a woe, Trumpet 6 is a woe, and Trumpet 7 is a woe. We will look at the first two of those in this lesson.

Trumpet 5

When Trumpet 5 sounds, we will find that we can divide this portion of the passage into 4 S's. The first S is **S**atan, the second S is **s**moke from the pit, the third S is **s**corpion locusts, and the fourth S is a **s**overeign (or a king) over those locusts. We'll examine those one at a time.

First, in v. 1, we are given a description of Satan himself. When the fifth angel sounded, we read about **a star that had fallen from heaven...** (9:1). Hmm, I thought you said this was about Satan. We find out in the next verse that a key was given to *him*, so now we know that the star is an individual. We are told that he *had fallen* to earth. Some translations read *fell to earth* but, correctly understood in the Greek, the correct reading is he *had fallen to earth*. Now we need to discuss some "angel-ology," so stay with me as we explore the Old Testament background. In Isaiah 14:12-14 we read these words:

> **How you have fallen from heaven, O Star of the Morning, Son of the Dawn. You have been cut down to the earth, you who have weakened the nations! But you said in your heart, "I will ascend to heaven; I will raise my throne above the stars of God, And I will sit on the mount of assembly In the recesses of the north. I will ascend above the heights of the clouds; I will make myself like the Most High."**

Scholars are nearly unanimous in their opinion that this is a passage that refers to a previously perfect angel named Lucifer, and all of those I's are things that Lucifer said he would do:

"I will ascend to heaven."
"I will raise my throne..."
"I will sit on the mount..."

"I will ascend above the heights…"
"I will make myself like the Most High."

How do you think that will work out? How many Gods are there in the universe? There is one, and when Lucifer said, "I will make myself like the Most High," and he gathered his legions around him, they were all cast out of heaven. So they all *had fallen* from heaven, and they *had fallen* to the earth. What happens next in Chapter 8? We mentioned this, but here I want to emphasize the first word. A *key* was given to him, and he opens—so that he can unleash the forces that are there—the bottomless pit, most correctly translated as the abyss. Where and what is the abyss, and why is it locked so that it needs a key? Those are good questions to ask, and we need some more angel-ology. In Jude 6, we are told this: **Angels who did not keep their own domain, but abandoned their proper abode, He has kept in eternal bonds under darkness for the judgment of the great day.**

A particular group of fallen angels has been kept in prison in the abyss because of what they did. Jude does not tell us what these angels did when they "abandoned their proper abode"—that's another study for another day—but unlike other fallen angels who are active on Earth, and who have been active on Earth for a very long time (fallen angels active as demons), these particular angels did not have that opportunity. When they sinned this great sin and abandoned their proper abode, God kept them in eternal bonds under darkness. They were kept in the *abyss*. Again, this is not *all* fallen angels; this is one group of fallen angels.

What more do we know about the abyss? We need to go to Luke's Gospel (8:28-31).

Seeing Jesus, he [a demon possessed man] cried out and fell before Him, and said in a loud voice, "What do I have to do with You, Jesus, Son of the Most High God? I beg You, do not torment me." For He had been commanding the unclean spirit to come out of the man. For it had seized him many times; and he was bound with chains and shackles and kept under guard; and yet he would burst his fetters and be driven by the demon into the desert. And Jesus asked him, "What is your name?" And he said, "Legion"; for many demons had entered him. And they were entreating Him not to command them to depart into the abyss.

There's that word again. Jesus had the authority to condemn demons to chains in the abyss, where one group of fallen angels was being kept prisoner. And they begged Him not to do that. They knew they wouldn't be allowed to possess this man any more, but they still wanted to be free to roam the earth and cause trouble. So that is what the *key* is about, and that is what the *abyss* is about.

In v. 2 (the <u>second S</u>) we have smoke from the pit (the abyss). We are told it is like a great furnace. Many of us have furnaces in our homes, and they're very sanitized, sterilized, sealed units. We can walk right up to them and they won't hurt us. In fact, I can even change the filter while my furnace is running, and it's completely safe. We don't experience a great FURNACE: big, open furnace. The smoke, John says, is like coming from a great furnace. It is so massive that there is huge pollution on the Earth so that the sun and air are darkened because of the smoke that comes from the abyss.

So that is Satan (first S) who is given the key to the abyss and smoke from the abyss (second S). The major portion of Trumpet 5 is the scorpion locusts (<u>third S</u>) in vs. 3-10. They come from the smoke, so as this smoke comes out of the abyss, within that smoke is this army of locusts with scorpion-like power.

Now these are not ordinary locusts. What do regular locusts eat? They eat crops. A swarm of locusts can devastate an entire field of crops in a matter of a few minutes. They are the dread of farmers because, if a swarm like that shows up, there is nothing a farmer can do but watch his or her crop be devastated. But these are not ordinary locusts. How do we know that? They are told *not* to hurt grass or green things or trees, which are the normal things that locusts would eat. Instead, they are given power to hurt—not kill—certain people. They do not have the power to kill; they have the power to hurt—to torture, but not to kill. And only certain people. They cannot touch those who are sealed with the seal of God on their foreheads.

Now who are the ones with the seal of God on their foreheads? They are at least the 144,000 who were sealed back in that interlude between Seal 6 and Seal 7 on the scroll. But I believe they are more than those 144,000, because we said that the service these 144,000 Jews would render to Jesus Christ is proclaiming the truth that Jesus is the Messiah the Jews have been searching for. I believe that anyone who would come and believe in Jesus Christ because of the witness of the 144,000 would receive the same seal. Now the passage does not say that, but I believe that is a good inference. If that be true, that means torture by these locusts is only the experience of unbelievers.

The locusts are allowed to torment for five months. Now some people are into numerology. They see a number in the Bible, and all of a sudden they want to build an entire theological system around it. Let's not do that,

Understanding the Revelation

OK? The normal life span of a locust is five months, so there you go—it's that simple. Let's not read anything into it beyond that.

Their sting is like the sting of a scorpion. It does not kill, but I am told that a scorpion sting is the most painful sting one could ever experience. It is nothing like a bee or wasp or hornet sting. It is incredibly painful. These stings are so painful, we are told people will seek death. They want to die because they are in so much pain. But they can't die. Now notice in vs. 7-10 the appearance of these scorpions:

The appearance of the locusts was like horses prepared for battle; and on their heads, as it were, crowns like gold, and their faces were like the faces of men. And they had hair like the hair of women, and their teeth were like the teeth of lions. And they had breastplates like breastplates of iron; and the sound of their wings was like the sound of chariots, of many horses rushing to battle. And they have tails like scorpions, and stings.

Did you notice the repeated use of the word *like* and at one point the phrase *as it were?* We said that means *something like this, but I don't know exactly how to describe it.* John doesn't know what words to use. He sees these locusts with their scorpion stings, and he gives all this imagery, and keeps using the word *like, like, like, like, like,* because he doesn't have the words to describe them. They are unlike any insect, anything he has ever seen in his entire life. So, I must conclude that this is a demonic army of locusts that is sent forth to harm—not to kill—but to harm, to torture.

Lastly (the <u>fourth S</u>) we have the sovereign or the king over the locusts. He is called in two different languages Abaddon and Apollyon. Both of those words mean destruction. I must conclude that the king over them is Satan himself. Now you say, "Well, Satan wasn't bound in the abyss." No, and it doesn't say that he came out of the abyss. We're told that he was given a key *to open* the abyss. The locusts come out of the abyss, and their king, Satan, is waiting.

In concluding this section of the passage, it is important also to note the limitations:

1. The key was *given* to him; he did not have a key to the abyss himself. He had to be *given* the key.

2. The locusts were limited. Power was *given* to them. They were not allowed to harm crops. There were certain people they were not allowed to harm. They were not allowed to kill.

3. They had five months—that's a long time to be tortured—but it was a finite time: five months.

What is the point? God limits the length and the depth of this torture. God is omnipotent, and Satan is not omnipotent. Can and does God use the forces of evil in judgment on the people who have not repented of their sin? Clearly, He does that right here, but there is a limit on what Satan and his army of scorpion locusts can do. But be warned, demons are real, they are dangerous, they are organized, and they are destructive. We must always be on guard against demon activity in our world. It is very real, but God is always the One sitting on the throne.

Before Trumpet 6 sounds, John tells us this: **The first woe is past; behold, two woes are still coming after these things** (9:12). Oh, goody. Wow! That was just the first of three woes: five months of scorpion locust torture.

Trumpet 6

Trumpet 6 sounds, and this time we have four C's: a **c**ommand, a **c**hronology, a **c**ount, and a **c**alamity. We'll look at those one at a time.

First, the command. There was a voice from the four horns of the *golden* altar. Gold represents how precious the altar is. Gold is the most valuable substance on Earth, and a symbol of the preciousness and value and significance of this altar in heaven. In heaven it represents Christ's perfect and finished work on Earth when He shed His blood to pay the price for all of our sins on the cross. The golden altar symbolizes the shed blood of Christ. If you study the book of Exodus, you will see that Moses was instructed to build two altars, and they both had four horns: projections at the four corners of the altar. So when we're told that this voice comes from the four horns of the altar, remember this. The four horns surround the entire altar. It means that all that Christ is, all His finished work surrounds this voice command. It is a command that says the arms of Jesus Christ are wide open to all who will come to Him in repentance. But to those who reject Him, *all* of Christ's authority and power is given in judgment. This voice is from the four horns of the altar. The command in that voice is to release the four angels who were *bound* at the great river Euphrates. These must again be demonic, fallen angels, because God's angels are not bound. They do His will; they are ministering servants. But these four are bound. And where are they bound? They are bound at the great river Euphrates, long recognized as the division between East and West in Eurasia. Vernon McGee says this:

> *The Garden of Eden was somewhere in this section. The sin of man began here. The first murder was committed here. The first war was fought here. He was where the Flood began and spread over the earth. Here is where the Tower of Babel was erected. To this area were brought the Israelites of the Babylonian captivity.*

Babylon was the fountainhead of idolatry. And 'tis the final surge of sin on the earth during the Great Tribulation period.[57]

They are *bound* at the River Euphrates. A couple chapters later we will discuss the drying up of the River Euphrates. For right now it is enough to know the general geography.

Some have speculated that these four angels are perhaps demonic princes of four powerful nations from which a great army will arise. We're not certain, but if we go back to the Book of Daniel, we read in Chapter 10 that Daniel was praying for understanding of a vision, and an angel was dispatched to meet with him and explain the vision. Here is a paraphrase of what the angel says, *I was dispatched the day you started praying, but I have been fighting against the Prince of Persia, and I had to fight with him until Michael the Archangel came and helped me. Then I overcame him, and then I was able to come to you.* That angel also describes the Prince of Greece. In angel-ology The Prince of Persia and the Prince of Greece are demons who influence governments for evil. I believe that every government that has ever existed on earth has one of those—demons who specifically try to influence the leaders of that nation for evil. Perhaps that's who these four angels who had been bound are, and now they are released. So perhaps four powerful nations will join together to form this army. That's the command.

The chronology (<u>second C</u>) is that they have been prepared for the hour, the day, the month, and the year. Right down to the very hour, God's eternal plan will be worked out. God knows the exact hour when all of this will take place. It will not happen one minute too soon; it will not happen one minute too late. It will happen exactly when God has planned it to happen, and that hour is known only to Him. But it is certain—it has been determined from the foundation of the world—because once again, God is the Sovereign who sits on the throne.

Next is the count (<u>third C</u>). We are told that there is an army of 200,000,000. It literally says twice 10,000 x 10,000. Do the math: 10,000 x 10,000 is 100,000,000, and twice that is 200,000,000. Is this a literal number? Notice what John says: **"I *heard* the number"** (9:16). He didn't guess, he didn't try to count. And if John heard the number, that means it's a literal number. In other places he says things like countless multitudes. He doesn't try to count them, and he is not given a number. Here he is a given a number—200,000,000—and it is the largest number in the whole Bible. To get an idea of the size of this army, it is almost double the combined Allied and Axis armies of World War II. That includes the United States and all of our allies, as well as all of the armies that joined with Hitler: Germany, Japan, and Italy. This is almost double that number.

Then comes the calamity (fourth C). This army of 200,000,000 had colors of fire, which would be red; hyacinth, which would be blue; and brimstone, which would be yellow. Did all the riders wear all three colors, or was it one color per rider, given how each horse could inflict suffering and death? We can't say for certain, but we know that the colors symbolize fire, smoke, and brimstone. However, notice that the primary focus is not on the *riders*, but rather on the *horses*. If we look in vs. 17 and 19, we'll see this:

The heads of the horses are like the heads of lions; and out of their mouths proceed fire and smoke and brimstone. For the power of the horses is in their mouths and in their tails, for their tails are like serpents and have heads; and with them they do harm.

All we're told about the riders is what they wore. We are told that the horses are the ones to watch out for. What is John talking about? I don't think Citation and Secretariat would be very war-like horses with fire and brimstone able to destroy. Many scholars have speculated that this is a description of modern weapons or tools of warfare, and that's certainly possible. It is a very plausible theory. John had never seen a rifle, a machine gun, or even a handgun. He had never seen a Humvee, a tank, or a jeep. He had never seen an F15 fighter jet, a stealth bomber, a drone, a missile, a rocket launcher, or a nuclear weapon. The weapons of war that John knew about were horses and chariots, so that would be his frame of reference to describe any weapon of warfare. It is certain that in John's day there was no Greek word for stealth bomber! Therefore, many scholars have speculated that he is doing his best in first century Greek to describe 21st or 22nd or 23rd century (whatever century it is) weapons of warfare. Others have speculated that this is a description of another demonic army, and that is another possible explanation. Scholars seem to be equally divided on this point. I lean toward the conclusion that John is trying to describe modern weapons of warfare, and this is an army of people. But regardless of what it is, notice that though the locusts *tortured*, this army *kills*. Previously when Seal 4 was opened, a fourth of mankind was killed. Now 1/3 of what is left is killed, and that means that half of the world's population is now dead. The current population of the world is 7.8 billion people, so if these events were to happen now, we are talking about 3.9 billion people dead. Charles Swindoll says:

Tragic images fill our minds as we try to imagine the chaos, confusion, grief, and overwhelming shock that will sweep the globe at that time. What humans have experienced in natural disasters, military strikes, and terrorist attacks will be completely forgotten in light of these unparalleled events.[58]

The last two verses tell us about the rest of mankind. Again, Charles Swindoll states: "What will happen to those who live through it? How will they respond? Surely they will turn to their righteous Redeemer in repentance for their wickedness…right?"[59] The opposite. John tells us that they did *not* repent from worshiping demons and idols. They are described as idols of gold and silver and brass and stone and wood, which can neither see nor walk. Warren Wiersbe says, "Here are dead sinners worshiping dead gods."[60] They do not repent of their murders or their sorceries. The Greek word is *pharmakia*, and it literally means drugs. These are drugs used to deaden the emotional pain. We would guess heroin, cocaine, and the like—hard drugs. Immorality of all kinds—and theft. I want you to notice the commandments that are violated here:

Commandments 1 & 2: You shall have no other gods before Me; you shall not make an idol.

Commandment 6: You shall not murder.

Commandment 7: You shall not commit adultery.

Commandments 8 and 10: You shall not steal; you shall not covet. (Coveting comes before stealing.)

Six out of ten! They won't repent of any of them. Every now and then I like to see what Eugene Peterson has to say in his very free paraphrase of Scripture called *The Message*. He says it this way:

The remaining men and women who weren't killed by these weapons went on their merry way—didn't change their way of life, didn't quit worshiping demons, didn't quit centering their lives on lumps of gold and silver and brass, hunks of stone and wood that couldn't see or hear or move. There wasn't a sign of a change of heart. They plunged right on in their murderous occult, promiscuous, and thieving ways.[61]

That's pretty pointed, isn't it? That's the rest of mankind.

ATM (Apply to Me)

1. God is sovereign. Never forget that. He's in charge. He allows armies of men or armies of demons to be part of this judgment, but He is in charge of every last thing. He knows the day; he knows the hour; He is in charge of it all.

2. If that's true, why doesn't God do something about sin? Right now! Well, what would you like Him to do, those of you who ask that question? What *exactly* is it that you would like God to do? Would you

like God to get rid of everyone who has ever sinned? No? So you want to be God, and you want to draw the line as to how God should and shouldn't judge? I want to remind you that there was a time when God did judge the whole world with a flood. We're told that every thought of man was only evil continually before the flood. Except for Noah and his family, everyone perished. Then we started over: *Oh, it's going to be great now.* Not! God did do something about sin 2,000 years ago at the cross. He provided deliverance, forgiveness, the penalty paid. That's what He did about sin, and in this book we see that finally He is dealing with the sins of mankind: those who will not repent.

3. On whose side do we want to be when those judgments fall? If you've never given your life to Jesus Christ, let me tell you there is no other way of salvation. *OK, I'll be a nicer person now so I can earn my way into heaven.* No, no, no, no. We can never earn our way into heaven; that's why the cross was necessary. If you've never surrendered your life to Christ and accepted His payment for sin, you are lost and without hope, and you will be on the wrong side when these judgments fall. If you've never given your life to Christ, do it today.

4. We have an awesome responsibility to warn people about these judgments. That's our job today: to send out the message that there is salvation in no one else but Jesus Christ. We dare not take the path expressed by the Universalist, which Harry Ironside describes so clearly:

> **There are universalists who believe that all punishment, whether in time or eternity, is with a view to the final salvation of the delinquent and that eventually all men will learn by judgment, if they refused to learn by grace, and will turn to God for salvation.**[62]

No, no, and no. We must reject that. There is one and only one way to eternal life, and that is through Jesus Christ. Reject it, and you will spend eternity separated from God. We must be serious about getting that message out.

Lesson 11

Read 10:1 – 11:14

A Heavenly Messenger and Two Earthly Witnesses

Out of the opening of Seal 7 we saw seven trumpets that were to sound. In Lesson 9 we studied the first four trumpets, and then in our last lesson we discussed Trumpets 5 and 6. In this lesson we would assume Trumpet 7 would come next. However, that would be wrong. Just as there was an interlude between Seal 6 and Seal 7, so also there is an interlude between Trumpet 6 and Trumpet 7. That is why we are studying all of Chapter 10 and the first 14 verses of Chapter 11. Trumpet 7 will sound at 11:15, which be our next lesson. So, all of this lengthy passage is one unit; it is another interlude.

There are some things that need to be mentioned about this interlude, this passage of Scripture. It explains some things that were not covered in detail as we studied Seals 1 through 6, the first interlude, Seal 7, and Trumpets 1 through 6. It looks back in time at some points, it looks forward in time at other points, and overall *it is not to be interpreted chronologically*. It is instead thematic, and it sets the stage for the second half of the tribulation. You see, we have reached the mid-point of the tribulation, which is to last for seven years. That means the mid-point is 3.5 years, and that length of time appears twice in this passage, which is the signal that we have arrived at the mid-point here just before the sounding of Trumpet 7.

One of the keys to understanding much of The Revelation is knowing Daniel's prophecy of the 70 weeks. In that prophecy Daniel was given a revelation of how long the tribulation would last. There would be 69 weeks leading up to the crucifixion of our Lord Jesus Christ. Now in that prophecy one week does not equal seven *days*, but instead one week equals seven *years*. Keep that in mind. In that prophecy Daniel was able to predict the date of our Lord's crucifixion. Following that came the parentheses of the church age between week 69 and week 70. Concerning week 70, which is yet future, Daniel wrote (Daniel 9:27):

> ...he [Antichrist] will make a firm covenant with the many for one week, but in the middle of the week he will put a stop to sacrifice and grain offering; and on the wing of abominations will come one who makes desolate, even until a complete destruction, one that is decreed, is poured out on the one who makes desolate.

So, at the beginning of the seven years of tribulation, the final week of Daniel's prophecy, Antichrist comes to power. He makes a covenant with the many (meaning the Jews, which we know because this revelation was given to Daniel in answer to his prayer about what would happen to the Jews), rebuilds the Jewish temple, and re-establishes daily sacrifices. But in the *middle* of this seventieth week of Daniel's prophecy (the three-and-a-half-year point), Antichrist breaks that covenant. In II Thessalonians 2:3-4 Paul explains to us what will happen:

> **...the man of lawlessness [Antichrist] is revealed, the son of destruction, who opposes and exalts himself above every so-called god or object of worship, so that he takes his seat in the temple of God, displaying himself as being God.**

That will happen at the mid-point of the tribulation. Having made a covenant with the Jews, Antichrist breaks that covenant, kicks the Jews and their sacrifices out of the temple, takes his seat in the temple and says *I am God; you must worship me.*

You have probably noticed that this lesson has already included teachings from other related passages in the Bible; that will continue through this lesson because, without those other passages, we cannot have a clear understanding and correct interpretation of the verses that are before us. With all of that in mind let us study the passage at hand.

A Heavenly Messenger

At the beginning of Chapter 10 John saw another strong angel. *Another* means there must have been a first (or more than one) strong angel(s). Indeed he previously used that description in 5:2; it was a strong angel who asked the question, **"Who is worthy to open the book?"** (We noted that the Lord Jesus Christ alone is worthy to open the scroll.) This particular strong angel in Chapter 10 is described as (pay attention to each one of these four things) **clothed with a cloud, and the rainbow on his head, and his face was like the sun, and his feet like pillars of fire** (10:1). John is obviously describing something he has never seen before. He does the best he can, and here is one artist's best attempt to put it into a picture:

You see a strong angel that seems to fill heaven and earth. You see the rainbow, the sign of the covenant that God would never again judge the world with a flood, surround his head. You see him clothed in clouds, you see a face shining like the sun, and you see his feet like pillars of fire. I can't say for certain if this is exactly what this angel looked like to John, but this artist's picture does match John's description. You will notice some things about this picture which we haven't mentioned yet, but now we will discuss them. He is holding an *open* scroll, he is raising his hand toward the sky, and one foot is on the land while the other is on the sea. John specifically said that the right foot was on the sea and the left foot was on the land. That must be significant because John says it three times in this chapter (vs. 2, 5,

8). It shows authority over all the Earth, because the Earth consists of land and sea.

The open scroll is called a little scroll. I am very glad that scholars agree that this is another interlude (between Trumpet 6 and Trumpet 7), because this little scroll is one of many about which they disagree in this chapter. Is this the same scroll as in Chapter 5, or is this a different scroll? In Chapter 5 the Greek word is *biblion*; here in Chapter 10 the Greek word is *biblaridion*. The words are similar, but different, which would argue for this being a different scroll. (The words of course both contain "bibla," from which we get our word bibliography.) Biblaridion means little scroll; biblion means scroll. Some scholars believe it is still the same scroll. It is now open—no longer sealed—because the seals have been opened. I believe, however, that this is something different, a further revelation of God's plan. Once again we shall not start a separate denomination over whether there is one scroll or there are two different scrolls.

The angel cries out with a loud voice, like a lion! (By the way, have you noticed how many times we keep encountering the two-word phrase "loud voice"? It is used in The Revelation 20 times! This is a noisy book! There aren't any still, small whispering voices. There are loud voices proclaiming what God is doing.) After the angel speaks (with a loud voice!) seven peals of thunder speak. John understood the words that were spoken by the seven peals of thunder. The last time you were in a thunderstorm did you understand anything the thunder was saying, other than *If you're outside, get indoors*? But John understands, and he prepares to write it down, which makes sense. But then he hears a voice saying *Stop! Don't write it down. Seal it up*. That might not seem right. Isn't this book called The Reveal-ation in which things are *revealed* to us? But not this. Scholars love to debate this one, each with his/her own opinion. There is one sect that even says they know exactly what the seven peals of thunder said, but they aren't telling anyone else! We must conclude that we don't know what the seven thunders said, and we won't know this side of eternity because it has been sealed up. It was a secret, and John was not to write it. But doesn't God want us to know everything? No. The following verse must be burned into our consciousness (Deuteronomy 29:29): **The secret things belong to the Lord our God, but the things revealed belong to us and to our sons forever.** There are things God has chosen to keep secret. It was that way in the days of Moses, and so it is here in the days of John. This is a secret which the Lord has chosen not to reveal.

Now, you might be wondering, who is this angel? Some say he is the Lord Jesus Christ. He is clothed in clouds. Who could be clothed in clouds but God alone? On Mt. Sinai when God gave The Law, He descended in a cloud. When He led the people of Israel through the wilderness, He led them during the day with a pillar of cloud. When He came and spoke with Moses directly, He came in a cloud. Since this angel is clothed with a cloud, the argument says, this angel must be the Lord, specifically God the Son. But scholars don't agree on this either. I believe he is not the Lord because John doesn't worship him. Back in Chapter 1, when he saw the glorified Lord Jesus Christ, he fell at His feet as though he were dead. But John doesn't worship this angel. Additionally, notice that the angel raises his hand and swears by Him who lives forever and ever (i.e., God) that there will be no more delay. When God swears by Himself, the wording is different. Consider these words in Genesis 22:16-17, where God is speaking to Abraham:

"By Myself I have sworn, declares the Lord, because you have done this thing, and have not withheld your son, your only son, indeed I will greatly bless you, and I will greatly multiply your seed as the stars of the heavens, and as the sand which is on the seashore; and your seed shall possess the gate of their enemies."

The writer to the Hebrews (6:13) says that when God made that promise, since He could swear by no one greater, He swore by Himself. But this angel does not swear by himself; he swears by Him who lives forever. So I conclude this is another strong, powerful angel, different from the one we met in Chapter 5. (Again, no separate denomination please over the identity of the angel.) What we can say with certainty is that he has the *authority* of God's throne. When he says there will no longer be any delay, time's up. When Trumpet 7 sounds, the second half of the tribulation begins and the mystery of God is finished.

What is this *mystery of God?* There is near unanimous agreement about this one. It is God's long tolerance of evil. Leon Morris says, "There is an answer to the perplexities of history. The mystery of God will be finished; prophecy will be fulfilled. The angel confirms this with an oath."[63] Walter Scott (not Sir Walter Scott, the author and historian) says:

Does it not seem strange that Satan has been allowed for 6,000 years to wrap and twist his coils around the world, to work evil and spoil and mar the work of God?... Is it not a mystery why God, the God of righteousness and holiness, allows evil to go unpunished and His own people to be crushed and broken on every hand? Truly this is the mystery of God.... God bears with evil till the hour of judgment arrives, when He will avenge the cry of His elect, and come out of His place to punish the wicked...evil, now tolerated and allowed, will be openly punished. The mystery is at an end. Christ is about to reign.[64]

When Trumpet 7 sounds, we are coming to the end of that mystery, and Christ will come to reign.

The instruction to John is that he is to take the scroll and eat it. Have you ever eaten a scroll? I'm certain the answer is no. But John ate this scroll, and eating it was symbolic of completely absorbing its message. By the way, the same instruction—to eat a scroll—was given to Ezekiel (Ezekiel 3:1-3). When Ezekiel did so, it was sweet. John's scroll was sweet in the mouth, but it caused indigestion in the stomach, just like the angel said. It was bitter. What does all that mean? Sweet in the mouth, bitter in the stomach. The future at the end of the story is bright, beautiful, wonderful, and perfect. Proclaiming that future is sweet. As we work our way through the second half of The Revelation, I can't wait to get to the end because proclaiming those last two chapters is so very sweet. But the judgment before we get there is very bitter, and proclaiming those events is not sweet at all. To quote Leon Morris again: "The more his heart is filled with the love of God, the more certain it is that the telling forth of woes will be a bitter experience."[65]

To conclude this chapter, *they* said to John (paraphrase), *You've got more work to do.* Until now the chapter has been John, the angel, and the seven peals of thunder. Now, instead of *he* said, the text reads *they* said. Who are *they*? I'm not certain. Possibly it refers to some other angel(s) or other voices of heaven. We are not told. The specific instruction is (10:11) **"You must prophesy again concerning many peoples and nations and tongues and kings."** What would he prophesy? The things in this second scroll which he has eaten: he has more work to do. Charles Swindoll says of this moment: "The recommissioning of John marks a watershed moment in the book of The Revelation. From this point on the judgments would become decidedly more severe."[66] We will see that play out beginning with our next lesson.

In Chapter 11 John is given further instructions. He is given a rod/staff, and someone (he doesn't say who) tells him to measure the temple, the altar, and the worshipers. What temple? In the Bible there have been three different temples. There was the grand, splendid, glorious temple which Solomon built; it was laid waste by Nebuchadnezzar. There was a rebuilt temple which you can read about in the book of Ezra; it was not nearly as splendid as Solomon's temple. It was also destroyed. When we get to the New Testament, we find the temple where Jesus worshiped, which was built for the Jews by Herod the Great. That temple was also laid waste when the Romans destroyed Jerusalem in 70 A.D. We looked at Daniel's prophecy, which tells us that Antichrist will make a covenant with the Jews which will include the rebuilding of the temple and the re-establishment of daily sacrifices. What good is that, daily animal sacrifices? Can the blood of goats, the blood of lambs, take away sin? No, it was just ritual before, and it will be just ritual again. *Oh, we're once again being good Jews.* Who takes away the sin of the world? Only Jesus Christ, the Lamb of God. So this temple that Antichrist will build, with all of its ritual and riches and its altar, is simply dead religion. Measuring in Scripture is a sign of measuring something for judgment; in this case it is symbolic of judgment that is about to come. So what John is measuring is that future temple that Antichrist will build for the Jews.

When John is told to measure the worshipers, it doesn't mean that John measured one of them and said, *Oh, he's 5 feet, 10 inches; there's a tall drink of water who is 6 feet, 5 inches (must have played in the NBA); there's a short one, only 5 feet, 6 inches!* That's not what he's doing. He is enumerating them and sizing them up for judgment as well. He is told not to measure the outer court, which was the place of the Gentiles. The nations will tread it under foot for 3.5 years (42 months)—there's that ½ of the tribulation time. When Antichrist sets himself up in the temple as the object of worship and abolishes the sacrifices at the midpoint of the tribulation, for the next 3.5 years the Gentiles will tread underfoot the entire temple area in Jerusalem. Therefore, this must refer to the second half of the tribulation. Remember I said that this interlude looks backward and it looks forward. Here this 3.5-year period (42 months) looks forward to what will happen when Antichrist takes his seat in the temple and says, *You must worship me alone.*

The Two Witnesses

Here is a topic in The Revelation where you could have ten different denominations, just based on the identity of the two witnesses! They are the next to be described. They are given authority to prophesy (preach) for 3.5 years, not written as 42 months, but rather 1,260 days. A Jewish year was 360 days, and math tells us that 1,260 days is 3.5 Jewish years. They are described as olive trees and lampstands. Time prohibits us from discussing all the details of that symbolism, but know that it comes from Zechariah: the witnesses have Holy Spirit power and they preach light. They have four powers:

1. The power to kill their enemies with fire from their mouths
2. The power to shut up the sky so that it does not rain
3. The power to turn water into blood
4. The power to smite the earth with every plague

We are told in 7:11 they will *finish* their work. After they have finished their work, the beast shows up. The beast is another name for Antichrist. This is the first time he is named this way in The Revelation, but he has been gathering power and authority, making a covenant with Israel and helping them rebuild their temple. Now he steps in and makes war against the two witnesses. Why does it take war against them to destroy them? Because they have power to make fire come out of their mouths and destroy their enemies. It takes a war against them to defeat them, and they are killed in Jerusalem. How do we know that? Look at 11:8…**their dead bodies will lie in the street of the great city which mystically is called Sodom and Egypt, where also their Lord was crucified.** Where was Jesus crucified? Jerusalem. Now, *mystically* the city is called Sodom and Egypt. We need to understand that in God's eyes Jerusalem will be seen as immoral and polluted as the city of Sodom and as worldly as the country of Egypt. That is the meaning of the mystic label. Remember those restored sacrifices? Again, all dead ritual—no relationship with God through Jesus Christ.

What does the world do when they are killed? Every people, tribe, and tongue celebrate. They send gifts to one another because they are so happy these two witnesses are dead. It's going to be Christmas, Mardi Gras, and Cinco de Mayo all rolled into one. People will whoop it up! Harry Ironside says, "The last voice on God's behalf has been silenced, and they will rejoice over the dead bodies of His witnesses."[67] How can the whole world know and see what has happened to these two witnesses? Satellites, television. Impossible in John's day, but we understand. We can have news from around the world in the blink of an eye. Their bodies lie in the street and burial is forbidden by the authorities.

Can you picture it on the news? Maybe something like this:

This is Christiane Amanpour reporting from Jerusalem, and I'm here to report that those two witnesses who tormented the earth are still dead. No one has dared even touch their bodies; they lie in the street, and happily they're still dead.

Then suddenly after three and a half days they are resurrected!

This is Christiane Amanpour reporting from Jerusalem. Yes, those bodies are still there; the witnesses are dead, dead, dead. Wait a minute, something is happening. They're coming back to life— We interrupt this news broadcast for some commercial messages; we'll be back quite a few minutes from now.

We're told that great fear comes upon those who were celebrating their deaths (I don't doubt it!). Finally they ascend to heaven, and their enemies see them ascend. (Jesus' friends saw Him ascend; here the enemies see the two witnesses ascend!).

In that same hour there was a great earthquake and 1/10 of the city fell. That is the only time we see this particular fraction in The Revelation. We have seen 1/2, 1/3, 1/4, but here it is 1/10 of the city that fell. It was a bad earthquake, but not one that devastates the entire city. Seven thousand people die. Some have speculated that the number is 1/10 of the population, but the text doesn't actually say that. The rest in the city were terrified. I would think so! We are also told they gave glory to God. Does that mean they came to saving faith in Jesus Christ? Charles Swindoll says:

> *We can't be sure how many of those people who suddenly give glory to the God of heaven will be exercising genuine saving faith. Throughout history numerous people have acknowledged the power and wrath of God without actually confessing Him as their personal Lord and Savior.*[68]

Now, who are the two witnesses? Again, this is where we could divide into ten different denominations! Many have speculated that one of them is Elijah, and I believe that is probably accurate. One of the things Elijah did during his ministry was that he was able to stop the rain. In addition, Malachi prophesied that before the great and terrible day of the Lord, He would send the prophet Elijah. Now some see that prophecy as completely fulfilled in John the Baptist, who certainly did come in the spirit and power of Elijah. His looks and his ministry are very similar, but when he was asked pointblank, *Are you Elijah?*, he said no. John the Baptist came in the *spirit and power* of Elijah, but here in Chapter 11 of The Revelation is literal Elijah. Elijah was seen on the Mount of Transfiguration with the Lord Jesus Christ. You might remember that Elijah did not die but was taken up to heaven in a whirlwind.

Some have speculated that the other witness is perhaps Enoch, the other man in the Old Testament who did not die. He walked with God, and God took him. He did not experience death, and the argument is that these two must experience death at some point because it is the fate of all mankind. Here that happens. That explanation is possible, and there is some validity to it. However, apart from the fact that Enoch did not die, there is no other reason to believe that he is the second witness. The better theory is that it is Moses, who was with Jesus and Elijah on the Mount of Transfiguration. The water being turned to blood, along with the other plagues, looks like Moses' ministry. And together Moses and Elijah represent the law and the prophets. Another reason to believe this is Moses is found in Jude 9:

> **Michael the archangel, when he disputed with the devil and argued about the body of Moses, did not dare pronounce against him a railing judgment, but said, "The Lord rebuke you."**

We know from the book of Deuteronomy that the Lord buried the body of Moses, but apparently after that there was a dispute about his body. Why would Satan care about the body of Moses? Because Satan knows this body will be brought back to life, seen on the Mount of Transfiguration, and put into use here in The Revelation. Michael the archangel makes sure the body is protected.

We cannot say with certainty who is right about the identity of these witnesses (other theories exist as well). Charles Swindoll sums it up well: "We can at least say with confidence that these two figures sum up the kind of miraculous and prophetic ministry that has marked other periods of biblical history."[69]

For how long do they prophesy? Three and half years, given as days. Is this the first half of the tribulation or the second half (remember that this interlude is not chronological)? I believe here we are discussing something that begins at the start of the tribulation and lasts until the midpoint, i.e., the first half of the tribulation. What have they been prophesying during that time? They explain the events of the seals and the trumpets, that they are judgments from God. They are warning people that time is short and they must repent of the sins. Some have speculated that the 144,000 Jewish evangelists (remember them?) were converted because of the preaching of these witnesses. We cannot say for certain, but it is a possibility.

That is the ministry of these two witnesses. Do not miss v. 14 at the end of this section: **The second woe is past; behold, the third woe is coming quickly.** Remember Trumpet 5 was the first woe, and now we find out that Trumpet 6 was the second woe (10:1-11:13 are the interlude of this lesson). I believe 11:14 connects with the end of Chapter 9 and the army of 200,000,000 we looked at in our last lesson. This phrase about the third woe is placed here because (if you look ahead you will see this) the seventh angel is about to sound.

ATM (Apply to Me)

1. John wasn't *forced* to eat the scroll, was he? He had to take it. Spiritual life begins and continues with taking the Word of God into our lives and our hearts. Harry Ironside says:

   It is only as we feed upon and digest the Word of God that we ourselves are nourished and built up in the truth of our most holy faith and are in a right condition of soul to use that Word for the help and instruction of others.[70]

   The inspired Word of God does us no good if all it does during the week is sit on the shelf. We must *take it* into our hearts and our lives.

2. God doesn't reveal everything, and I must be content with that. There are things God has chosen to keep secret. He is God, and I am not, and I certainly must acknowledge that.

3. The future of eternity is sweet for those who belong to the Lord. If you know the Lord Jesus Christ as Savior, the sweetness of what is ahead is beyond anything that anyone could describe in earthly language. It is wonderfully sweet.

4. If you do not know the Lord Jesus Christ, there is nothing but bitter, horrible judgment.

5. Therefore, when we share the gospel, our message must first be balanced. We must proclaim the sweet: forgiveness of sins, reconciliation with God, a relationship with Him. Our message must include all those wonderful truths, but it also must be balanced with a warning that judgment is the only thing awaiting those who reject Jesus Christ. I am bound by Holy Scripture to proclaim both.

6. Next, our message must be bold; there is no place for a wimpy message: *Well, I believe this way, but if you want to believe another way, you'll get to heaven, too.* NO! There is one and only one way to salvation, and that is in Jesus Christ.

7. Next, our message must be biblical. When you hear a preacher or teacher preaching or teaching the Word of God, test everything against what the Scriptures say.

8. Finally, our hearts must be burdened for those who do not know Jesus Christ.

All of that is how to make a difference as *we* serve as witnesses in this world of sin.

Lesson 12

Read 11:15 – 12:17

The Seventh Trumpet

Six trumpets have sounded judgment upon the earth, followed by a second interlude; that interlude was the subject of our last lesson. We also noted that we have reached the mid-point of the seven years of tribulation. We are ready for Trumpet 7 to sound.

When Trumpet 7 is blown, there is again a loud voice. Remember that the phrase *loud voice* is used 20 times in The Revelation. It is a noisy book as these judgments fall on Earth. God wants no one to miss it—loud voices. These are not things that are whispered. Here there are loud voices (plural) speaking in anticipation of what will happen. They do not describe what *has* happened, but they tell us what *will* happen in the unfolding of God's plan as we enter the last 3.5 years of the tribulation, leading to the consummation of history.

Declaration of The Kingdom

Loud voices said, **"The kingdom of the world has become the kingdom of our Lord, and of His Christ; and He will reign forever and ever"** (11:15). The kingdom (singular) means the kingdom that has been under the control of Satan. Vernon McGee says, "Satan's kingdom is going to be subdued, but not by some saccharine-sweet talk on brotherhood and love. It is going to be delivered to the Lord Jesus Christ, and He is going to rule."[71] Do you believe that? Amen! That is what has been revealed to John. Charles Swindoll says:

> *The words emphasize the great transfer of power from wicked humanity under the spiritual bondage of Satan (the kingdom of the world) to Christ and the saints under the sovereign headship of God the Father (the king of Our Lord and of His Christ). However, to effect this change, the kingdom of darkness must be judged and the kingdom of light must cast its brilliance upon the face of the earth.*[72]

Decree of Judgment

There is to be reward given to prophets, saints, and those who fear God's name. One commentator puts forth the view that prophets refers to

Old Testament believers, saints to New Testament believers, and those who fear God's name are those who come to Jesus Christ during the tribulation. Certainly, *saints* is a New Testament synonym for believers, and those who fear God's name could mean those who come to faith in the tribulation days. However, *prophets* appears to be an odd choice of word to refer to all Old Testament believers, and it is not used that way elsewhere in Scripture. I believe this is a more general description: prophets, saints, those who fear God's name means all believers of all ages. The phrase is followed with the words **to…the small and the great** (11:18). There will be reward given to *all* those in the Old Testament who did put their faith in the *coming* Lord Jesus Christ; there will be reward given to those in the New Testament and the Church age who have put their faith in the Christ who *has come* to save us. However, along with that will be judgment.

Next John sees the temple of God, and it is open, symbolizing unbroken fellowship with God that will be ours in eternity. Then in the temple he sees the Ark of the Covenant, followed by lightning, thunder, and a hailstorm. What is all that about? The Ark of the Covenant contained two very important tablets of stone on which were written the Ten Commandments. God is symbolically saying, *I gave My moral law in writing on tablets of stone, and then in My written Word I gave My moral instructions to the world so the world will know the basis on which I will judge. I also gave those tablets and those instructions as an act of love, because everyone on Earth obeying those commandments would mean a fantastic life. What a wonderful world it would be! I didn't give these commandments to tell people to stop having fun. I gave these commandments so they could have fun by living righteously together. But now judgment is coming, and those commandments are how I will judge.* The paraphrase is mine, but I believe it captures the symbolism and spirit of what God is saying: the lightning and the thunder and the hailstorm are symbols of the beginning of the end of God's last judgments.

Overview of Chapters 12-14

That brings us to Chapter 12, and I must say at this point that Chapters 12 through 14 are the most challenging to understand in the entire book of The Revelation. A basic foundation, properly understood, will make these chapters more accessible. Stay with me here.

1. What is Woe 3? Trumpet 7 is to be the third of 3 woes. Remember that before Trumpet 5 sounded, an eagle flying in heaven said, **"Woe, woe, woe, to those who dwell on the earth, because of the remaining blasts of the trumpet of the three angels who are about to sound!"** (8:13). At the end of Trumpet 5 and its judgment (9:12), we were told the first woe was past, and two more were about to come. After Trumpet 6 there was a similar verse (11:14) saying the second woe was past, and the third woe was coming quickly. Although those two verses describe

specifically Woe #1 and Woe #2, corresponding to Trumpets 5 and 6, there is no wording in The Revelation which says, "This is the third woe." We must infer what it is. I believe the third woe is the seven bowls of wrath, which are the last judgments. Remember this diagram from Lesson 9:

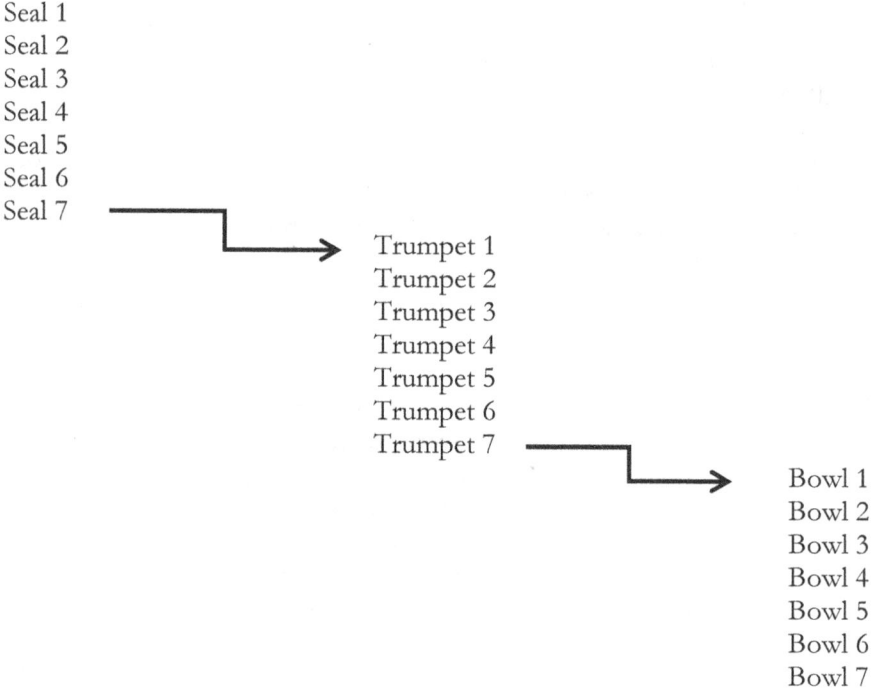

Seal 1
Seal 2
Seal 3
Seal 4
Seal 5
Seal 6
Seal 7 ⟶ Trumpet 1
Trumpet 2
Trumpet 3
Trumpet 4
Trumpet 5
Trumpet 6
Trumpet 7 ⟶ Bowl 1
Bowl 2
Bowl 3
Bowl 4
Bowl 5
Bowl 6
Bowl 7

The seven seals start the judgments, the seven trumpets come out of Seal 7. Trumpet 5 is Woe 1; Trumpet 6 is Woe 2. In this lesson Trumpet 7 sounds, and out of that come the seven bowls of wrath, but those bowls don't begin to be described until the start of Chapter 15. But we are here in Chapter 11 for the sounding of Trumpet 7. That means 15:1 follows the end of Chapter 11 chronologically, and it begins Woe 3.

2. That returns us to the question of Chapters 12 through 14, and there are two keys to unlock their mystery. The first key is that they are *not* chronological, neither within the entire book nor within themselves as a unit. The second key is that they contain supplemental material that helps explain many of the other events described before *and* after them. There is also some history, some of it going back even before the world began.

3. As we read through these chapters, we will meet a cast of key characters who will be very involved in the events of the last days of the Earth.

4. These chapters elaborate on the *why* and the *how* of the events of the entire book.

5. There are seven sections in Chapters 12 through 14, and they are easy to find. Here is how they are introduced:

12:1	A great sign
12:3	Another sign
13:1	And I saw
13:12	And I saw
14:1	And I looked
14:6	And I saw
14:14	And I looked

If you circle each of those in your Bible, you will clearly see the beginnings of seven sections of supplemental material, given as signs, that help to shed light on what *has happened* in Chapters 1 through 11 and what *will happen* in Chapters 15 through 22.

In a perfect world we would have time to consider all of Chapters 12 through 14 in one lesson. We will instead spread out the study of these chapters through three lessons. This lesson will examine the first two signs—those starting at 12:1 and 12:3. We will find that these two signs are closely related. There is overlap, and there are places where one draws information from the other.

Sign 1: A Woman

She is with child and then she gives birth to a child. We don't immediately know the identity of the child, but if we peek ahead to v. 5, we will find that the Child is to rule all the nations with a rod of iron. So, the Child is clearly the Lord Jesus Christ Himself; about that there can be no question. Who then is the woman? There has been speculation through the years, some of it quite odd. Some have suggested that she is the Church. Does that sound right? No. Which is true: the Church gave birth to Jesus Christ, or Jesus Christ gave birth to the Church? The second statement is clearly the answer, so the woman cannot be the Church. Some have speculated that she is Mary, the mother of Jesus. As we study the context of the entire chapter, we will find that label does not work because it does not fit all the things the woman experiences. Mary Baker Eddy, the founder of Christian Scientism, claimed she was the woman, the child was her teachings, and the dragon was all those who oppose her teachings. As I said, there have been odd interpretations through the ages.

Who then is it who brings us the birth of our Lord Jesus Christ? From whom does Jesus come in human genealogy? Of course, the answer is Israel: the woman is symbolic of the nation of Israel. Further evidence of that is found in the description of the woman in v. 1: **a woman clothed with the sun and moon under her feet and on her head a crown of twelve stars.** Do you remember the dreams of Joseph all the way back in Genesis? In his second dream he said this about what would soon become the nation of Israel, i.e., his mother, his father, and his brothers (Genesis 37:9): **"Lo, I have had still another dream; and behold, the sun and the moon and eleven stars were bowing down to me."** This description reinforces the fact that the woman is Israel, who gives birth to the Savior of the world, our Lord Jesus Christ.

Sign 2: The Dragon

The second sign (vs. 3-17) is Satan. Although he interacts with the woman, most of the chapter is actually about him. He is seen as a dragon with seven heads, seven diadems, and ten horns. The diadems are royal ruling crowns, not the wreath-crowns of athletic games. The fact that there are seven represents the completeness that he has in his authority to deceive the nations. (We will discuss the ten horns in a future lesson.) In v. 9 he is also called the serpent of old, the devil and Satan. There is no question as to his identity.

In v. 4 he sweeps away 1/3 of the stars and they are thrown down to Earth. Remember that these chapters are not chronological. Right here we have gone back before the foundation of the world. This is an explanation of what happened to Satan. In Lesson 10 we looked at

Scripture from Isaiah, and we want to look at a portion of it again. This is a description of the one known as the angel Lucifer before he fell (Isaiah 14:12-14):

How you have fallen from heaven, O star of the morning, son of the dawn! You have been cut down to the earth, you who have weakened the nations! But you said in your heart, "I will ascend to heaven...I will make myself like the Most High."

A passage in Ezekiel (28:14-16) further describes what happened to him:

You were the anointed cherub who covers, and I placed you there. You were on the holy mountain of God; you walked in the midst of

the stones of fire. You were blameless in your ways from the day you were created, until unrighteousness ["I will make myself like the most High" from Isaiah] was found in you. By the abundance of your trade you were internally filled with violence, and you sinned; therefore I have cast you as profane from the mountain of God.

Those two passages give the details of what is summarized and elaborated on here in v. 4. It wasn't just Satan who was cast from the mountain of God; it was also 1/3 of the angels who followed him in his rebellion against God. Those angels have become demons. It is comforting to know that means that of the total number of angels in the universe, 2/3 did not fall, so they outnumber the demons two to one. Nevertheless, 1/3 of the angels is a great fall.

He (Satan) wants to destroy the Child after His birth. Of course, he does. He has been at war with the plan of God going all the way back to sin in the garden, when Eve was told that her seed would bruise the head (i.e., destroy his power) of the serpent, the devil, the dragon; and for 6,000 years he has tried to stop that from happening. It was Satan who placed into the mind of Cain that he should kill his brother: if Abel is dead and Cain is a murderer, how can the seed of the woman bruise the serpent (Satan)? What did God do? He gave Eve another son by the name of Seth. If you trace the line of Jesus all the way back to Adam and Eve, you will find it goes through Seth. In Noah's day everyone was judged, and Satan was probably rejoicing because he knew no one could bruise him on the head if there was no one alive. But God kept eight people alive on the ark.

The line of the promised one who would bruise the serpent on the head goes through Abraham, Isaac, and Jacob. Satan put it into the mind of Esau to kill his brother Jacob, but Jacob fled for his life, and God protected him. Satan put it into the mind of Pharaoh to kill all the Israelites (the descendants of Jacob) at the Red Sea, but God parted the sea and they crossed on dry ground. At one point after the death of Solomon there was such infighting among the descendants of David, that there was only one remaining descendant of David alive—a baby named Joash. He was rescued from the executioners and ultimately became king. Satan knew the One who was to bruise him on the head would come from the line of David, and if Satan could destroy the line of David, there would be no one to destroy him. In the book of Esther Satan put it into the mind of Haman to annihilate the Jews, but God intervened through Esther and Mordecai.

When we come to Jesus' actual birth, there is Herod, lying about why he wants to know where the One born King of Jews can be found. He tells the wise men, *I want to go and worship Him, too. (I want to kill Him* would have been the truth.) So, Satan put it into his heart to kill all the male children two years old and under, but God warned Mary and Joseph in a dream to flee to Egypt.

You see, this war to stop the head bruiser started all the way in Genesis 3, and it continues even today. Satan hated the nation of Israel, he hated the line of David, he hated the idea that there would be Someone who would bruise him on the head, and he did everything in his power to stop the Messiah from being born. I want to tell you he failed!

He still hates Israel today, though. Look at the world. How many friends does Israel have? Iran is trying to develop a nuclear weapon so they can wipe Israel off the map. God will not allow that. The hatred for Israel continues today on every side, but God is still on Israel's side, even though they rejected and killed their Messiah. It would be wise for forward-looking nations to be on Israel's side, not against them.

So, this Child is born, and Herod failed to kill him. Now if you look at 12:5 you will find the following: **She gave birth to a son, a male child, who is to rule all the nations with a rod of iron; and her child was caught up to God and to His throne.** We have His birth, and we have His ascension. Is anything missing in there? The entire Gospel of John, right? But John had already described all those events in his Gospel. The emphasis here is not on Jesus' ministry on earth, not even His crucifixion and resurrection. It is on who He is: from the nation of Israel, born and ascended to God and to His throne. That is the shortest summary of the life and ministry of Christ you will ever see; everything in the middle is omitted.

The woman (remember, she is Israel) fled into the wilderness, and the period of time is 1,260 days. That should look familiar: it is 3.5 years. I will explain when and why that happens just a few paragraphs from now, but right now we continue with the dragon because there is war between Michael and his angels and the dragon and his angels (that's 1/3 of the angels; we know them as demons). Satan is thrown down to Earth and (here it is again) there is a loud voice. This voice says *HURRAY!* (my paraphrase). Why? Because the accuser has been thrown down.

What does that mean? Until this point in time (the mid-point of the tribulation) Satan could be before God, having access to Him. We find in the book of Job that Satan said to God that Job feared God only because God had blessed him so much. He *accused* Job of only being righteous because of God's blessing. He was proven wrong; Job stayed true to God, no matter what. In the first two verses of Zechariah 3 there is a brief description of Joshua the high priest (not the Joshua of the book which bears his name) standing before God, and Satan is there also. Throughout history and up until this point in the tribulation he has had the opportunity to stand before God and accuse people of faith, including you and me, making accusations (*Did You see what Keith did, that sin he committed this week?*). The good news is his accusations against Christians are worthless because of the blood of the Lamb and the testimony of faith in Jesus. (Even when believers are murdered, they overcome [v. 11]). But now, here in v. 9 Satan can't accuse any more. So the heavens say with a loud voice, *HURRAY!*

Now, if you've been paying close attention, you've possibly been asking yourself this question: What is the difference between 12:4 (Satan and 1/3 of the stars swept out of heaven) and 12:9 (Satan thrown down to the earth)? Are they the same thing? What is all that about? To answer those questions we need to look at four falls of Lucifer, who began as perfect (we read that no blame was found in him until he rebelled against God). There are four falls of Lucifer, leading to his ultimate end, which is the lake of fire:

1. The first fall is described in 12:4, and it is the same as what we read in Isaiah and Ezekiel: from glorified angel to demonic accuser. Until 12:9 he has authority to accuse believers before God.

2. Then in 12:9 he goes from demonic accuser to restriction on Earth. He can no longer be in heaven accusing believers; he has lost that access, which is why there is rejoicing in heaven.

3. The third step is from Earth to 1,000 years of bondage in the abyss, which will be described in 20:3.

4. His ultimate end will be described in 20:7, which is from the abyss to the lake of fire.

So, there are four stages of his fall, and that explains the difference between 12:4 and 12:9. Notice that we have had to piece together multiple Scriptures from the Old Testament and from here to understand this chapter. But one main purpose of this vision is to describe how there came to be a Satan in the first place.

We continue. In v. 13 we see that he persecuted the woman (remember she is Israel). He failed to kill her offspring, so now he will persecute Israel. She is given wings of the great eagle to fly to a place of protection (v. 14). We don't know exactly what that means or where that place of protection is, but we know that his goal to wipe out Israel one more time will fail; she will be protected. For how long? A time, times, and half a time. Why can't it just say a certain number of years? Actually, it does. A time is one year, times is two years, and half a time is of course 1/2. Add them together and the total is 3.5 years. Remember I said we would explain v. 6 (Israel's protection for 1,260 days = 3.5 years)? Here it is. It is the same description in both v. 6 and v. 14.

Satan, in order to chase after her, poured out a flood of water (v. 15), and the earth drank up the water. Symbolic or literal? Unknown. If literal, the meaning is obvious. (The wings of the eagle could even refer to airplane wings and a great airlift to carry Jews to safety.) If symbolic, then it symbolizes great persecution that Satan tries to unleash on Israel, but the forces of Earth stop it from happening. In any event, Satan takes one last shot at wiping out God's chosen people. Now he is enraged (v. 17). Donald Grey Barnhouse says:

> *The animal [the dragon] that was dangerous enough when he roamed through the whole forest is now limited to a stockade, where, made with the restrictions which he sees around him, and raging because he feels the end near, he throws the insane strength of the death struggle into all his movements.*[73]

He goes off to make war with the rest of her offspring, those who keep the commandments of God and hold to the testimony of Jesus. Obviously, these are believers he makes war against, either a portion of Israel for some reason not protected in the wilderness, or Gentile believers who are Israel's spiritual seed because of their faith. This is looking forward to the last 3.5 years of the tribulation and what is about to happen. If you think the first 3.5 years were horrible, this is what Satan is about to unleash because he is *enraged*.

ATM (Apply to Me)

1. Don't let discouragement about Satan's influence in this world overwhelm you. Do you ever get discouraged about that? I do. I see it in politics, I see it in the media, I see it in some of what goes on in education. I see it in crime and hate and racism. I see it everywhere when I look around.

2. Don't let it overwhelm you, because we overcome by the blood of the Lamb, and we overcome *only* by the blood of the Lamb. The time is coming for God to give reward to those who know Jesus Christ. Stay true to Him, follow Him with all of your life, with all of your heart, with all of your soul, with all of your strength. We overcome.

3. On the world stage Satan is behind the hatred of Israel. We must understand that. Why is there so much hatred for Israel? They are attacked, they defend themselves, and world leaders condemn Israel. That is because Satan is behind it. He still hates the nation of Israel, the mother of the One who is our Savior, who came to rule the nations with a rod of iron.

4. Finally, "His Kingdom cannot fail, He rules over earth and heaven. The keys of death and hell are to our Jesus given."[74] Remember that we serve a victorious Lord, One who is Victor over sin and death and Satan because He alone has the keys of death and hell. **He will reign forever and ever** (11:15).

Lesson 13

Read 13:1 – 18

A Beastly Story

Remember that Chapters 12 through 14 are supplemental material. They are not chronological to fit in with what comes immediately before or after them. Some of Chapter 12, we noted in our last lesson, went back in time to before the foundation of the world. This was an opportunity for John, and for God in giving him this revelation, to introduce certain characters and to explain certain things. That is where we find ourselves in this lesson. Remember that chronologically Chapter 15 follows Chapter 11 (11:19). Chapter 15 will pick up with the seven bowls of wrath, which come out of Trumpet 7.

We noted that Chapters 12, 13, and 14 are divided into seven sections, with seven signs given to John:

12:1	A great sign
12:3	Another sign
13:1	And I saw
13:12	And I saw
14:1	And I looked
14:6	And I saw
14:14	And I looked

In our last lesson we looked at Chapter 12, consisting of the first two signs: a woman (Israel) and a dragon (Satan). Because of Satan's great hatred for anyone or anything God loves, there was significant overlap between those two signs.

In this lesson we are studying the two signs of Chapter 13, each introduced with the words *And I saw* (13:1,11). We will see three characters, one of whom we already met. He is the dragon: we were told very clearly that he is Satan.

The first *And I saw* introduces a beast; he is Antichrist. The second *And I saw* introduces a second beast. Later in The Revelation he will be given the label/title of false prophet. Keep those two characters in mind throughout this lesson: Antichrist and the false prophet.

Some people have suggested a false or fake evil trinity here between the dragon (Satan), Antichrist, and the false prophet. There certainly are three agents of evil, but I do not want to go so far as to call it a trinity. The Holy Trinity of the one God we worship—Father, Son, and Holy Spirit—is a mystery that our minds cannot fully comprehend. The Lord our God is One. There is one God. The Father is God, the Son is God, the Holy Spirit is God, but there is one God—One in Three, Three in One. Our human minds cannot fully grasp that concept, but it is what the Scriptures clearly teach. However, I can grasp Chapter 13. I can understand this group of three. There is Satan, and there are his two agents, Antichrist and the false prophet. I prefer to use the term triumvirate of evil, as these three agents work together to bring about worship of Satan. You will notice also that for most of this chapter Satan is in the background; the most important character is Antichrist, while Satan is mentioned very little.

Now before we launch into our study of the two beasts, it is important for us to once again go back to the book of Daniel. If you do not understand Daniel, you cannot understand The Revelation; if you do not understand The Revelation, you cannot understand Daniel. The two prophetic books work together. We have discussed this before, but I want to look at it again because we have reached the mid-point of the tribulation. In Daniel 9:27 we read:

> **...he [Antichrist, now identified as the first beast of The Revelation] will make a firm covenant with the many [Israel] for one week [7 years], but in the middle of the week [after 3.5 years] he will put a stop to sacrifice and grain offering; and on the wing of abominations will come one who makes desolate, even until a complete destruction, one that is decreed, is poured out on the one who makes desolate.**

At the beginning of the time of the tribulation this man (Antichrist) rises to power, he makes a covenant with Israel, he rebuilds their temple, their worship and sacrificial system are re-established, and they think it is finally utopia. But their dreams of that are short-lived, because halfway through the seven years of the tribulation he breaks his covenant with them; he ends their sacrifice and grain offerings. In Chapter 13 we will see some of the other things he does. Keep Daniel in mind during this study.

Sign 3: The First Beast

He comes out of the sea; in the Scriptures sea represents the nations. Some have taken that to mean he must be a Gentile because he comes from the nation**s**, not from Israel. Others say he must be a Jew; otherwise, the nation of Israel will not follow him when he makes a covenant with them to rebuild their temple and re-establish their worship.

There is a man by the name of Max Nordau; he was the brains behind a series of eleven Zionist Congresses in the early 20th century. Nordau, a Jew, said this at one of those conferences (remember this is before the re-establishment of the nation of Israel in the 1940s): "We are ready to welcome *any man* as our Messiah who will lead us back to our own land and establish us there in prosperity"[75] (my italic emphasis). That represents the feeling of many Jewish people. So, I don't believe we can say for certain whether this man is a Jew or a Gentile. We must not read too much into the fact that he comes out of the sea.

He has ten horns with ten diadems, he has seven heads with blasphemous names, he is like a leopard, he has feet like a bear, and a mouth like a lion. Have you ever seen anything like that? Certainly not. John did his best to tell us what he saw, and what he is telling us is that in the eyes of God this beast is indescribably horrible. The dragon (Satan) gives him (Antichrist) power and thrones and authority. Once again, we need to go back to Daniel, but keep those animals in your head—leopard, bear, lion. Watch what happened when Daniel prophesied about kingdoms that would come on earth, starting with Daniel's day (Daniel 7:4-7):

> **The first [beast] was like a lion and had the wings of an eagle...And behold, another beast, a second one, resembling a bear...After this I kept looking, and behold, another one, like a leopard...After this I kept looking in the night visions, and behold, a fourth beast, dreadful and terrifying and extremely strong...different from all the beasts that were before it, and it had ten horns.**

Daniel saw four major kingdoms. The first (lion) was the one in which he was living, Babylon. The second (bear) was Media-Persia, and the third (leopard) was Greece. The fourth beast, which he cannot/does not name (he only says that it was dreadful and terrifying and extremely strong) was Rome. That is the beast we are encountering here. Did you notice that the Revelation 13 beast had characteristics of all the other three beasts?

How do we know this beast of Chapter 13 is Rome, effectively come back to life? Later on (17:9) we find out that the seven heads represent seven hills. Rome was known as the city of seven hills, and people were proud of that description. This will be some form of a reconstituted Roman empire, and the ten horns will be ten nations brought together. Warren Wiersbe tells us this about the symbolism:

> *The three animals...remind us of the four beasts Daniel saw in his dream: a lion (Babylon), a bear (Media-Persia), a leopard (Greece), and a "terrible beast." John saw these animals in reverse order since he was looking back, while Daniel was looking ahead. The final world empire will be rooted in all the previous empires and unite in one their evil and power. Added to the ferocity of these beasts will be Satan's own power, throne, and authority!*[76]

How in the world can that ever happen? It's hard to unify Europe. There was the old Common Market. Now we have the European Union, but then we had Brexit, and now other countries are considering leaving the EU. Every time Europe tries to unite, it fails. Some people say it can never happen and thrive long-term. Vernon McGee said this many years ago: "Many have said that it is impossible to get Europe together. It *is* impossible until God is ready—and Satan is going to supply the man."[77] That is what all these animals are about and how it all comes together.

The first beast has actually been active since 6:1-2. We met him on a white horse going forth to conquer. He has been rising to power, but he has been doing it through peaceful means. He has been persuading people to follow him. As tribulation has come on earth, people have looked for someone to follow who will take care of them and provide for them. He makes a covenant with Israel, and they gladly follow him. So he has been active, but he has been masquerading as a man of peace, saying, *I will provide peace; I will take care of everything.*

Here we find out he had a fatal wound in one of his heads. That is mentioned in v. 3 and v. 12. It is further described in v. 14 as a wound of the sword. Verse 3 and v. 14 tell us he was healed of his fatal wound. Does this mean that this man (Antichrist) was actually killed dead, or did he just appear to be dead? Is he just pretending to have been resurrected when he never really died? Did he actually die and come back to life? Scholars disagree. Certainly he is trying to mimic our risen Lord and Savior who did die on the cross for the sins of the world and did rise again. I can tell you that v. 3, which says **as if it had been slain,** is the exact same phrase that was used to describe the Lord Jesus Christ all the way back in Chapter 1: **a Lamb as if it had been slain.** So it appears he died and then came back to life. However, some have said that is symbolic; he died politically and then got his power back. (Do you remember what I said at the start of this book about interpretations of The Revelation differing based on how much is seen as literal, and how much is seen as symbolic?) In any event, whether literal or symbolic, he has become more popular, more powerful than ever before. We are told the whole earth was amazed (v. 3): everyone looked in wonder at the beast.

They worship Satan (v. 4), who is the source of the beast's authority, and they worship the beast. Here is what they say about him: **"Who is like the beast, and who is able to wage war with him?"** (13:4). Harry Ironside says:

> *This coming one is the Grand Monarch of the New Humanity cult. He is the coming Imam of the Muslims. He is the long-expected last incarnation of Vishnu awaited by the Brahmins; the coming Montezuma of the Aztecs; the false Messiah of the apostate Jews; the great Master of all sects of yogis; the Ultimate Man of the evolutionists; and the Übermensch of Nietzsche.*[78]

The whole world will say, *He's the one we've been waiting for. Who is like him? Who could ever wage war against him?* And the whole world will worship him. There will be wonder, there will be arrogant words, there will be blasphemies (he will speak against God and God's Name and God's tabernacle and against those who dwell in heaven). He will be able to do all that for 42 months—there's that 3.5-year time again. That is how long his authority will last. This looks ahead to Chapter 15, when we enter the second half of the tribulation.

He will wage war with the saints to overcome them. That means there will be believers on Earth at this time. He will rule the world, and everyone except believers will worship him. How are they described? They have their names written in the Lamb's Book of Life from before the foundation of the world. They will not worship him because they will know better.

Two things are mentioned in v. 10, captivity and the sword: **If anyone is destined for captivity, to captivity he goes; if anyone kills with the sword, with the sword he must be killed.** We understand the first part about captivity, but to whom does the second half refer (people who kill with the sword)? Bible commentaries are mostly silent about that question, noting only the use of captivity and sword! But Leon Morris was brave enough to offer us this interpretation:

> *If it is in the providence of God that the Christian is for captivity, then to captivity he will surely go. But the second part has to do with requital. The man who kills with the sword will be killed as he has killed...The truth of Christ cannot be defended by violence.*[79]

Christians should not at this time defend themselves with the sword. The one who uses the sword will be killed with the sword.

Did you notice we have seen wonder (1-3), worship (4-5, 8), words (6), and war (7,10)? (I am indebted to Warren Wiersbe for that alliteration.) You might also notice that I have omitted v. 9. What about that verse? Well, it's very short and simple: **If anyone has an ear, let him hear.** That is of course a great warning. Notice what it *doesn't* say. Do you remember the phrase at the end of the letters to all seven churches in Chapters 2 and 3? **He who has an ear, let him hear what the Spirit says to the churches** (2:7, 11, etc.). Those who hold to the pre-tribulation rapture position—the taking out of all believers and the taking of the Holy Spirit (who indwells believers) out of the world before the tribulation—tell us why 13:9 is different. The argument is that the rapture occurred at the beginning of Chapter 4, so the Spirit and churches are not mentioned here in Chapter 13. That is certainly possible. However, if you have done any debating, you know that arguments from silence are not the strongest arguments. Yet the omission of Spirit and churches here in 13:9 would be consistent with the pre-tribulation rapture position.

Sign 4: The Second Beast

That brings us to the second beast, who is introduced with the same words as the first beast: *And I saw.* He is, as we have already noted, the false prophet, and that specific label shows up later in The Revelation. He comes out of the earth. If you combine that with the first beast coming out of the sea, perhaps the symbolism is as simple as the whole Earth being the domain of Satan. One comes from the sea, one comes from the earth, and the three of them work together.

He has two horns like a lamb. Isn't that a nice picture? He looks like a sweet little lamb. He probably talks in very warm tones, and people love hearing him talk. He gets excited when he needs to; he can rouse crowds when he needs to. But notice (v. 11) he spoke like a dragon. We are reminded of Jesus' words in Matthew 7:15. **"Beware of the false prophets, who come to you in sheep's clothing, but inwardly are ravenous wolves."** Now that applies to any false prophet, any heretic through the church age, but this is the ultimate fulfillment of that warning from our Lord Jesus Christ Himself. He (the second beast) exercises the same authority as the first beast, and he makes the Earth worship the first beast. Notice that in v. 12 that fatal wound of the first beast is mentioned again. That is the third time we read of the fatal wound. When you see something mentioned three times, it must be extremely significant.

119

The first beast was a political leader; the second beast is a religious leader. John Phillips says this about the false prophet:

His arguments will be subtle, convincing, and appealing, His oratory will be hypnotic, for he will be able to move the masses to tears or whip them into a frenzy. He will control the communication and media of the world and will skillfully organize mass publicity to promote his ends. He will be the master of every promotional device and public relations gimmick. He will manage the truth with guile beyond words, bending it twisting it, and distorting it. Public opinion will be his to command. He will mold world thought and shape human opinion like so much potter's clay. His deadly appeal will like in the fact that what he says will sound so right, so sensible, so exactly what unregenerate men have always wanted to hear.[80]

This is a dangerous, dangerous man. Think of all the great orators who have been able to move people in powerful ways through the centuries. Think of Abraham Lincoln, Reagan, Churchill for good; Hitler for evil. All of them would be nothing in comparison to what you see in this chapter.

He will perform signs, i.e., he has power to do miracles. The one that is specifically mentioned is fire coming down from heaven. Those signs will deceive people because he is a deceiver by nature. How can he do that? Remember Pharaoh's magicians, who imitated the miracles of Moses. This is the same kind of thing with the same source of power: Satan.

He has an image made of the first beast, and then the image breathes and speaks in v. 15. If you have read the prophets and the Psalms, you will know they all said the same thing: idols don't and can't walk or speak. But this one does, and that also causes people to wonder and be in awe. If you refuse to worship (v. 15), you're dead. Charles Swindoll says, "These two monstrous emissaries of evil will be the most persuasive and dynamic political and religious leaders in all of time."[81] Harry Ironside predicts the way the world will go mad (he comes from a pre-tribulation view):

Let every Christian suddenly be taken away from this scene, and you will have gross darkness covering the earth. With the preservative power of righteousness gone, the masses of men will be given up to corruption and violence. Read the account of the days before the Flood, and you will have some sense of the chaotic condition that will prevail.[82]

How long does Antichrist have? 1,290 days. Daniel tells us from the time (the mid-point of the tribulation) the regular sacrifice is abolished and the abomination of desolation is set up, which is the image of the beast, there will be 3.5 years (1,290 days). Satan will finally get what he has always wanted—worship from the whole world—but he only gets it for 3.5 years.

Then he makes life even more difficult. Everyone must be marked with the name or the number of the beast in order to buy or sell. The number of his name is 666, and it is the number of a man. There have probably been about 666 interpretations of that number over the last 2,000 years. Emperor Nero, Emperor Constantine, Mohammed, the popes, Martin Luther, Napoleon, Abraham Lincoln, Hitler, FDR, JFK, Mikhail Gorbachev, Saddam Hussein, Osama bin Laden have all been suggested. I want to talk about two of those; you might have at least heard the first one. (You need to understand that this is junk.) There is a phrase, *Vicarius Filii Dei*, meaning Vice-regent of the Son of God. The people who say the pope is Antichrist tell us this phrase is on the crown of the pope (the pope wears a tiara for many formal occasions). If you take the Roman numerals in Vicarius Filii Dei and convert them to our numbers (both v and u come from the same Latin letter, so each is 5), you get this:

V(5) + i (1) + c (100) + i + u (5) + i + l (50) + i + i + d (500) + i = 666

Wow, you might say, that is really convincing, but there are major flaws here. First, the phrase *Vicarius Filii Dei* appears only once, and that is from a document supposedly written by Constantine that is widely regarded as a forgery. Second, it has never appeared on any crown of any pope. Every pope gets to choose his own crown and what he wants written on it. Some of those crowns have been preserved for posterity, and not one of them contains this phrase. In fact, it is a phrase the Catholic Church never uses to refer to the pope, so if anyone tells you this is the evidence that the pope's name is equal to 666, don't believe it.

Here is another way to convert names to numbers that someone invented:

A = 100

B = 101

C = 102

D = 103

etc.

Z = 125

Notice we don't get to 126 (26 letters in our alphabet) because we started with 100, not with 101. Then if you take the six letters of Adolf Hitler's last name, they are these numbers:

H = 107

I = 108

T = 119

L = 111

E = 104

R = 117

Those total 666. Hitler was Antichrist! Well, Hitler is dead. He took poison, and then just in case it didn't work, he shot himself in the mouth. That was the end of the evil Adolf Hitler.

So, I thought I'd have a little fun with numbers and my own name.

My 3 names each have 5 letters. 3 x 5 = 15, and 1 + 5 = 6. That's one 6.

The letters in Kunda are in positions 11, 21, 14, 4, and 1 in the alphabet. Add them together, and 11 + 21 + 14 + 4 + 1 = 51. Again 5 + 1 = 6. That's two 6's.

I needed a third 6, and I really had to stretch for the last one. My middle and last names have 2 L's (50 each = 100), and 1 D (500). 500 + 100 = 600. That's the third 6.

So, the number of my name is 666! Give me your name, nicknames, maiden name, titles, degrees; I'm confident I can come up with a way for your name's number to be 666. The important thing is that the text says, **Let him who has <u>understanding</u> calculate the number of the beast** (13:18, my emphasis). People won't be able to have that kind of understanding or wisdom until they see who the person is. The number we should be concerned about today is not 666. We should be concerned about the number of people we know who have not yet come to personal faith in the Lord Jesus Christ, and who desperately need to hear that there is salvation in no one else. How many of your friends have not yet heard the gospel? *That* is the number to be concerned about. Those who are alive when all of these events happen will have the opportunity to apply wisdom and understanding to the situation.

Three and a Half Years

Before we move on to ATM, I want to say some things about the 3.5-year periods that keep recurring. It has been represented as time, times, and half a time; it has been represented as 1,260 days; and it has been represented as 42 months. The following chart will bring clarity to which events happen during the first 3.5 years and which happen during the latter 3.5 years of the tribulation:

FIRST 3.5 YEARS	SECOND 3.5 YEARS
2 Witnesses	Israel in wilderness
	Outer court of temple overrun
	2 beasts in charge of all
	Antichrist's blasphemies
7 seals & 6 trumpets	7th trumpet (3rd woe) = 7 bowls of wrath

In Lesson 11 I explained why the 2 witnesses have their ministry during the first 3.5 years. Of course, the 7 seals and the first 6 trumpets all come during the first 3.5 years, with Trumpets 5 and 6 bringing Woes 1 and 2. In Lesson 12 we discussed how Israel being protected in the wilderness and the outer court of the temple being overrun come during the second 3.5 years. Then in this lesson we looked at the 2 beasts in charge of everything and Antichrist's blasphemies, which match up with Daniel's prophecy of those things beginning at the midpoint of the tribulation, meaning they also happen during the second 3.5 years. We have heard Trumpet 7 sound, but we have not yet come to the 7 bowls of wrath which come out of Trumpet 7, so they will also occur during the second 3.5 years. Not everyone agrees on which half of the tribulation each 3.5-year period describes, but that is what makes the most sense to me. Once again, remember that these seven signs in Chapters 12 through 14 are supplemental material. They are thematic and topical; they are not chronological.

ATM (Apply to Me)

(The first sentence of each of the first three in the list are quotes from Charles Swindoll.)

1. "Satanic wonders are often impressive, but they are always deceptive."[83] If you hear about some supernatural event, check it out; be

skeptical; make sure it is of the Lord before you affirm it as something that is good and godly. Do not be deceived.

2. "Wherever anything or anyone other than God is worshiped, Satan is pleased."[84] You might say, *I would never worship an idol; I don't even know where there is an idol I could worship.* There can be idols we don't see that are worshiped ahead of Jesus Christ: career, hobby, sports, money, relationships. If any one of those or anything else in our lives is more important than our relationship with the Lord Jesus Christ, that's an idol. Whenever that happens, Satan is pleased.

3. "Even when God's power is at its greatest, God's power is greater still."[85] Did you notice the little phrase *It was given…*? Four times that phrase appears in this chapter, showing that certain authority was given to Antichrist or to the false prophet. I believe that refers to power that came from Satan, but it was always limited by the leash on which God holds Satan. The time was always limited as well. God's power is the greatest power.

4. II Thessalonians 2:9-10 **[Antichrist is] the one whose coming is in accord with the activity of Satan, with all power and signs and false wonders, and with all the deception of wickedness for those who perish, because they did not receive the love of the truth so as to be saved.**

Warren Wiersbe says:

The world would not receive Christ, but it will receive Antichrist. The world would not believe the truth, but they will believe the lie. Jesus spoke (and still speaks) gracious words of salvation, and men turn a deaf ear, but they will listen to the blasphemous words of "the beast." The world will not worship the Christ, but they will bow down to Antichrist.[86]

Early in the morning of the day I preached this message, one of our dear saints in my church was promoted to heaven. She had received Christ as her Savior *80 years earlier.* I can say with confidence that the second she drew her last breath on Earth, she was in the glorious presence of her living Lord. When your time on Earth is up, where are you headed? If you know it will be a promotion, Hallelujah! But if you're not sure, become sure today. You do not know the future; today could be your last opportunity. What side do you want to be on when all of these events unfold? If you have never surrendered your life to Jesus Christ, today—right now—can be your time of salvation.

Lesson 14

Read 14:1 – 20

Salvation and Judgment

Salvation and judgment. It's a theme we have seen throughout the book of The Revelation, and the contrast is extremely strong in this chapter.

I have mentioned that chronologically 15:1 follows the end of Chapter 11 which is 11:19. Remember that Chapters 12 through 14 are supplemental material; they are not chronological in the overall flow of The Revelation, but they help explain some of the *why* and the *how* of things that are transpiring. If you miss that fact, you can get into some very odd interpretations of Scripture by trying to fit these chapters into the overall chronology. We have also seen some other events that are *not* part of the tribulation, and we saw how prophecy from both the Old Testament and from the Gospels fits together.

We noted that Chapters 12 through 14 are in seven sections, seven visions/signs, which are introduced as follows:

12:1	A great sign
12:3	Another sign
13:1	And I saw
13:12	And I saw
14:1	And I looked
14:6	And I saw
14:14	And I looked

Two lessons ago we looked at the visions (or signs) starting at 12:1 and 12:3, and then in our last lesson we looked at those starting at 13:1 and 13:11. 12:1 was the sign of the woman, who is a symbol of Israel giving birth to the Christ, the Savior of the world, and 12:3 began the sign of Satan. The two signs in Chapter 13 were Antichrist and the false prophet. In this lesson we are looking at the last three signs. We will study them separately and in detail.

125

Sign 5: The 144,000

John saw the lamb standing on Mount Zion (14:1). Who is the Lamb? We have met Him many times in this book. He is the Lamb of God who takes away the sin of the world, the One who died for our sins, the One who is risen, the One who has conquered death. With Him are 144,000 who are sealed on their foreheads. Have we seen them before? Yes, we have; it was in 7:1-8. We saw a detailed description of who they are. They are 144,000 Jews, and we saw that their tribes were even enumerated: 12,000 from each of 12 tribes. They are very clearly Jews. We haven't heard of them since Chapter 7, but here they are again. Some people speculate that this is a different group of 144,000. You have to really stretch your imagination to come to that conclusion. We are told here that they are sealed on their foreheads, just like the 144,000 back in Chapter 7. It is clear this is the same group.

So why do they show up here? They're here because there's a good chance that many of us have probably been wondering what has happened to the 144,000. Well, here they are, standing on Mount Zion with the Lord Jesus Christ. Now where is Mount Zion? We need to understand that in Scripture there are two different Mount Zions. There is a heavenly Mount Zion. In Hebrews 12:22 you can read about being in the presence of God on Mount Zion, and it is clearly a heavenly Mount Zion. However, there are many references in Scripture to a place on Earth near Jerusalem. I believe (some disagree, but we won't start a separate denomination over this) the Mount Zion described here in Chapter 14 is on Earth.

The 144,000, it says in the passage, are sealed. What does that mean? It means they are secure. How many were there back in Chapter 7? 144,000. Did you notice how many there are here? 144,000, not 143,999. There are still 144,000. They were sealed for protection, and how many did Jesus Christ lose? None. They are also special. What do we mean by that? Look at vs. 2 and 3, where John heard the sound of harpists playing on their harps and they (that's the 144,000) **sang a new song before the throne and before the four living creatures and the elders; and no one could learn the song except the one hundred and forty-four thousand who had been purchased from the earth.** No one else can sing this song! Only the 144,000 can sing it because they're special. What is that song? I don't know because I'm not part of the 144,000, so I haven't heard it, and therefore I can't tell you. I can't learn it because *they are special*. We should have no problem with the fact that they get to learn a special song.

We noted back in Chapter 7 that they are Jews who have come to recognize Jesus as their Messiah, and they are powerful evangelists proclaiming that truth. (We tried to imagine what it would be like to have 144,000 Jewish Billy Sundays or Billy Grahams, and what kind of difference that would make on Jewish people around the world.) We are told they are spotless and that they are blameless. If you look in v. 4, you will see they have not been defiled with women; they have kept themselves chaste. Verse 5 says no lie was found in their mouths. Have you ever known somebody who was just a habitual liar? The joke is you can tell when that person is lying—his/her lips are moving. Maybe you have seen some politicians like that! This group of 144,000 doesn't lie. This group has not been defiled with women; we are told they have kept themselves chaste. The word is literally virgin, and it is typically a word that was used of women, but when it applied to men it meant celibate. Why would you apply it to men? Because it says they have not been defiled with women. The implication here is that the 144,000 are men and that they are celibate. Like so many things in The Revelation, is this literal or is this symbolic? Does this mean literally that they were celibate and that none of them ever married? Some people say yes, that is exactly what it means. Others say no, this is symbolic, because in Scripture purity in sexual relations is often used as a symbol of purity in our relationship to the Lord. The Lord called Israel an adulterer when it went after foreign gods, so this is symbolic of a pure relationship with the Lord. Whichever interpretation is correct, I can certainly conclude that they have led holy lives, and purity in their spiritual lives would also mean purity in their physical lives. Remember also that to take a wife and have relations with her is not <u>unholy</u>; it is <u>holy</u> and it would not be considered defilement. (Again, we won't start a separate denomination over whether this is literal or symbolic.)

When are they standing on Mount Zion? If they are standing at the mid-tribulation point, then they are to be sealed and protected for 3.5 more years, which will be the worst of the tribulation. That certainly is a possibility. However, since Chapters 12, 13, and 14 are not chronological, this is something that might look ahead to the *end* of the tribulation. It shows us their final destiny: to be privileged to stand with the Lord Jesus Christ on Mount Zion at the final end of it all, and there will still be not 143,999 but 144,000. I favor that interpretation.

Sign 6: Three Angels

You will see that three angels are mentioned: one each in vs. 6, 8 and 9. We will identify them as number 1 angel, number 2 angel, and number 3 angel. When number 1 angel shows up, John says, **"And I saw another angel"** (14:6). What does he mean by another angel? We haven't seen any angels in this chapter, but we have seen plenty of angels throughout The Revelation, so this is *another* angel. This number 1 angel has an *Eternal gospel.*

This is the only use of the word gospel in the entire book of The Revelation: 14:6. How long is eternal? Forever because the gospel is forever. And who is it for? It's for every nation, every tribe, every tongue, and every people. It's not just for the Jews, it's not just for those born near the land of Palestine in the Middle East, it's not just for those in Antarctica (that would be a really small number!), it's not just for the United States, and it's not just for South America. It's for *every* nation, tribe, tongue, and people. There is *one* gospel for the whole world. There is no other gospel. Everyone must be saved by the blood of Jesus Christ.

The angel said to worship Him who made the heaven, earth, sea, and springs of water. Why would he say that? Certainly, that's true, but wouldn't it likely say something about the blood of Jesus? Why the emphasis on Creator worship? I believe it is because rejection of Christ *starts* with rejection of worship of the Creator, leading to worship of the creation. Out of worship of creation comes ridiculous theories that everything that is here—you and I and the massive complex detail with which our bodies function—all happened by chance. Natural selection. There was this Big Bang and then there was primordial soup, and all of a sudden there was life (they don't know where that came from), and then there was just a one-celled amoeba, and it crawled up on land and it grew lungs and then arms and legs and finally it became smart enough to be man. Do you believe that junk? That's the prevailing thought being taught in many of our schools today as if it were truth. It's a fat lie of the devil and in the last time it will be even worse. That is why the angel said to worship Him and not His creation. However, if you start with Him as Creator, then you'll know He is also the One who has the authority to judge (people like to avoid discussing that), which is what He is doing in this book. You must escape the judgment by knowing the Lord Jesus Christ. Worship of the One who made the earth, sea, and springs of water is the starting point to believing and accepting the eternal gospel.

Number 2 angel doesn't have the *eternal gospel* but he has the prophecy of *eternal doom.* He says, **"Fallen, fallen is Babylon the great"** (14:8). It's prophetic and looks forward to something that we will look at in detail when we get to Chapters 17 and 18. This is another section that looks ahead. Remember Chapters 12 through 14 are not chronological. Some look back, some look ahead. This looks ahead. For right now I can say that Babylon here in The Revelation represents the entire world system financially and religiously that is opposed to God. We will see its judgment in Chapters 17 and 18—religious Babylon and commercial Babylon fallen. Eternal doom.

Number 3 angel talks about *eternal consequences.* In our last lesson we looked at the two beasts, Antichrist and the false prophet. This angel says that to worship the beast or receive the mark of the beast means that the person who does so will be tormented with fire and brimstone, and that their smoke goes up for a little while. Now wait, no, it doesn't say that, does it? It says their smoke goes up *forever and ever*, and they have no rest day and night. You can't be any clearer than that, can you? Hell is real. It's a place to be shunned. We can't escape it in our own goodness, but we can do so through the power of the blood of Jesus. We can have forgiveness so we don't wind up there. It's real.

Now I want to say something about the reality of hell. There is a sad situation in many pulpits today. Consider this statement: *I do not believe in a literal hell.* I don't subscribe to that statement, but a few years ago there was a survey done by a Northwestern University professor. He surveyed pastors and ministers across this country.[87] He asked them, *Do you believe in the literal hell?* Do you know what percentage of pastors and ministers agreed with the statement *"I do not believe in a literal hell"*?

Congregational Church 96%

Episcopalian Church 96%

Methodist Church 92%

Presbyterian Church 85%

Baptist Church 50%

Lutheran Church 30%

Those numbers are frightening. I'll bet you're wondering how that can happen. How can that be, because Scripture is so clear? Once you deny that the Bible is the Word of God, and you say that only some of it is the Word of God, who becomes the final authority? You do. You decide which parts you want to believe and which parts you don't want to believe. So, if you don't like those verses about hell, you decide they are just not true—they're not part of the Word of God—it's just something that someone put in there to scare people. Well, it *should* scare us because it's real. You see, the teaching that the Bible isn't really the Word of God has permeated many seminaries and Bible colleges for those are preparing for ministry, and that heresy has filtered down through their students into the pulpits across America. That's why you get numbers like this. Do you wonder why our country is in the shape it's in? There is no fear of God because there's no fear of judgment. I hope your church believes in *the whole Bible for the whole world.* (By the way that's the motto of Asbury Theological Seminary.[88])

Is it fun to teach about hell? No, of course it's not fun. But it's real. And it's in God's Word, and I am compelled to teach the whole of Scriptures. So those were *eternal consequences* for those who received the mark of the beast.

But do you know what? There are also some good eternal consequences here in this passage, and they are about the perseverance of the saints. (Saints is a synonym for believers in Scripture. Saint does not equal super Christian. All believers are saints in Scripture.) The ones who don't worship the beast, the ones who don't receive the mark of the beast, the ones who keep the commandments of God and keep their faith in Jesus Christ, there are eternal consequences for them too. Oh, wonderful consequences. Yes, many of them will be martyred. Others will starve. Can you imagine living during that time, if you can't buy or sell anything unless you have the mark of the beast? How will you eat? The only food you might be able to find is what you could beg or what you could grow yourself. Maybe you can find a group of people in a commune somewhere who can help each other out, but there will be a good chance you will be found out and martyred. However, about those who are martyred John says **Blessed are the dead who die in the Lord from now on. They rest from their labors and their deeds follow them** (14:13). Sometimes you might hear those words used at a funeral. Certainly, that is true of believers today: blessed are the dead who die in the Lord. But in context John is talking about what happens during the tribulation: great blessing and rest for those who died in the Lord.

Sign 7: Angels with Sickles

We now consider 14:14-20, the last of the seven signs of these three chapters. We see Jesus sitting on a white cloud holding a sharp sickle. How do we know it's Jesus? Look at the description in v. 14: **...behold a white cloud and sitting on the cloud was one like a son of man, having a golden crown on His head.** Does that sound familiar? Having a golden crown on His head? Some might say this is an angel. No, it's the Lord Jesus Christ Himself who is the Son of Man. It's a title Jesus often used of Himself. He's wearing a crown, the crown of righteousness. We also encounter three more angels, and we shall label them angels number 4, number 5, and number 6. We find them in vs. 15, 17, and 18.

Number 4 angel comes from the temple and he says to Jesus, **"Put in your sickle and reap, because the hour to reap has come, because the harvest of the earth is ripe"** (14:15). He swings His sickle, and the Earth is reaped. What all that means, we will look at in a moment in some detail. But first I want to move through the rest of this section and then we'll go back and look at possible interpretations. Number 5 angel is from the temple, and he is holding a sharp sickle also. Then number 6 angel arrives: he has the power of fire and comes from the altar. (Remember what the altar in heaven represents. It is a symbol of the shed blood of our Lord Jesus

Christ who is the one perfect all sufficient and sacrifice for all time who takes away all sins for all who put their faith in Him.) What does it mean that He has power over fire? Fire represents judgment. He has the power of judgment over those who have rejected the one all- sufficient sacrifice. They choose to send themselves to hell because they will not come to Christ and be saved. Number 6 angel then calls out to number 5 angel and says to use his sickle to gather the ripe grapes of the earth. Then the clusters from the vine are put into the wine press of judgment. The last verse of the chapter tells us about massive bloodshed. That is probably looking ahead to the great battle where hundreds of millions will try to destroy the Lord Jesus Christ, and there will be massive defeat for all of them.

As we seek to understand what these angels are doing, it is important at this point in our study that we return to consideration of what is commonly called The Rapture. Paul wrote about it in I Thessalonians 4:16-17:

The Lord Himself will descend from heaven with a shout, with the voice of the archangel, and the trumpet of God; and the dead in Christ shall rise first. Then we who are alive and remain shall be caught up together with them in the clouds to meet the Lord in the air, and thus we shall always be with the Lord.

Bible students have been debating (and sometimes arguing over) when this event will occur for many centuries. We know it *will* occur because it says so in God's Word. But there is no place in The Revelation where we find this event described in the same way. I have already mentioned that many believe The Rapture occurs at the beginning of Chapter 4, before The Tribulation (We discussed that in Lesson 5). Others believe that vs. 14-16 here in Chapter 14 describe the event, so let's take a closer look at those verses specifically, which are a harvest or reaping of the Earth. Therefore, some people believe it fulfills the following words of Jesus from Matthew 13:24-30.

"The kingdom of heaven may be compared to a man who sowed good seed in his field. But while men were sleeping, his enemy came and sowed tares also among the wheat, and went away. But when the wheat sprang up and bore grain, then the tares became evident also. And the slaves of the landowner came and said to him, 'Sir, did you not sow good seed in your field? How then does it have tares?' And he said to them, 'An enemy has done this!' And the slaves said to him, 'Do you want us, then, to go and gather them up?' But he said, 'No; lest while you are gathering up the tares, you may root up the wheat with them. Allow both to grow together until the harvest; and in the time of the harvest I will say

to the reapers, "First gather up the tares and bind them in bundles to burn them up; but gather the wheat into my barn.""

I *don't* believe the verses before us here in Chapter 14 are describing the same event. Matthew Chapter 13 talks about separating wheat and tares, which refer to apostasy in the church mixed with true biblical teaching. A perfect example would be the heresy that is taught about hell by so many ministers and pastors that we looked at earlier. Certainly, Jesus will reward the wheat (those who have been true to the Word of God), and He will figuratively burn up the tares who spread heresy. But the only thing the passages have in common is a general reference to harvest. No separation of wheat and tares is even hinted at here in Chapter 14.

More closely related to Revelation 14 are these words of Jesus from Mark 4:26-29.

"The kingdom of God is like a man who casts seed upon the soil; and goes to bed at night and gets up by day, and the seed sprouts up and grows—how, he himself does not know. The soil produces crops by itself; first the blade, then the head, then the mature grain in the head. But when the crop permits, he immediately puts in the sickle, because the harvest has come."

This passage in Mark is the only place in all four Gospels where the work sickle is used. Jesus is clearly talking about *good* crop, and so, it is argued, the sickle here in our study is the harvesting of believers in The Rapture. That argument is a strong one. We will say more about the timing of this event in a moment.

All of that discussion assumes that vs. 14-16 describe one event, while vs. 17-20 describe a different event. However, the other interpretation is that all of vs. 14-20 is simply a double metaphor—both sickles describe the same event, and that event is judgment. Evidence for that view is found in Joel 3:12-14 (my underlining):

Let the nations be aroused and come up to the valley of Jehosha-phat, for there I will sit to judge all the surrounding nations. Put in the sickle, for the <u>harvest is ripe</u>. Come, <u>tread, for the wine press is full</u>; the vats overflow, for <u>their wickedness is great</u>. Multitudes, multitudes in the valley of decision! For the day of the Lord is near in the valley of decision.

Notice that the sickle of the harvest and the treading of the wine press appear together in the same verse, so a strong case can be made that they are describing the same act of judgment by God, meaning none of the verses in Revelation describe The Rapture. They are rather a foreshadow of what is about to happen during the last 3.5 years of The Tribulation. (By the way, if you've ever heard evangelists use this text about multitudes in the Valley of Decision who need to decide whether to follow Jesus, that would be a misapplication of the text. The Valley of Decision is clearly not where men decide about God; it is where God decides about man.)

So, we are faced with these two competing views of the passage. The scholars who believe The Rapture is being described here, commonly called a mid-tribulation Rapture position, also tell us that the Church will escape only the second half of The Tribulation, which is specifically God's wrath. They point to I Thessalonians 5:9 (my underlining): **God has not destined us for <u>wrath</u>, but for obtaining salvation through our Lord Jesus Christ.** But look at these words from all the way back in Revelation 6:16 (my underlining): **"Fall on us and hide us from the presence of Him who sits on the throne, and from the <u>wrath</u> of the Lamb."** This is from the opening of the sixth seal, which is close to the *beginning* of The Tribulation. So, the argument about God's wrath only being the second 3.5 of the tribulation years fails.

So, what are we to conclude? *If* these are separate events (the harvest and the grapes), then it is likely that the first does indeed describe the rapture, but in different terms from I Thessalonians 4. But there are unanswered questions with this view. Why is the Church not mentioned as a witness during the first 3.5 years? Two witnesses are mentioned, but they are probably Elijah and Moses. The 144,000 are sealed for protection and ministry of evangelism, but they are clearly Jews. The only mention of the Church would be the martyrs in Seal 5, but they are under the altar in heaven. What about a ministry the Church would have on Earth? If, however, you put The Rapture at the beginning of Chapter 4 or somewhere in Chapter 4 or 5, you are faced with the difficulty that no passage in Revelation 4 or 5 (before the opening of the scroll of judgment) reads anything like I Thessalonians 4. To get there, you must conclude that John represents the Church, and when he is called to *Come up here* in Revelation 4, he is symbolic of the entire Church. You can understand why scholars have different interpretations!

But now let's talk about the timing, and this is critical. Remember what we said about Chapters 12 through 14. They consist of seven different signs John saw, and they are *not* part of the overall chronology, nor are they chronological by themselves. We have traveled back before the creation of the world, and we have looked ahead to the final reward of the 144,000. So, it is possible that The Rapture *is* described here, but the timing of it could be *anywhere* in the overall chronology. That doesn't answer the question of when, but it might just bring about some unity of thought about the meaning of vs. 15-16. *Or* if this is all one event, which is what Joel probably suggests, then the double metaphor simply reinforces just how desperate things are about to get on Earth. However, that removes the closest thing in all the book of The Revelation to describing the rapture!

I'm certain many readers have an opinion. You've been taught certain things, and some readers might have really strong convictions about this. That's good, and I respect you for that. But let's recognize, please, that brilliant Bible scholars who are all dedicated to the truth of God's Word do not all agree. (They're not the liars who don't believe the Bible and who deny the reality of hell.) These are people who are dedicated to the Word of God. So whatever position you hold, please hold it with humility, and above all please hold it with love for your brothers and sisters in Christ, because there will be disagreements. What binds us together is the truth that our Lord Jesus Christ is coming again; that's the point of unity.

Although we can't say with certainty exactly how this is going to happen, don't miss the vital truth right here. At the very least the wine press descriptions tell us the judgments in The Revelation are certain to get worse, and that's where our next lesson will take us.

ATM (Apply to Me)

1. Have you seen the balance in this chapter—eternal gospel and rest from their labors vs. doom, gloom, judgment? That's the gospel, my friends. I'm sure many readers have heard it said that in order to tell you the good news I have to tell you the bad news. There would be no *need* for the good news if there weren't bad news. The bad news is I'm a sinner. We're all sinners, we're sinners by nature and we're sinners by choice. What do we deserve because we have rebelled against the Creator, the holy God of the universe? We deserve to be judged for eternity, suffering for our sins. None of us can ever say we've been good enough to earn our way into heaven, because the standard is perfection. But the good news is we don't have to earn our way into heaven. We not only can't, we don't have to. Jesus on the cross paid the penalty for our sins. Which sins? All of them! When you put your faith and trust in the Lord Jesus Christ, you have the assurance of eternal life, eternal reward. and rest from your labors. That's the good news. Enjoy the balance here in Chapter 14, because the next few chapters get pretty ugly. When those seven bowls of wrath start to be poured out, there will not be any interludes of mercy. The last 3.5 years of the tribulation, Oh my! You do not want to be anywhere near the Earth during those 3.5 years.

2. Despite what the heretics say, hell is real. We do not want to spend eternity there. Vernon McGee says: "After almost a century of insipid

preaching from American pulpits, the average man believes that God is all sweetness and light and would not discipline or punish anyone."[89] The Revelation tells a different story. We have to remember that. There's a heaven to be gained and a hell to be shunned, and we are surrounded by people who have not yet come to saving faith in Jesus Christ. We have a mission to be true to God's Word, to proclaim the bad news *and* the good news, and to let people know there is salvation. Hell is real. Do you want your family members there? Do you want your friends there? Do you want your neighbors there? Hell is real.

3. I want to conclude with the positive. This is important. Jesus keeps and preserves His own now, just as He says He will keep the 144,000 in the last days. If you have given your life to the Lord Jesus Christ, He has you in His hand and He will never let you go. Think of Peter who denied even knowing the Lord three times. Did He let Peter go? Did He give up on him? No. He will never let you go. He loves you so much, He loved you with a cross, and He's got you. Saving, helping, keeping, loving, He is with me to the end. He's got you and He's got me, and He'll never let us go!

Lesson 15

Read 15:1 – 16:16

6 Bowls

We have moved through a series of judgments that started with seven seals. Remember our diagram:

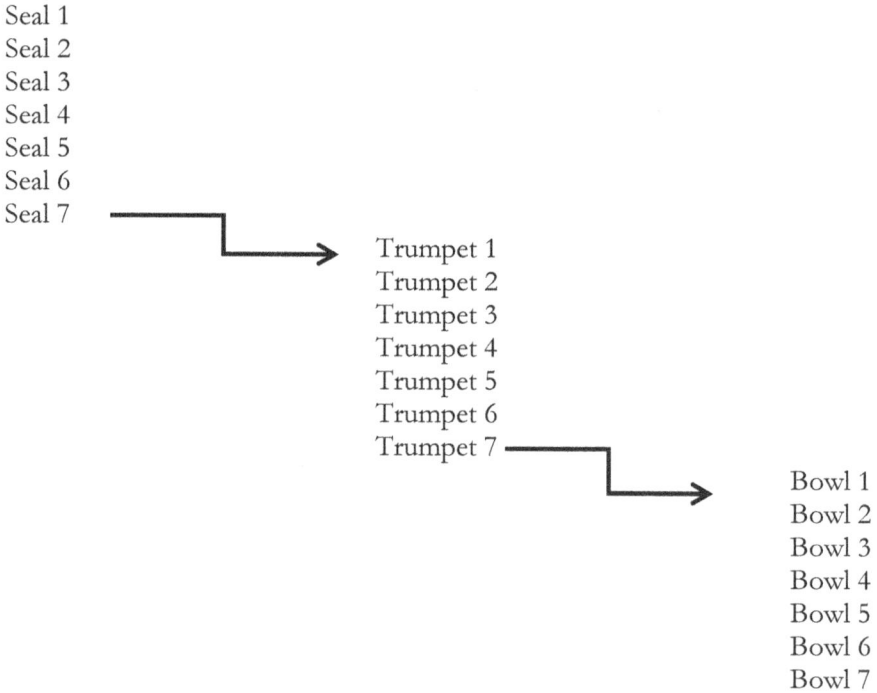

Seal 1
Seal 2
Seal 3
Seal 4
Seal 5
Seal 6
Seal 7 ⟶

Trumpet 1
Trumpet 2
Trumpet 3
Trumpet 4
Trumpet 5
Trumpet 6
Trumpet 7 ⟶

Bowl 1
Bowl 2
Bowl 3
Bowl 4
Bowl 5
Bowl 6
Bowl 7

Six seals were opened, followed by an interlude. When Seal 7 was opened, out of that came seven trumpets of judgment. Six of those sounded, followed by another interlude. When Trumpet 7 sounded, from that came seven bowls of wrath. Now, it's been quite a while since our lesson where Trumpet 7 sounded. At the time we noted that Chapter 15:1 follows the end of Chapter 11:19 chronologically. In our last three lessons we looked at seven different visions/signs that John saw between the end of Chapter 11 and the start of Chapter 15. We noted that they are not chronological either among themselves or within the overall flow of The Revelation. We have seen that at one point they went all the way back before the world was created, and they have also looked forward to the glorious end of history. John saw a woman, who represented Israel, and we saw her giving to the world the Christ child, the Messiah, the Savior. We saw a vision about Satan. In Chapter 13 we saw Antichrist and the false prophet, two beasts. In our last lesson we looked at the victory of the 144,000 prophets; it showed us their final destiny of glory; we saw a proclamation of the eternal gospel, the fate of Babylon, and eternal consequences and rewards for those who did or did not receive the mark of the beast. The seventh sign was of the harvest of grain and of grapes that occupied much of our discussion in the previous lesson.

Prelude to The Bowl Judgments: 5 S's

That brings us to the bowl judgments. Chapter 15 is the *prelude* to Chapter 16. It's the setting of the scene for what is about to happen. Chapter 15 can be divided into five sections: they are five S's (I am indebted to David Jeremiah for this alliteration). The first one is a *sign* that is described as great and marvelous. The second one is something like a *sea* of glass. John uses the words *as it were*; that's an idiom that means it wasn't actually a sea of glass but was what it looked like. Third is the *song* of Moses and of the Lamb. Fourth are *seven* angels with *seven* bowls. Fifth is *smoke*. This is the shortest chapter in The Revelation, just 8 verses.

Charles Swindoll tells us[90] we have:

A snapshot scene of coming judgment in v. 1

A glorious scene of triumphant joy in vs. 2-4

A dreadful scene of wrathful doom in vs. 5-8

Remember this is just the prelude to the actual judgments, which are the bowls of wrath that come beginning in Chapter 16. But first let's look at each of these five S's in Chapter 15.

The first S is a sign that is described as great and marvelous. We know those are wonderful words that describe who God is. God is great, God is marvelous. God is described as great and God is described as marvelous in many, many, many places in Scripture, but that phrase *great and marvelous* occurs only two times in the whole Bible, and they're both right here in Chapter 15 (vs. 1 and 3). This sign must have been particularly significant to John. What was it? Seven angels with the last—emphasis on *last*—plagues. In them the wrath of God is *finished*. Now you might be thinking of Jesus' words on the cross, where he said, "It is finished." That is a different Greek word, one that means paid in full. The Greek word here for the wrath of God being finished means completed, done, accomplished; the wrath of God is over.

The second S was something that *looked like* (the meaning of *as it were*) a sea of glass. That tells me that he couldn't figure out exactly how to describe it, so he used a metaphor. We have seen a sea of glass metaphor before in a vision of heaven (Chapter 4). This one is different because it is mixed with fire. Why is that, and how can you have a sea mixed with fire? That's all part of the metaphor. It is possibly symbolic of the fire through which the martyrs passed who are now in glory. It is also possibly symbolic of the fire of the final judgment that is about to fall. I believe it's symbolic of both. We are told that the martyrs who are there have come victorious from the beast, his image, and the number of his name. Remember that everyone was required to get his name or the number of his name on their hands or foreheads, and everyone was required to worship the beast. These martyrs are people who said *no*, I will not worship the beast, I will not bow down to the beast, I will not receive his number. Leon Morris says "It is worth noting that in the early church the day of a man's martyrdom was often called the day of his victory.[91]" Because someone who was about to be promoted to heaven by being martyred for Christ had been victorious over every temptation to give in to compromise and to renounce his faith, the one who stayed true even to the point of martyrdom was considered a victor. That's how such a person is described here. They are victorious and they are standing on (or perhaps next to) the sea of glass, holding harps. Why are they holding harps? Because there needs to be some accompaniment for the third S.

The third S is the song of Moses and the song of the Lamb. The text of the song of the Lamb appears here, but what is the song of Moses? We think of Moses the lawgiver, we think of Moses the one who brought the Ten Commandments and all of the law to the people of Israel, and we think of the one who led them for 40 years, the one who before that had gone to Pharaoh and said, **"Let my people go"** (Exodus 5:2 and multiple other places). What is the song of Moses? There are two songs with which Moses is associated. One is in Exodus 15 and the other in Deuteronomy 32. This surely refers to one or both of those two songs or at least to a portion of them. You might be familiar with Exodus 15:1. **I will sing to the Lord for He is highly exalted; the horse and its rider He has hurled into the sea.** The following verse (15:2) says, **The Lord is my strength and song, and He has become my salvation. This is my God, and I will praise Him; my father's God, and I will extol Him.** Those are words that were appropriate at that point for their deliverance from the hand of Pharaoh and from the armies of Egypt. But they are also appropriate for us. The Lord is my strength and song, and He, through the Lord Jesus Christ, has become my salvation. So perhaps that is the song of Moses, along with some of the verses that follow. The other possibility is the song of Moses is Deuteronomy 32. This is a very long chapter and a very long song. I am indebted to David Jeremiah, who points out that the last part of this particular song in Deuteronomy 32 is extremely relevant to what is going on at this point in The Revelation. There is a strong possibility that this is what is meant by the Song of Moses here in Chapter 15. Study these words from Deuteronomy 32:39-43.

> **"See now that I, I am He, and there is no god besides Me; It is I who put to death and give life. I have wounded, and it is I who heal; and there is no one who can deliver from My hand. Indeed, I lift up My hand to heaven, and say, as I live forever. 'If I sharpen My flashing sword and My hand takes hold on justice, I will render vengeance on My adversaries, and I will repay those who hate Me. I will make My arrows drunk with blood, and My sword shall devour flesh, with the blood of the slain and the captives, from the long-haired leaders of the enemy.'" Rejoice, O nations, with His people; for He will avenge the blood of His servants, and will render vengeance on His adversaries, and will atone for His land and His people."**

It is a song describing God's final judgment. We cannot say for certain which song/chapter/book is meant, but those verses in Deuteronomy 32 certainly fit at this point of The Revelation.

We do know, however, the song of the Lamb because it's given for us right here in vs. 3-4. Notice first that we give praise to God for His great and marvelous works. There's that phrase again—great and marvelous—the second and last time it appears in the Bible. There are four W's (David Jeremiah's alliteration again). His <u>works</u> are *great and marvelous*. The song goes on to praise God for His righteous and true <u>ways</u>. The things that He does are righteous and true; they are never false, and they are never unfair. Then there is praise to God for His <u>worth</u> [holiness] in v. 4. He is perfect and He must judge sin because He is holy. Fourth, at the end of v. 4 His <u>worship</u> is <u>worldwide</u>. **All the nations will come and worship before You.** His works, His ways, His worth, and worldwide worship. That is the song of the Lamb. If you look at the very end of v. 4 (**Your righteous acts have been revealed**), you will see the theme has circled back to God's righteous acts (<u>works</u>). This song of the Lamb is bookended by the mighty works of God—the *great and marvelous* works of God. What a wonderful, wonderful song: the song of the Lamb.

The fourth S is the seven angels who come out of the temple. Did you notice that? They come out of the temple. They are wearing white linen and golden girdles. Take all of that together—where they come from and what they are wearing—is all a sign of their purity and their holiness. Their work in the temple is holy, and now their judgments are also holy. One of the four living creatures gives them the seven golden bowls of the wrath of God. We met the four living creatures who served around the throne of God very early in The Revelation. Here one of them steps forward and gives to the angels the seven golden bowls of the wrath of God.

Following that is the fifth S, and that is smoke. It is smoke from the glory of God, and it is smoke from the power of God. Notice that no one enters the temple until the seven plagues are finished. One commentator notes that is "because of God's presence in His manifested glory and power during the execution of these judgments.[92]" In other words no one, nothing in heaven or on Earth, will stop these judgments. Leon Morris notes, "When God's good time has come, nothing can stop the final judgment.[93]" So that is Chapter 15, the shortest in the entire book, and it is the prelude to Chapter 16, in which these bowls of wrath are actually poured out.

You might remember that back when we were ready for Trumpet 5, Trumpet 6, and Trumpet 7, there was a message from an eagle that said **"Woe, woe, woe to those who dwell on the earth because of the remaining blasts of trumpet of the three angels who are about to sound."** (8:13) Then after the Trumpet 5 sounded and there was judgment, we were told the first woe had passed and there were two more coming. After Trumpet 6 sounded we were told the second woe was past and behold, the third woe was coming quickly. However, we get no such words anywhere in The Revelation that specifically label the third woe. Instead, when we think there ought to have been some great calamity come on Earth, we had the intervening material of seven signs in Chapters 12, 13, and 14. Now we see the seven bowls of wrath, which come out of Trumpet 7. Though Scripture does not tell us specifically, I believe these seven bowls of wrath are the third and final woe. Along with that they are the last of the judgments.

Bowls 1 - 6

In the first 16 verses of Chapter 16 we will look at the first six bowls of judgment. First John heard a loud voice. (Have you heard that phrase before?! Yes, this is a noisy book.) Sometimes the loud voice is that of an angel, but I believe it's probably the voice of God Himself here in Chapter 16. He says, **"Go and pour out the even bowls of the wrath of God into the earth"** (16:1). Do you understand? *It is time* for these judgments. They will be the worst things that have ever happened on planet Earth. No natural disaster, no manmade disaster, no war, no weapon, no terrorist attack, no explosion, no crime spree: nothing that has ever happened on Earth comes anywhere close to what is about to happen as these seven bowls, the final wrath of God is poured out. They go by us in fairly rapid succession.

The first angel pours out his bowl, and there are boils and sores on those who had the mark of the beast or who had worshiped the beast. *But I had to receive the mark in order to buy and sell. I was just being a good citizen.* That excuse won't work. The mark of the beast is the mark of judgment. Was there anyone left on Earth at this point who hadn't received the mark of the beast? Had they all been raptured and/or martyred by this time? If there are believers remaining, then they would be exempt from the boils and the sores. Does that sound familiar at all? Do you remember what happened in Egypt? One of the plagues of Egypt was that all the Egyptians had this type of plague come upon them, but Israel was protected. So, if there are any true believers left, they would be exempt.

Bowl 2 is poured out in the very next verse, the seas become blood, and every living thing in the seas dies. Now just use your imagination. Earlier we saw where 1/3 of the sea became blood in one of the judgments, but now it's all of the Atlantic, all of the Pacific. Do you know your oceans? All of the Indian Ocean, all of the Arctic Ocean, all of the seas, all the salt water became blood. Of course, everything died. Can you imagine being a shark, dolphin, a little sea bass? You wouldn't have a chance. Can you imagine the stench from that? Can you imagine what it would be like living on earth with all the seas becoming blood? Think of the ecological cycle of evaporation, condensation, precipitation. What would happen to that? Would there be good water coming down in the form of rain? One of the primary sources of water—the seas—is now blood, and everything would be disrupted. But there's more.

The third angel pours out his bowl, and now all the fresh water becomes blood (16:4-7). *Well, I'd be okay; I'd just go to the grocery store and get myself some bottled water.* Certainly not. Where do you think that bottled water comes from? There would be no water left to drink except what people had stored. Did you notice the phrase **angel of the waters**? (16:5). There's an angel of the waters. He is certainly the angel who poured out this bowl of judgment, but he must also be the angel who is responsible for the fact there is drinkable water on earth. We note from him, and then in the response from the altar, that *they* shed the blood of the saints and prophets, and *they* receive what *they* deserve, which is specifically blood to drink. This angel of the water says, **"Righteous are You…because You judge these things"** (16:5). The altar (remember the altar in 9:13, where the four horns of the altar spoke) speaks again; remember it represents the shed blood of Christ. If you reject the shed blood of Christ, then you are under judgment. The altar says God's judgments are true and righteous. I'm reminded of Egypt in regard to some of these things. Around the time Moses was born Pharaoh decided it would be a good idea to drown all the male Israelite babies. What happened to his army? It was drowned in the Red Sea. I'm reminded of the book of Esther, where Haman decided it would be a good idea to build a massive gallows to hang Mordecai on. What happened to Haman? He was hanged on the gallows he had prepared for Mordecai. There is poetic justice in Scripture, and that is what is reinforced here. They shed the blood of the saints and prophets, and now they get what they *deserve*—blood to drink. That's Bowl 3.

Bowl 4 is poured out on the sun, and it brings intense heat to scorch men with fire. There are different ways God could make the heat of the sun do that. Right now that heat is good and wonderful; it's just the right amount of heat the Earth needs, but God could change that in an instant. All He has to do is remove a few layers of atmosphere, and all of a sudden that atmosphere that protects us from the sun's heat is gone. Or He could simply move the sun closer to the earth. You say that would surely disrupt everything. It couldn't possibly happen because everything would be out of whack. Who made the sun and the Earth and everything else? If He wants to move the sun closer to the Earth, He can do that. Whatever He does, there is intense heat to *scorch* the Earth.

So boils (horrible sores), no water to drink, and then when you need water the most there won't be any during intense heat scorching people on earth. Charles Swindoll says:

> **One might expect that the next verse would describe how all those sore-afflicted, starving, thirsting, burning men and women of earth will raise their hands and cry out to God for mercy. Surely a loving God would hear the cries of their hearts, relent up His just wrath, and bring times of refreshing and renewal—even at this late stage.**[94]

Do they? Look at vs. 9 and 11. People do not repent or give glory to God, but rather they blaspheme His name; they curse God. If that's the way the people on earth respond, we understand why there won't be just four bowls of judgment.

The first four bowls have dealt with judgment on the natural world; God has completely withdrawn His hand of provision. In doing so He has said in essence, *Hey, you know how you don't want to come before Me? You don't want to bow before Me, you don't want to submit to Me, you don't want to recognize me as Creator; you want to make up scientific (so called) fantasies about how everything in the world got here by chance? You don't need Me? You don't want Me? I'm the One who has been providing for mankind since the creation the world, making sure it sustains life.* God has withdrawn His hand a provision because man has worshiped the creation rather than the Creator. Next, we turn to a different type of judgment—the political world.

Bowl 5 is poured out on the throne of the beast, and his kingdom is darkened. Where is the throne of the beast? We saw that part of the way he controls his kingdom is by ruling from Rome, but we also saw that his image was set up in Jerusalem. So, it is one of these two places. Specific locations aren't important. How big is this kingdom, and does this refer to everything he is ruling? If it does, it refers to the whole world; this is worldwide darkness. Some scholars have speculated that this refers to the area immediately surrounding his throne. I think it's worldwide because it says his kingdom, and he has taken over the whole world. It is quite possible, though this is not stated, that the darkness is symbolic of his waning power, that he is already losing his grip as we get closer to his final judgment. We cannot say for sure, but we know people gnawed their tongues in pain. Pain from what? Pain from their sores back in Bowl 1; the sores are still there. Did you notice these people did not repent of their deeds, but rather they blasphemed the God of heaven because of their pain and sores? Presumably, the scoring heat of the sun has for a moment disappeared because we have darkness, but the sores persist. The *did not repent* phrase is repeated.

Bowl 6 is poured out, and the Euphrates River dries up (v. 12). The reason for that is to prepare the way for the kings of the east. There will be a massive army that will align together against Jesus Christ. We are given an explanation of what Satan will do to help that happen. Three unclean spirits that look like frogs emerge—one from the dragon (Satan), one from the beast (Antichrist), and one from the false prophet. (By the way, this is the first time he is given the label of false prophet. I mentioned previously we would see that title actually show up, and here it is. It's used again later as well). From each one of this unholy triumvirate of evil—Satan, Antichrist, and the false prophet—an unclean spirit goes forth. John saw them symbolically looking like frogs, and they use miraculous signs to deceive the kings of the world to order to gather them together for the war of the great day of wrath. They gather together at a place called Har-Magedon; today we call it Armageddon. We will see in a moment that at this point the action freezes, because some other things have to be described before that Great War.

Did you notice we went from v. 14 to v.16? What about v.15? There is a parenthesis in the middle of all these bowls of wrath. It is a warning, and there is a promise. It is the one positive thing in this chapter: one important promise. The warning is: **"Behold, I am coming like a thief."** [Don't be caught off guard.] **Blessed is the one who stays awake and <u>keeps his garments</u>, lest he walks about <u>naked</u> and men see his shame** (my underlining). The reference is probably to the captain of the temple, who would make his rounds during the night to see if the guards were awake and alert. If one was found asleep, he was either beaten or his garments were removed from his body and set on fire, thus leaving him naked and ashamed for falling asleep on the job. To keep one's garments spiritually, a person has to always be alert (i.e., stay awake) to the dangers of Satan and the dangers of evil, and a person must be ready for the Lord's return, so that we are not surprised like people are when a thief comes and some are not ready. The blessing for the one who stays awake is the positive promise.

Conclusion

We leave the story with the kings of the earth gathered at Armageddon, and we will pick it up again in Chapter 19. More interlude material? Yes. But in order to understand the chronology of The Revelation, you have to understand where this explanatory material is, where these interludes are, where the parentheses are. Otherwise, you can get lost and not know what's going on. So freeze right here. Chapter 19 will come back to the armies of the earth that will gather at Armageddon. The next two lessons will deal with specific judgments of evils on earth.

But make no mistake, these seven bowls of wrath which are described first in 15:1, they are the *last*. Now how fast will all these bowls be poured out? How will people on earth know they are in the second half of the tribulation? In the last 3.5 years they come zoom, zoom, zoom, and zoom—one right after the other. They could be spread out over some period of time; however, it is not too long because no one would survive, and there would be no one left to mass together in an army. We can say with certainty that we have now come very close to the end of the tribulation. Vernon McGee says:

> *Remember that the Book of Revelation is Christocentric, that is Christ centered. Don't let the four horsemen carry you away, or don't be distracted by the blowing up the trumpets...and don't let your interest center on these bowls of wrath. Let's keep our eyes centered on Christ. He is in charge; He is the Lord. In this book we have the unveiling of Jesus Christ in His holiness, in His power, and in His glory...Remember that way back in Chapter 5 the Lord Jesus was the only One found worthy to open the seven-sealed books...He is in command to the end of this book.*[95]

ATM (Apply to Me)

1. Christ had the wrath of God poured out on Him at the cross so that we will be spared from the future wrath of God. If you have never accepted Christ's provision when He paid for all of our sins on the cross, do it today to avoid the wrath of God.

2. The saints in heaven, martyred or promoted through another death, rejoice in the triumph of God as He deals once and for all with the problem of suffering and sin. Read David's prayer in Psalm 7:9: **Oh let the evil of the wicked come to an end; but establish the righteous: for the righteous God tries the hearts and minds.** That prayer is being answered in complete finality, and every saint who has ever lived rejoices.

3. Someone once said that Dwight Moody reduced the population of hell by two million. In precise and perfect theology only Christ reduces the population of hell by saving people. What is meant is that many people gave their lives to Christ because of his ministry. I don't know the actual number, but I know it's a large one. We want to do everything we can to reduce the number of people who will face those judgments. There's urgency to living as a Christian in this world and being a consistent witness for Him.

4. 15:3-4 is a great model for worship in prayer. That's where we saw the works of God, we saw the ways of God, we saw the worth of God, and we saw how His worldwide worship. If you don't know how to pray in worship, there's a good outline. It's a very practical thing we can use on a daily basis.

5. Do not confuse the longsuffering of God with indifference toward sin. Do you remember what Peter wrote in his second epistle? (II Peter 3:3-4):

Notice first of all that in the last days mockers will come with their mocking following after their own lusts, and saying, where is the promise of his coming? For ever since the father fell asleep, all continues just as it was from the beginning of creation.

God is longsuffering and He is patient, but when the judgments are about to fall, time's up. There's no escape; we must never confuse the patience and longsuffering of God with indifference toward sin. He *will* have the final word.

Lesson 16

Read 16:17 – 17:18

It Is Done (Religious Babylon Is Judged)

I must ask you to please pay close attention in this lesson. The symbolism here and the depth of what God has revealed to John are extremely important, not just for John's day, but for the Church of all time, including today.

Let's review where we are. The Lamb of God opened the seven seals on the scroll of the judgment, and from the seventh seal came seven trumpets. From the seventh trumpet came the seven bowls of the wrath of God, the seven last plagues of judgment. They are Woe 3. We are told that in them the wrath of God is complete. In our last lesson we looked at the first six bowls: a plague of boils, the seas becoming blood, the fresh water becoming blood, scorching heat, darkness, and the Euphrates River dried up to prepare the way for the great Battle of Armageddon.

Bowl 7

As we come to 16:17, Bowl 7, once again we hear a loud voice. This one comes out of the temple from the throne. Now, whose voice would come out of the temple from the throne? No one other than God's, and God says, **"It is done."** The judgments are done. There is lightning and thunder and the most massive earthquake ever. In California they talk about The Big One. They don't know anything about The Big One. This in Chapter 16 is *the* big one. Along with that massive earthquake, there are hailstones weighing about 100 pounds each. Just let your imagination run wild for a little bit. The largest, heaviest bowling balls weigh 16 pounds. Imagine what it would be like to have a bowling ball fall on you. Now imagine something more than six times that weight falling out of the sky. You talk about hail damage on your roof? That one would wind up in the basement! Are you wondering about the size of those hailstones and saying, "Well, that's impossible." First of all, who made the hail? Second, let's look at two Scriptures.

> **As they [armies of 5 Amorite kings] fled from before Israel…the Lord threw large stones from heaven on them as far as Azekah, and they died; there were more who died from the hailstones than those whom the sons of Israel killed with the sword** (Joshua 10:11).

146

He has done it before and He will do it again. When Job was questioning God, God asked Him a long list of cross-examination questions. The Lord said to Job (Job 38:22):

Have you entered the storehouses of the snow, or have you seen the storehouses of the hail, which I have reserved for the time of distress, for the day of war and battle?

God is in control of all of this. He has reserved those hundred-pound hailstones for the last days. In our last lesson we saw how men didn't repent during the bowl judgments. Here again they blaspheme God, this time because of the hail.

Next, we read that the great city, a symbolic Babylon (we'll see what that means as we get into our lesson) was split into three parts, and Babylon the Great was remembered before God (16:19). We must freeze the action here because Chapters 17 and 18 are once again a parentheses. We will pick up gain in Chapter 19 with the coming Battle of Armageddon. But between the end of Chapter 16 and the beginning of Chapter 19, we have two chapters dealing with the judgment of Babylon. Here we look at Chapter 17, and in our next lesson we will look at Chapter 18. The precursor to this showed up all the way back in Chapter 14. Do you remember that in Chapters 12, 13, and 14 we had supplemental material? John had seven visions, two of those visions/signs had three angels each, and one of the angels in one of those visions said this (14:8): **Fallen, fallen, is Babylon the great, she who has made all the nations drink of the wine of the passion of her immorality.** That was a look forward to what is described in Chapter 17 and in Chapter 18. In fact, in Chapter 18 we will see those exact words repeated: **Fallen, fallen is Babylon the great** (18:2).

The Harlot Woman

As we come to Chapter 17, we see two main characters. The first is a woman who is called a harlot woman. In order to understand what we are talking about we need to establish her identity. It's easy because the passage tells us. She has a name on her forehead: "**Babylon the great, the mother of harlots of the abominations of the earth**" (17:5). Roman harlots used to wear their names on their forehead; readers in that day would have made the connection. That word *abominations* occurs only five times in the entire New Testament. Two of them are right here in this chapter; three of the five are in The Revelation. She is clearly contrasted with the woman we met in Chapter 12, who was Israel and who was portrayed as good. She was the "mother" of the Messiah, i.e., the nation that gave us the Messiah.

The Beast

The other main character in this chapter is the beast. Remember the identity of the beast from Chapter 13; he is Antichrist. So those are the two main characters here in this chapter. The beast is Antichrist, and the harlot woman is Babylon the great, mother of harlots and of abominations.

Meaning of "Babylon"

Now, why Babylon? My goodness. Do you know that Babylon is mentioned more than 250 times in the Bible? Stop and think about that. Jerusalem is mentioned more than that of course. But New York City is not mentioned. Your hometown is probably not mentioned. But Babylon is mentioned more than 250 times.

It's important for us to understand that *there are two uses of Babylon in Scripture*. One is Babylon the city/empire. It was Babylon that overran the southern kingdom of Judah and took people into exile. That's where Shadrach, Meshach, and Abednego were thrown into the fiery furnace while in exile in Babylon. It is where Daniel saw the handwriting on the wall at Belshazzar's feast, the last night of existence for that empire. That's one way that Babylon was used—a city and a real empire that existed in time.

However, the other way Babylon is used in Scripture is as a symbol of the world's commercial values and the world's heretical religious system that have influenced mankind for evil for over 3,000 years. The harlot woman here is that heretical *religious system*. This chapter is about her judgment. If you look at 17:1, this angel says to John, **"I shall show you the judgment of the great harlot."** What is this heretical religious system that has incurred God's wrath so greatly that it is singled out for judgment in this chapter? In order to answer that question, I need to take us all the way back (stay with me; this is deep), to just after the great flood that destroyed the entire Earth and judged mankind. Eight people were left on Earth: Noah, his wife, his three sons and their wives. God blessed Noah and his sons and said to them, **"Be fruitful and multiply,** (don't miss this) **and <u>fill the earth</u>"** (Genesis 9:1, my underlining). The command is to *fill the Earth*. In Chapter 10 we learn that the beginning of Nimrod's kingdom was Babel in the land of Shinar. Nimrod was a grandson of Ham, who was a son of Noah; in other words Nimrod was a great-grandson of Noah. We shall trace what Nimrod did and what this has to do with Babylon, starting with Genesis 11:1-3:

> It came about as they journeyed east, that they found a plain in the land of Shinar and settled there. And they said to one another, "Come, let us make bricks and burn them thoroughly....And they said, "Come, let us build for ourselves a city, and a tower whose

top will reach into heaven, and let us make for ourselves a name; lest we be scattered abroad over the face of the whole earth."

Was God pleased with that? No, He was not. Why? Because He said, **"Be fruitful and multiply and <u>fill the earth</u>"** (Genesis 9:1). They were supposed to spread out and *fill the whole Earth*, but these descendants of Ham, starting with Nimrod, decided *We don't want to spread out and fill the Earth; we want to build a tower*. Why? To make a name for themselves in clear defiance of God. Our lives should glorify God, not us, and this was direct disobedience to God's command to fill the Earth.

Now what does all that have to do with this judgment in The Revelation? Let's unravel the mystery of Babylon that followed. I am indebted to Harry Ironside, who has laid this out in very detailed form so we can understand how we got from Nimrod to where we are today and why, at the last judgment, Babylon (a religious system) is singled out for judgment. This is a very lengthy quote, so pay close attention:

Nimrod, or Nimroud-bar-Cush, as he is called on the monuments, was a grandson of Ham, the unworthy son of Noah, whose character is revealed in his exposure of his father's shame. Noah was a preacher of righteousness. Ham, on the other hand, seems to have been all too readily affected by the apostasy that brought the Flood because he shows no evidence of self-judgment. He became the founder of a race that departed from the living God and led the way into idolatry, worshiping and serving the creature (let's make a name for ourselves) more than the Creator.

Ancient lore now comes to our assistance and tells us that the wife of Nimroud-bar-cush was the infamous Semiramis the First. She is reputed to have been the foundress of the Babylonian mysteries and the first high priestess of idolatry. Thus, Babylon became the fountainhead of idolatry and the mother of every heathen and pagan system in the world. The mystery religion that originated there spread in various forms throughout the whole earth, and, as we shall see, it is with us today.

Building on the primeval promise of the woman's Seed who was to come (you might remember that promise from Genesis 3), Semiramis bore a son, whom she declared was miraculously conceived! When she presented him to the people, they hailed him as the promised deliverer. This was Tammuz. Thus was introduced the mystery of the mother and the child, a form of idolatry that is older than any other known to man. It was Satan's effort to delude mankind with an imitation so like the truth of God that they would not know the true Seed of the woman when He came in the fullness of time.

From Babylon, this mystery religion spread to all of the surrounding nations as the years went on. Everywhere the symbols were the same, and everywhere the cult of the mother and the child became the popular system, and their worship was celebrated with the most disgusting and immoral practices. The image of the queen of heaven with the babe in her arms was seen everywhere, although the names might differ as languages differed. It became the mystery religion of Phoenicia, and the Phoenicians carried it to the ends of the earth. Ashtoreth and Tammuz, the mother and child of these hardy adventurers, became Isis and Horus in Egypt, Aphrodite and Eros in Greece, Venus and Cupid in Rome, and many other names in more distant places. Within one thousand years, Babylonianism had become the religion of the world, which had rejected the divine revelation.

Linked with this central mystery were countless lesser mysteries, the hidden meanings of which were known to only the initiates, but the outward forms were practiced by all of the people. Among these mysteries were the doctrines of purgatorial purification after death; salvation by countless sacraments such as priestly absolution; sprinkling with holy water; the offering of round cakes to the queen of heaven; dedication of virgins to the gods, which were literally sanctified prostitution; and weeping for a period of forty days before the great festival of Istar, who was said to have received her son back from the dead, for it was taught that Tammuz was slain by a wild boar and afterward brought back to life. To him, the egg was sacred, depicting the mystery of his resurrection, even as the evergreen was his chosen symbol and was set up in honor of his birth at the winter solstice, when a boar's head was eaten in memory of his conflict and a Yule-log burned with many mysterious observances. The sign of the cross was sacred to Tammuz, symbolizing the life-giving principle and the first letter of his name. It is represented upon vast numbers of the most ancient altars and temples, and did not, as many have supposed, originate with Christianity.[96]

That ought to stun us for just a moment as we reflect on it. Did you catch the 40 days of mourning leading up to Istar from which we get our word Easter, the egg, the Yule-log, the evergreen tree? All of those symbols come out of Babylonianism. This is the mystery that is revealed and judged here in Chapter 17. It even influenced the Jews after they were taken into exile. Many times we read about their idol worship and their going after false gods, and how it ended with their exile. Read what Ezekiel wrote (8:14-15, my emphasis) after the Jews were taken into exile:

He (the Lord) brought me to the entrance of the gate of the Lord's house which was toward the north; and behold, women were sitting there weeping for *Tammuz*. And He said to me, "Do you see this, son of man? Yet you will see still greater abominations than these."

There's that word again: abominations. That entire system that goes back over 3,000 years to Nimrod has permeated the earth and influenced every worldwide religion negatively in some way. Armed with all of that information, we are now ready to look at the woman harlot, who is mystery Babylon.

Mystery Babylon: 3 P's

(Thank you to David Jeremiah for this alliteration.) The first P is her *position*, interestingly described in two ways. *First*, in v. 1 she sits on many waters. In v. 15, that's interpreted for us so we don't have to guess: the waters are peoples and multitudes and nations and tongues. The fact that she is sitting on them means she is ruling over peoples, nations, and tongues, which means she has influenced the entire world with her false religion that she is. At this point, it turns out that Karl Marx was right when he described religion as the opium of the people. This religion will unite all of mankind in those last days as things on Earth turn bad. *Second*, in v. 3, when John saw her for the first time, she's sitting on the beast. Remember, the beast is Antichrist. So there will be an evil alliance of the beast with this worldwide heretical religion. Charles Swindoll says:

The representation of a final godless, humanistic, and nationalistic worldwide religious system is what she represents. In the same way that we might refer to Wall Street to describe the entire American financial system, Revelation uses Babylon to refer to the end-times religious/political/economic empire of the Antichrist.[97]

That is her position: on many waters (nations) and on the beast (Antichrist).

The second P is her *prosperity*. Did you notice the description? Clothed in purple and scarlet, adorned with gold and precious stones and pearls, having in her hand a gold cup full of abominations and of the unclean things of her immorality. This worldwide religion will be rich. There will be wealth. I believe it will take over all of the great temples and cathedrals and palaces that have ever been built. It will be rich. How will that be possible? If you are a pre-tribulation rapture person, the Church—the true Church—will be

gone. If you believe a Church will remain on earth, its wealth, its possession, and its buildings will be confiscated. Either way, only mystery Babylon
will possess the wealth, and everything this worldwide religion teaches will
be heresy. How do we know that? She is **full of abominations and of the
unclean things of her immorality** (17:4). "The attractive cup is revealed
as no more than an enticement to men to join the glittering harlot in her
evil ways. It is her method of seducing them from God,"[98] says Leon Morris. Harry Ironside adds:

> *It will be a union of Christless professors inheriting all of the hu-
> man and demonical mysteries of Babylon. In other words, all sects
> will be swallowed up in the one distinctively Babylonish system
> that has ever maintained the cult of the mother and the child. This
> system will for the first part of the tribulation period dominate the
> civil power.*[99]

We have seen her prosperity; we have seen her position. The third P is
her *power*. She is **drunk with the blood of the saints, and with the blood
of the witnesses of Jesus** (17:6). That means the worldwide religion that
will unite people will have zero tolerance for belief in the true God and in
Jesus, God the Son. The fact that she is drunk with their blood means she
enjoyed killing believers in Jesus Christ. She enjoyed martyring them. John
says, **"When I saw her, I wondered greatly"** (17:6). He is absolutely
astonished. The source of her power is the beast. The beast, as we have
said, is Antichrist from Chapter 13. In 17:3 we are told that he is **full of
blasphemous names.** In other places, we have read that there were blasphemous names on his horns or on his head, but here we are told that he is
full of blasphemous names. In other words, there is no place for anything
about the true God.

The beast has seven heads, and the seven heads are interpreted for us
two different ways. *First*, the heads are seven mountains on which the
woman sits. What is the seven-hilled city? From history, it's Rome, of
course. That means Rome will be the center of the worldwide government
that will institute this worldwide religion. Worldwide rule and religion will
be administered under the power of Antichrist from Rome. The great city,
Babylon, here identified as Rome, will ultimately be split into three parts by
an earthquake. *Second*, the heads are not only seven mountains, but they are
also seven kings. There are details given: five have fallen, one is, the other
has not yet come; and when it comes, it will be short-lived. Some see this as
emperors of Rome: five who had come, one alive at John's time, and then
the seventh of course being Antichrist. However, here is a list of emperors
up to the time of John:

Augustus (31 B.C.–14 A.D.)

Tiberius (14–37)

Caligula (37–41)

Claudius (41–54)

Nero (54–68)

Galba (68–69)

Otho (January–April 69)

Aulus Vitellius (July–December 69)

Vespasian (69–79)

Titus (79–81)

Domitian (81–96)

The people who hold to this interpretation conveniently leave some of them out (by not including all ten before Domitian) so they can just have five, followed by Domitian, the "one who is," who was alive in John's day. I find no scholarly reason to choose that interpretation. There were not just five previous Roman emperors. Rather, it seems more likely that they represent past, then present, and future empires that opposed, or in the case of John's day were opposing, God. They would be Egypt, Assyria, Babylon, Media-Persia, and Greece. Those are the five that would have fallen, and Rome is the "one that is" in John's day. The seventh one is the final world government that comes at the end of time. That is the one that is not yet. Not everyone agrees with that interpretation, but that is my best understanding. The beast is an eighth king or kingdom, but he is one of the seven. (We will figure that out in the next paragraph, how he is the eighth and one of the seven.) The ten horns are ten kings, and they are most likely ten European kings and nations that will be united under the beast. Remember that this kingdom will remain only for a little while (17:10). Again, Charles Swindoll says:

> **The original tower of Babel dream of a worldwide government with one ruler, one language, one religion, and one economy will finally be realized for a brief season—figuratively speaking, "for one hour.**"[100]

In other words, its rule will be short compared to other kingdoms of the past.

About the Beast

Now let's figure out what it means that the beast is the eighth, but he's one of the seven. We are told that the beast was, is not, and is about to come up out of the abyss (17:8). Do you remember the mortal wound of the beast from Chapter 13? He was alive, then he died, and then he came back to life. Because of that, he would first be the seventh king; then he would come back to life as the eighth, just as we refer to Grover Cleveland as the 22nd and 24th President of the United States with Benjamin Harrison in between. No other U.S. President has ever done that. Joseph Biden is the 46th President, but there have only been 45 men to hold the office because Grover Cleveland is 22nd and 24th. So, the beast is seventh before his death and eighth after his resurrection. One tool of Antichrist's reign will be the heretical religion of Babylon that started with Nimrod and influenced the entire world. We are probably talking about the first 3.5 years of the tribulation. How do we know that? Because 17:1 talks about the *judgment* of the harlot woman, who is mystery Babylon. In 17:16, we read about that judgment. The ten horns (ten nations) and the beast will hate the harlot (and *all* religion) and will make her desolate and naked and will eat her flesh and will burn her up with fire. When will that happen? At the midpoint of the tribulation. That's when Antichrist breaks his covenant with Israel; we saw that when we looked at the book of Daniel. Antichrist sets up an image of himself and everyone must worship the image. No other religion, not even religious Babylon, will be tolerated. God will use Antichrist and this ten-nation coalition to judge this ungodly religious system and eliminate it from the Earth after more than 3,000 years.

Conclusion

Why all the fuss about Babylon? God made all things by the command of His voice (*Let there be, and so there was*), so He alone is worthy of worship. God, in love, gave us His Book so we might know what is true and what is not. And God sent His Son, born of a virgin, to die in our place, and God raised Him from the dead to prove Him true and to conquer death. So, in creation, redemption, and revelation, God has shown that there is to be worship of Him alone, trust in Him alone for salvation, and belief in His Word alone for instruction. But, influenced by religious Babylon, the world has gone after religion instead of pursuing relationship with God in Christ in its attempts to have a works-based salvation, all of which can be traced back to mystery Babylon. Charles Swindoll says:

> ***Satanic strategy appears to be impressive and effective, but is, in truth, impotent and deceptive. Satan, the father of lies, and his host of demons have encouraged human beings to pursue purpose, meaning, and eternal life by means of human effort.***[101]

Do you doubt that? Watch any TV show, watch any movie, and notice what you hear when someone asks *Are you going to heaven?* What is the normal response? *I hope so, I hope I've been good enough.* It permeates our society, it permeates our world, this works-based religion. *I hope I can be good enough.* I always want to jump through the TV screen and on to the set and scream *You can't be good enough!* I can't be good enough. None of us can be good enough. That's why Jesus came to die in our place.

ATM (Apply to Me)

1. While the false religious system known as Babylon is called a harlot, remember that the Church of Jesus Christ—all who believe in Christ—is called the *Bride* of Christ! Could there be a greater contrast of women symbolically? The harlot woman; the Bride of Christ. Remember who we are, brothers and sisters. We belong to Jesus.

2. Given all this danger of false teaching, is working together with other churches a good thing or a bad thing? Keith, I don't want to get mixed up with a church where they don't believe the truth. Yet, shouldn't we work with our brothers and sisters in Christ? To answer those questions I want to briefly outline the essentials of what Jude calls **the faith** (Jude 3).

I. First is the Bible. We believe the whole Bible. We believe all of it, every word of it. It's all the inspired God-breathed Word of God. It's all true. Mankind doesn't get to decide which parts they like and which parts they don't, or which parts are God's Word and which parts are not. That would be heresy. We must affirm with one voice that the Bible is the Word of God. It is all the Word of God, *all true*; it is the final authority for faith and practice.

II. God, who has revealed Himself in his Word, is Triune. He is Father, Son, and Holy Spirit—Three in One, One in Three. He is eternally existent, all powerful, the Creator of all things.

III. Jesus Christ, the Second Person of the Trinity, God the Son, was born of a virgin, became a Man but never ceased to be God. He is the God-Man. He died on the cross, not as a martyr, but as a substitute for our sins and rose again to conquer death and give the promise of eternal life.

IV. Salvation is not earned. It can never, ever be earned. We can never be good enough. That's why we don't say *I hope so* when someone says, *Are you going to heaven?* We can know that we know that we know. For that to happen we must be born again. There has to be a supernatural event happen in our lives. It must be a spiritual birth, what John's gospel calls being born again, and what Peter in his epistles also called being born again. It's not a matter of rearranging the intellectual furniture and saying, *Yes, I like the philosophy of Christianity*. It's a spiritual birth, a rebirth. That's how we know we are going to heaven.

V. We affirm with one voice that Jesus Christ is coming again to judge the world and establish a new heaven and a new earth. There are differences of opinion of how all that will play out. We've already seen passages in The Revelation being interpreted in different ways. The point of unity is Jesus Christ is coming again. He is really personally, visibly, coming again.

VI. Marriage is between one man and one woman. God gets to define marriage; culture doesn't get to define marriage. Hollywood doesn't get to define marriage. The Supreme Court doesn't get to define marriage. The President doesn't get to define marriage. God gets to define marriage. If you go all the way back to the book of Genesis, He made them male and female. Marriage is a covenant before God between one man and one woman.

If you can find me someone who deviates from number II, III, IV, V, or VI, I will tell you it is because they have first deviated from number I. You take away number I and every kind of heresy can, and always does, follow. In a previous lesson we talked about the number of pastors and ministers in different denominations and the ridiculously high percentage who do not believe in a literal hell. Why is that? Because they rejected number I. The Bible is the final authority for faith and practice. One member of my church came to me after I preached the message about believing in a literal hell, and he said, "I was playing golf with a pastor from another church this week and I said to him 'I couldn't believe the percentages of pastors who don't believe in a literal hell.'" This pastor said to him, "Well, I'm one of them." There it is. The heresy is everywhere. God bless my church member who then said to him, "Well, then I guess Christ died in vain!" You see, if there is no hell, there is no penalty and judgment for sin, and if there is no penalty or judgment for sin, there is no need for a Savior, and if there is no need for a Savior, then Christ's death was a waste. How do you get there? You reject number I.

So about working with others, we cannot unite with people who will not affirm these fundamentals of the Christian faith. **The faith** of Jude 3: Jude says we are to *contend for it*. Now, find me someone who will affirm all of these things, no matter what denomination, no matter what label, and that person is my brother or sister in Christ, and I can work with that person. Is working together with other churches a bad thing? No, it's a good thing if we have a common core of beliefs. If not, then it is a bad thing, because then we move toward Babylonianism where anything goes.

3. Finally, a warning. Don't follow the lies of Babylon, or you will fall along with it. This religious philosophy, the woman harlot, has influenced the world going all the way back to its start with Nimrod. An entire chapter here in The Revelation is devoted to the judgment of that religious system. I hope that after this lesson you have a clear understanding of why that is.

Lesson 17

Read 18:1 – 24

Seduced by Wealth (Commercial Babylon Is Judged)

We are into another symbolic chapter, and we will see what Babylon stands for here as we move through this lesson.

Let's review where we are. When we studied the pouring out of Bowl 7, we saw massive armies gathered together, ready for battle. The Euphrates River was dried up, and there was a giant earthquake. At that point we had to freeze the action for Chapters 17 and 18, which describe specific judgment on Babylon. They are the last interlude in The Revelation. In our next lesson, which is Chapter 19, we will pick up the story (following 16:16) of that army massed for Armageddon.

Remember we said in our last lesson that Babylon is mentioned more than 250 times in the Bible, meaning it is an extremely significant name. We noted there are two uses of the word. It refers first to both a city and an empire; the city of Babylon was the capital of the Babylonian empire. It is the empire that overran the southern kingdom of Judah and laid waste the city of Jerusalem. That is one use of Babylon—a literal place.

Babylon is also used in Scripture as a symbol of the world's commercial values and heretical religious systems that have influenced mankind for evil for more than 3,000 years. In our last lesson we saw the harlot woman, who is symbolic of that heretical religious system. It was a deep, challenging lesson to follow, but if you paid close attention, I believe you probably learned many things. Here in Chapter 18 the symbol is different; Babylon is the world's commercial value system. How do we know that? As you read the chapter, did you notice all the emphasis on things, possessions, finance, commerce?

Some people have speculated that Babylon will actually be rebuilt as a city and that it will become the commercial center of the world. The belief is that the destruction described in this chapter refers to the fall of that rebuilt Babylon. To test that theory, let's look at what the prophets Isaiah and Jeremiah had to say about literal Babylon:

(Isaiah 13:19-22) **Babylon, the beauty of kingdoms, the glory of the Chaldeans' pride, will be as when God overthrew Sodom and Gomorrah. It will never be inhabited or lived in from generation to generation; nor will the Arab pitch his tent there, nor will shepherds make their flocks lie down there. But desert creatures will lie**

158

down there, and their houses will be full of owls, ostriches also will live there, and shaggy goats will frolic there. And hyenas will howl in their fortified towers and jackals in their luxurious palaces. Her fateful time also will soon come and her days will not be prolonged.

(Jeremiah 50:30) **The desert creatures will live there [Babylon] along with the jackals; the ostriches also will live in it, and it will never again be inhabited or dwelt in from generation to generation.**

The voices of those two prophets tell me that God is *not* talking about a rebuilt Babylon; Isaiah and Jeremiah make it very clear that the city will never be rebuilt or inhabited. We must conclude that, just as the harlot Babylon in our last lesson was a symbol of one world religion united under Antichrist, here it is used to symbolize the world's commercial values.

The fall of "Babylon" was foreshadowed back in 14:8, which was a single verse looking ahead to what would be described in detail in Chapters 17 and 18. **Fallen, fallen is Babylon the great, she who has made all the nations drink of the wine of the passion of her immorality** (14:8). Then 18:2 begins with **Fallen, fallen is Babylon the great...** (the repetition of the words from 14:8 is the important clue that ties Chapters 17 and 18 to that verse). They are the chapters where we learn the *details* of the fall of these two horrible systems: the world's pagan religious system and the world's commercial greed are destroyed as part of God's overall judgment on the world. I am indebted to Warren Wiersbe[102] for his outline of the chapter:

> The voice of condemnation (1-3, 5-8, 24)
> The voice of separation (4)
> The voice of lamentation [the largest section of the chapter] (9-19)
> The voice of celebration (20-23)

We will study each section/theme separately.

The Voice of Condemnation

John saw another angel. Has he seen quite a few of those? Definitely! In our last lesson we saw that it was one of the angels who had the seven bowls of wrath who showed John the coming judgment on religious Babylon. Here he does not say it was one of those seven angels, but rather he says it was another angel. However, he describes him in some detail. He comes down from heaven, he has great authority, and he is illumined with the Lord's glory, just as Moses' face shown with the Lord's glory when he returned from meeting with God on a mountain. He says he is announcing condemnation on Babylon for many sins: **...she has become a dwelling place of demons, and a prison** [not a prison like we think of the word, but a haunt] **of every unclean spirit, and a prison of every unclean and hateful bird** (18:2). This is a triple symbol, with all three parts describing the same evil: demons, unclean spirits, hateful birds. Do you remember Jesus' parable about the different kinds of soil? The farmer sewed seed, some landed on rocky ground, and the birds came and snatched it away. The birds were a symbol of enemies of the gospel snatching away the Word of God so it couldn't take root in a person's heart. The birds here are symbolic of the same thing, included as part of a triple symbol: the world's financial system—the way people think about money—has been triply influenced by Satan's deception. For that Babylon is condemned. As a result, nations, kings, and merchants have been affected and seduced and corrupted by her; for that Babylon is condemned. Her sins have piled as high as heaven (think about that and how high a pile of sins this symbol portrays), and for that Babylon is condemned. God remembers those sins. Do you know what God does with our sins when we accept Christ as Savior? He *forgets* them, Hallelujah. But He *remembers* Babylon's sins.

Babylon is also guilty of pride and self-glorification, saying **I sit as queen and I am not a widow and will never see mourning.** (18:7) Queen means *I have everything I want, and I'm in charge of everything, and I can rule.* Widow would be a symbol of poverty, which Babylon says she is *not. I am rich; I will never see mourning; I need nothing.* For her pride and her self-glorification Babylon is condemned.

The condemnation will be in one day: plagues of pestilence, mourning, famine, burned up with fire (v. 8). Remember all of this is symbolic; Babylon is a symbol of the world's financial system. Think about what each of those symbols would mean as those kinds of judgments fall on that financial system. *Oh, that couldn't happen.* For anyone who would say that, notice the next words: **God is strong**, three little words in v.8. If God decides it's over for the financial system, it's over!

Finally, if we look ahead to v. 24, we see that the blood of prophets and saints who have been martyred is on the head of Babylon. It probably refers to those who will lose their lives because of Antichrist requiring people to receive the mark of the beast in order to buy or sell, and those refusing being put to death, or if they can't buy or sell, starving to death. Their blood is on the head of this financial system, and for that Babylon is condemned. Verse 6 tells us the payback is *doubled.* That is the voice of condemnation.

The Voice of Lamentation

We will skip over v. 4 for right now and see that there are three groups of people who lament the fall of Babylon. First, kings will weep and lament *from a distance*. The fall of the world's financial system will cause kings to openly weep, but they will do their best to keep their distance. (*It's not my fault*. Do you hear that in politics? In the United States we've run up over 20 trillion dollars in debt, but it's always *It's not my fault!*). It's never the leaders' fault! People will be starving, but *It's not my fault* will echo around the world. Kings will weep and lament, but they will keep their distance.

Second, merchants of the Earth will weep and mourn because no one buys their cargo. But they also stand at a distance, doing their best not to be affected by what is going on around them. The things they buy and sell are listed here in some detail. First are things with intrinsic value: gold, silver, precious stones, pearls. Then come things for adornment: fine linen, purple, silk, scarlet. After that are listed manufactured items: things made from citron (a very costly wood), ivory, bronze, iron, marble. That is followed by seasonings (cinnamons and spices), fragrances (incense, perfume, frankincense), food (wine, olive oil, fine flour, wheat, cattle, sheep [the last item also including their wool]), and other items (horses, chariots, slaves, human lives). Even included are human lives that were bought and sold in that day and still are today in illegal slave trade.

John wrote at a time when Rome was *rich* on paper. Many people had wealth, and almost everyone who wasn't a slave owned slaves. The estimate among historians is very wide; it ranges from 5,000,000 to 60,000,000 slaves in the Roman empire. The accurate number is certainly somewhere between those, but in any event think of millions of slaves spread throughout the Roman empire, how many human lives were in bondage to slavery.

About indulgence there are horrible examples. A man by the name of Apicius, a famous chef, squandered a fortune of $1.3 million in refined debauchery, and he committed suicide when he had only $130,000 left (numbers converted to today's economy) because he could not live on such a "pittance." Caligula, one of the emperors, spent $2.6 million on luxury in one day. Emperor Nero declared that the only use of money was to squander it, and in a very few years he did just that: $23.4 million. At just one of his banquets the Egyptian roses alone cost $45,000.

As for the items that are mentioned that could no longer be bought or sold, silver is high on the list. It came mainly from Carthagena in Spain, where 40,000 men toiled in the silver mines. Dishes, bowls, jugs, fruit baskets, statuettes, whole dinner services, were made of solid silver. Women would bathe only in silver baths, soldiers had swords with silver hilts and scabbards with silver chairs, and poor women had silver anklets. Even slaves had silver mirrors. Tables made of the expensive wood, named as citron (which came only from a certain part of Africa, having a beautiful grain and a wonderful color), could cost anything from $5,000 to $19,000. The very wealthiest people owned many of those tables. It was a time of indulgence, so John's readers would have known exactly what it meant for Babylon to fall.

The third group of people who lament over Babylon are shipmasters, passengers, and sailors—those who trade in what others made (we call them middle men.) These importers and exporters cry out and throw dust on their heads. They also weep and mourn and stand at a distance, doing their best to not let the fall of Babylon affect them.

All three groups together said, **"Woe, woe, the great city"** (18:19). Notice the double *woe*, the Greek word *ouai* (oy!), which doesn't even need translation! Notice they are lamenting the loss of profit and wealth. The great city has fallen, and it will happen in one hour! (vs. 17, 19). Is that a literal time, or is that God's way of saying it will be very quick? Either way it is meant to tell us that it *will* be quick. Could that really happen? Let's think hypothetically (events of 2020 make this *not* hypothetical!). What if there were a worldwide pandemic? What might that do to the world's financial system? We saw firsthand how many were affected financially in 2020, and that was with a recovery rate of 98% from the coronavirus in the United States. Now think about the plagues and "natural" disasters of The Revelation. How long would the world's financial system be able to hold up? It would collapse in a very short time. God is saying that system, with its emphasis on wealth and greed, will all be judged, bringing the voice of lamentation.

The Voice of Celebration

It is interesting that this comes next; some in this chapter *celebrate* the fall of Babylon, the world's financial system. They are in heaven, and they are rejoicing (v. 20). Specifically mentioned are saints (that means all New Testament believers). Prophets and apostles are also mentioned. Why? Because they are the ones through the centuries who have tried to get people to understand that putting money first never works, that we must put *God* first in our lives. Because God has pronounced judgment, they are saying, *Hurray!* Does that not sound very loving? Understand that God's holiness and justice are proved here. Leon Morris says, "It is a passionate cry uttered out of the deep conviction that right must triumph and which eagerly welcomes that triumph."[103] That is the cry of rejoicing.

John sees something *like* a great millstone (picture a millstone used for grinding: John compares what he saw to that). John says it was thrown by a strong angel; I believe he was impressed that an angel could lift something big! What would happen if something like a giant millstone were thrown into the sea? There would be a massive splash, followed by ripple after ripple after ripple. This is a very accurate symbol of how financial systems fall. The United States, and ultimately the world, saw it in the days of The Great Depression. So, it will be in those last days.

The results? A long list of "no mores" is given in v. 23. No more music (flutes, trumpets specifically are mentioned). Of course. In order for the arts (visual or performing arts) to flourish in any culture, there must be peace and there must be prosperity. There will be neither, so the musical arts will be no more. No more craftsmen. No one will be buying anything, so there will be no reason to make anything. Therefore, no commerce. Also, no light of a lamp. Cities, formerly bright with light, will go dark. No weddings. **The voice of the bridegroom and bride will not be heard** (18:23). No one will even want to get married. I know how much the Lord loves a wedding between two people who are committed to Jesus Christ. He Himself was at a wedding in Cana in Galilee (John 2), and I don't believe He was there out of obligation. I believe He was there because he loved seeing two people committing their lives to each other in marriage. It is such a wonderful event. Hear the words from this amazing wedding hymn by Adelaide Thrupp:

Lord, Who at Cana's wedding feast didst as a guest appear,
Thou dearer far than earthly guest, vouchsafe Thy presence here;
For holy Thou indeed dost prove the marriage vow to be,
Proclaiming it a type of love between the Church and Thee.

The holiest vow that man can make, the golden thread in life,
The bond that none may dare to break, that bindeth man and wife;
Which, blest by Thee, whate'er betides, no evil shall destroy,
Through care-worn days each care divides, and doubles every joy.[104]

There will be no such joy and love and mutual commitment during these days. The words "[not] any longer" are found six times at the end of this chapter; the KJV translates the phrase as "no more." Music, craftsmen, light of a lamp, weddings—all of them not seen *any longer*. Donald Grey Barnhouse says:

The angels' words announce most impressively the vanishing forever of all the joys and delights of the great city, the music and the song, the hum of industry, the brightness of its illumination, and above all, the rejoicings of the bride and the bridegroom, which in the Bible stand for the highest of all human joys.[105]

There is one more verse here in this section. It discusses Babylon's sorceries (Greek word *pharmakia*, from which we get the word pharmacy), meaning drugs that have seduced and deceived people. Do we not see a drug crisis in the United States and around the world? It is yet one more reason for the voice of celebration because of God's judgments, here on the pharmakia.

The Voice of Separation

We can now return to v. 4, which we skipped. The instruction to believers is to come out of her (Babylon) for three reasons. First, don't participate in her sins because they will pollute you. Second, by not participating in her sins you will not receive her plagues. Third, the specific sins of idolatry, pride, and worship of pleasure are things believers should not have in their lives. Harry Ironside says, "Commerce is the goddess of the current feverish age, and to her everything must be sacrificed."[106] Believers are called to live differently and cannot put money first.

Why Is Commercial Babylon Singled Out?

In our last lesson we answered why there was such an emphasis on the judgment of religious Babylon; here we shall answer the same question about commercial Babylon. There is a thread that runs through the entire Bible from Genesis to The Revelation about honesty, integrity, fairness, and compassion in financial dealings. Widows and orphans, who were most vulnerable in Bible times, and in many respects still are today, are especially noticed by God when they are cheated and mistreated. Dishonest gain is also particularly loathsome to God. To illustrate this point, consider the following Scriptures, illustrating God's concern for financial justice.

Leviticus 19:10
You shall not glean your vineyard bare, nor shall you gather the fallen of your vineyard; you shall leave them for the poor and for the sojourner. I am the Lord your God.

Leviticus 19:11
You shall not steal; you shall not deal falsely; you shall not lie to one another.

Leviticus 19:13
You shall not oppress your neighbor or rob him. The wages of a hired servant shall not remain with you all night until the morning.

Leviticus 19:35-36
You shall do no wrong in judgment, in measurement of weight, or capacity. You shall have just balances, just weights, a just ephah, and a just hin: I am the Lord your God, who brought you out from the land of Egypt.

(Do you understand what dishonest merchants did? Unjust balances meant that if you, as a cheat, were buying from someone, your "one-pound" weight actually required 18 ounces of goods to make it balance, and of course you only gave payment for a pound. And if you were selling to someone, your different "one-pound" weight would balance as soon as 14 ounces were on the other side, but you would charge the person for a full pound. It was the ancient forerunner to the butcher putting his thumb on the scale!)

Leviticus 23:22
When you reap the harvest of your land, you shall not reap your field right up to its edge, nor shall you gather the gleanings after your harvest. You shall leave them for the poor and for the sojourner: I am the Lord your God.

Leviticus 25:14
If you make a sale to your neighbor or buy from your neighbor, you shall not wrong one another.

Deuteronomy 15:2
Every creditor shall release what he has lent to his neighbor. He shall not exact it of his neighbor, his brother, because the Lord's release has been proclaimed.

(Debts were to be forgiven every seven years.)

Deuteronomy 24:14-15
You shall not oppress a hired servant who is poor and needy, whether he is one of your countrymen or one of your aliens who is in your land in your towns. You shall give him his wages on his day before the sun sets, for he is poor and sets his heart on it; so that he may not cry against you to the Lord and it become sin in you.

Deuteronomy 25:14-16
You shall not have in your house two kinds of measures, a large and a small. You shall have a full and just weight; you shall have a

full and just measure, that your days may be prolonged in the land which the Lord your God gives you. For everyone who does these things, everyone who acts unjustly is an abomination to the Lord your God.

Proverbs 11:1
A false balance is an abomination to the Lord, but a just weight is His delight.

Proverbs 16:8
Better is a little with righteousness than great revenues with injustice.

Proverbs 17:5
He who mocks the poor reproaches his Maker; He who rejoices at calamity will not go unpunished.

Proverbs 19:17
Whoever is generous to the poor lends to the Lord, and He will repay him for his deed.

Proverbs 21:6
The getting of treasures by a lying tongue is a fleeting vapor and a snare of death.

Proverbs 22:16
Whoever oppresses the poor to increase his own wealth, or gives to the rich, will only come to poverty.

Isaiah 1:17-19
Learn to do good; seek justice, correct oppression; bring justice to the *fatherless*, plead the *widow's* cause.

Amos 2:6-7
Thus says the Lord: "For three transgressions of Israel, and for four, I will not revoke its punishment, because they sell the righteous for silver, and the needy for a pair of sandals—those who trample the head of the poor into the dust of the earth and turn aside the way of the afflicted.

Amos 5:12
I know your transgressions are many and your sins are great, you who distress the righteous and accept bribes, and turn aside the poor in the gate.

Micah 6:8
He has told you, O man, what is good; and what does the Lord require of you but to do justice, and to love kindness, and to walk humbly with your God?

Malachi 3:5
"I will be a swift witness against the sorcerers, against the adulterers, against those who swear falsely, against those who oppress the hired worker in his wages, the widow and the fatherless, against those who thrust aside the sojourner, and do not fear me," says the Lord of hosts.

Moving to the New Testament:

Matthew 6:24
[words of Jesus] "No one can serve two masters, for either he will hate the one and love the other, or he will be devoted to the one and despise the other. You cannot serve God and money."

Mark 8:36
[words of Jesus] "What does it profit a man to gain the whole world and forfeit his soul?"

I Corinthians 6:9-11
Do not be deceived: neither the sexually immoral, nor idolaters, nor adulterers, nor men who practice homosexuality, nor thieves, nor the *greedy*, nor drunkards, nor revilers, nor *swindlers* will inherit the kingdom of God. And such were some of you.

Colossians 4:1
Masters, treat your slaves justly and fairly, knowing that you also have a Master in heaven.

James 5:1,4
Come now, you rich, weep and howl for your miseries which are coming upon you. Behold, the pay of the laborers who mowed your fields, and which has been withheld by you, cries out against

you; and he outcry of those who did the harvesting has reached the ears of the Lord of Sabaoth.

I am certain there are readers who are asking, *What about the sluggard; what about the human sloth? What about the lazy who want to live off others?* They are also condemned in Scripture:

Proverbs 10:4
A slack hand causes poverty, but the hand of the diligent makes rich.

Proverbs 13:4
The soul of the sluggard craves and gets nothing, while the soul of the diligent is richly supplied.

Proverbs 14:23
In all toil there is profit, but mere talk tends only to poverty.

II Thessalonians 3:10
When we were with you, we would give you this command: if any- one is not willing to work, let him not eat.

Greed and dishonesty are condemned; laziness is also condemned. So where does Babylon exist today? Everywhere. The CEO salaries of some companies, contrasted with what their employees receive, is downright criminal. The typical annual pay package for CEOs at the biggest U.S. com- panies topped $12.3 million in 2019. It would take 169 *years* for the typical employee at most S&P 500 companies to earn that much money, and that assumes a salary of $73K per year. Does that sound fair?

Government officials often live the high life while others struggle in poverty. There is an old joke about the former Soviet Union. A man walks into a store and asks, "Do you have any fish?" He is told, "You're in the wrong store. This is the store that doesn't have any beef; the store that doesn't have any fish is across the street." That was the typical condition of the masses, while the ruling class had everything they wanted. However, it's not just the old Soviet Union. I read recently about a major city in the Unit- ed States (you would recognize the name if I gave it). The mayor's *wife* has a staff of 14 people, costing the taxpayers $2 million per year. But the mayor said that because of the pandemic 22,000 workers might have to be fur- loughed. I know where to start! People in power love to live the high life, paid for by the taxes of everyone else. Babylon.

There are business owners and repair technicians who overcharge for their services. Have you ever been a victim of one of them? We need and expect small business owners to be straight with us. We had an elder candidate whose name came up recently at my church who owns his own business. One of our [then current] elders explained how he had done business with that man and found him to be one of the most honest men of integrity he could possibly wish for. That got our attention; we wanted that kind of man on our board of elders, and today he is. God is honored by men and women who have *not* been corrupted by commercial Babylon. Perhaps you have seen both types, even in your church.

Remember that the sloth is also condemned. These are people who can work but prefer to live off the tax revenues paid by everyone else.

Conclusion

Just like religious Babylon, commercial Babylon is singled out for judgment at the end of the age, and now we have seen why. It will fall in one hour, either literally or certainly very quickly. If you have ever wondered where and when there will be justice in this vastly corrupt area, here it is. God will judge godless commercialism and greed.

ATM (Apply to Me)

1. If you have much because God has blessed you with wealth, give to Him as an act of worship, and help those who need a hand up as an act of service.

2. If I *pursue* wealth, I will end up spiritually poor.

3. If I pursue Christ, I will end up spiritually rich, regardless of my financial situation. Where would you rather end up: spiritually poor or spiritually rich?

4. Balance about the importance of money is essential. Is money important? Jesus talked about it often, so it *must be* important. Don't ever let anyone tell you money is not important; it is *very* important. The way we use it has to be so carefully balanced. Charles Swindoll says:

Not every luxury places us in Babylon's embrace. However, Babylon begins to woo us where luxury starts to possess us. On that axis, everything shifts. When that happens, the green ghost of greed invades our dwelling and haunts our once-contented minds, like the farmer Jesus mentioned in Luke 12:16-21, who substituted the material for the spiritual. That man, said Jesus, was an outright fool.[107]

You see, compromise with worldliness is fatal.

Postscript

I want to tell you one more story before we conclude this lesson, the true story of Michael Larson and the old game show, *Press Your Luck*. It had a rectangular board where different squares around the board changed every half second or so between valuable prizes and Whammies. One square was lit at a time, changing rapidly. Whatever was lit when you stopped the board was what you won, but if you hit a Whammy you lost everything. Michael Larson had decided he wanted to be a contestant on the show, and in preparation for his appearance he had recorded hours of footage from previous episodes. He then slowed the recordings to the slowest speed possible to look for patterns in the way the squares changed and what square was lit. He discovered there were two patterns that always led to either $4,000 plus an extra "spin" (which was what a turn at the board was called) or $5,000 plus an extra spin being lit. So, when he became a contestant, he looked for only those two patterns, and time after time he was able to stop the board on one of those two squares. His goal was to win $100,000, so every time he added more money and an additional spin, the host asked him if he wanted to stop. Of course, he always said no. (When his time on the show finally aired, it had to be spread out over two episodes.) While he was playing, the producers in the control room came to realize he had gamed the system, and there was nothing they could do to stop him—they were beaten. Eventually Michael Larson won over $110,000 (a typical winner would win between $5,000 and $10,000 if he/she was really lucky). He then invested his winnings in some businesses, including a restaurant. He also heard about a contest on the radio, where you could win $30,000 if you had a dollar bill that matched a certain serial number, so he went to the bank and withdrew a large sum of money in $1 bills in an attempt to win. He went through every one and none matched. One day while he was away, his house was broken into and $50,000 was stolen. Because he wasn't careful about following all the tax laws for his businesses, he ultimately had to flee the state where he lived because the government was after him for tax liability. Before he reached the age of 50 he died of throat cancer. A tragic story of someone who made Babylon his god.

Warren Wiersbe: "Are we citizens of Babylon or citizens of heaven?"[108]

Lesson 18

Read 19:1 – 21

Armageddon

The prophet Zechariah (14:4) wrote:

In that day, his feet will stand on the Mount of Olives, which is in front of Jerusalem on the east, and the Mount of Olives will be split in its middle from east to west by a very large valley, so that half of the mountain will move toward the north and the other half toward the south.

The Mount of Zion, where Jesus is to plant His feet when He returns, is the exact same mountain from which He ascended in Acts Chapter 1. His return, as told here, is the crowning moment in The Revelation. What is The Revelation about? It is about the second coming of Christ. We have studied many different things that have led to that event. And now here, we have the Lord Himself returning to earth. We know that when the Lord ascended 40 days after His resurrection, the apostles looked up to the heavens, and an angel came and said, **"Why do you stand looking into the sky? This Jesus…will come in just the same way as you have watched Him go into heaven"** (Acts 1:11). He is coming to that mountain, Mount Zion, according to Zechariah, and that is where this passage is taking us.

First, we need to review a little. You might remember that in 14:8 we read these words: **"Fallen, fallen is Babylon the great, she who has made all the nations drink of the wine of the passion of her immorality."** That was part of a vision that included an angel prophesying/foreshadowing the fall of Babylon. Chapters 17 and 18 are where that fall is described in detail; we looked at the fall of religious Babylon in Chapter 17 and the fall of commercial Babylon in Chapter 18, as both of those heretical and self-centered systems were judged. As we come to Chapter 19 we will find 6 A's (with thanks to David Jeremiah for the alliteration). We have Alleluias over the fall of Babylon (an immediate follow-up to Chapters 17 and 18); Announcement of the marriage, Appearing of Christ, Armies of Christ, Authority of Christ, Avenging of Christ. We will study those one at a time.

Alleluias over Babylon (1-4)

John heard a loud voice. Are you surprised that he heard a loud voice? I've reminded us multiple times: this is a loud book, with 20 loud voices! This time he says *as it were…* That is his way of saying *it sounded like*. Like what? A great multitude in heaven. It was *one* voice sounding *like* a great multitude. That was the best he could do to describe it. It was obviously very powerful, and the voice said "Hallelujah!" Do you know that word? It occurs often in the Old Testament and is usually translated from Hebrew into *Praise the Lord* in English. But here it is allowed to stay transliterated as the word *Hallelujah*. In the entire New Testament, all 27 books, this word occurs just four times, and they are all right here in this chapter. This word has been saved for this chapter and this chapter alone. Following the Hallelujah we are told that the Lord's judgments are *true* and *righteous*. They are not based on what some slick lawyer might be able to do, not based on what some crooked judge might do who has been bribed; they are *true*. They are based solely on truth, and they are 100% *righteous*. There is perfect justice with God, and there is rejoicing because Babylon, the great harlot, has been judged. That's what we looked at in Chapters 17 and 18. She had corrupted the earth and shed the blood of believers. She not only had heretical false religion and a commercial system that emphasized greed, consumerism, and possessions, but she also was responsible for the blood of believers in martyrdom. So, there is rejoicing because the power of God has vanquished evil. Have you ever asked, *Why doesn't God do something about evil?* Well, here it is. God is doing something about evil, and those who are in heaven rejoice in this *loud* voice. In v. 3 there is another Hallelujah, and this time it is because her smoke goes up forever and ever. Never again will the Earth be led astray by this false religion that came from Babylon, that started 3,000 years ago and spread and corrupted the true faith of our Lord Jesus Christ, and that led the world to worship the creation rather than the Creator. Never again will the greed of commercial Babylon infect the world's values. Her smoke goes up forever and ever. The 24 elders and the 4 living creatures (by the way, this is the last time the 24 elders are mentioned in The Revelation), fall down and worship God, and they give an *Amen* to it all. Then they give a third Hallelujah. Why? Because the power of God has vanquished evil!

Before we move on, I want to go back to v. 1. Did you notice this? **Salvation and glory and power belong to our God.** Wait a minute. I thought this was all about judgment. It is. But notice what word comes first in that sentence. *Salvation*. What is God's *best* for every person on Earth? *Salvation*. God is **not wishing for any to perish but for all to come to repentance** (II Peter 3:9). That is His *best* plan: *salvation*. Salvation *comes* from Him, and He wants everyone to experience that. But we get to choose how God's power is manifested in our lives. Will it be salvation? Or will we reject that, so it will be judgment? Once again, the choice is clear. Notice that His holiness is behind it all. It was His holiness that came up with a plan of salvation in the first place. It was His holiness that knew there had to be a penalty paid for sin, and He sent His only Son to do that: to die on the cross on our behalf, to pay the penalty for sin. But for those who reject it, His glory, His power, His perfect truth and righteousness will judge sin. So those are the three Alleluias over Babylon, tying these verses to Chapter 17 and 18.

Announcement of the Marriage (5-9)

This time there is a voice from the throne. This is not the voice of God, because the voice says, **"Give praise *to* our God"** (19:5). John again uses the words *as it were* (meaning it sounded like) and now he is overwhelmed. He gives us three metaphors. He says the voice was like a great multitude, like many waters, and like mighty peels of thunder. Think of that description. I can't imitate that kind of voice. But that's how John describes it. It was unlike anything he had ever heard. What does this voice say? The fourth and final Hallelujah of the Bible. **For the Lord God, the Almighty, reigns** (19:6). Only an *omnipotent* God, an all-powerful God, could take sinful mankind and turn us into what we are about to see in the marriage: a perfect, pure, and spotless bride.

Those who hear this voice are told to rejoice, be glad, and give the glory to Him. He is the one who had the plan before the foundation of the earth concerning the problem of sin. The omnipotent God is the one who could make possible the marriage of the Lamb, which has now come. His bride has made herself ready. The *bride* is the Church: the *Bride of Christ*.

There are other metaphors that Jesus used, and that Scripture uses, to describe the relationship of Christ and the Church. In John 10 Jesus called Himself the Shepherd, and He calls us the sheep. In John 15 He called Himself the Vine, and He calls us the branches. In Ephesians 2 Paul refers to Him as the Cornerstone, and us as building stones. Peter (I Peter 2) calls Him the High Priest and calls us a kingdom of priests; that is, we don't have to go through some human priest to come before God to confess our sins. And in Ephesians, Chapters 1, 4, and 5, He is called the Head and we are called the body. But here in Revelation 19, in fulfillment of other Scriptures, the Church is called the *Bride of Christ*. She is given bright and clean wedding garments made of fine linen. Ladies, those of you who have gotten married at some point in your lives, if I could ask you how many of you wore linen on your wedding day, there would probably be very, very few who would say you did. I can think of many beautiful things that wedding gowns are made of, but linen probably isn't one of them. But here, the clean and bright fine linen is symbolic of the purity of the bride: the perfect bride of Christ, washed clean by the blood of Christ. There is also a very curious statement; it says the linen is the righteous acts of the saints. How did we get a wedding dress of *righteous acts*? We know we aren't saved by righteous acts; we are saved by grace through faith in Christ alone. We sing *Rock of Ages*: "Nothing in my hand I bring, simply to Thy cross I cling."[109] So what is this about the righteous acts? Some translations say it is the righteousness of God, which of course is the righteousness that is found in Christ. But the word is plural: the *righteousnesses*, best translated *the righteous acts*. It is adornment for the fine linen wedding dress. You've probably seen movies and TV shows where there are generals or other officers, and on their chests they always have awards. Each one is symbolic of some good thing they have done, or some act of bravery, or some promotion they've gotten. The more of those you see on that officer, the more impressed you are. That's what John is talking about here. The righteous acts of the saints are not for salvation, but they are the adornment of the wedding apparel. Vernon McGee puts it this way: "Through the ages, believers have been performing righteous acts which have been accumulating to adorn the wedding gown."[110] Then he adds, "By the way, what are you doing to adorn that wedding gown? What are you doing for the Lord today?"[111] That's what righteous acts means.

Then the angel does something else curious: he tells John to *write*. John *has been* writing it down! But there have been certain places along the way where he has been reminded to be sure he does so. The first was all the way back in Chapter 1, where in vs. 11 and 19 he was told to **Write what you see** in his first vision of the risen Lord. Of course, he was told to write the letters to the seven churches in Chapters 2 and 3. In 10:4, however, he heard a voice of the thunders and he was about to write it down, and he heard a voice saying, "Seal up what the thunders said. Don't write that." In 14:13, he was told to write concerning those who were being martyred, **Blessed are those who die in the Lord from now on.** And here he is told again to write what are true words of God: **Blessed are those who are invited to the marriage supper of the Lamb.** These are true words of God. This book was *written* by the instruction of God.

We've had the *marriage* of the Lamb; now we have the marriage *supper* of the Lamb. Now let me ask you, who is invited to a wedding? Is the bride invited to the wedding? Is an invitation sent out to the bride? No, the bride and the groom send out invitations to friends. So, if the bride is the Church, who are those who are *invited* to the marriage supper? The prevailing thought is that this must refer to Old Testament believers. They are not the Church, but they are people who believed in God, and who put their faith in the coming of a Savior. Some have speculated that if the rapture happens at the beginning of the tribulation, and the Church is taken out of the world, then anyone who had come to faith during the tribulation would also be invited. In any event they are *blessed.*

Appearing of Christ (11-13)

We are now ready to finally pick up the story of the army massed at the plain called Har-Magedon (16:16) or Armageddon. You might remember that as the bowls of wrath were poured out, the Euphrates River was dried up, and the armies of the Earth were called together *at the plain called Armageddon.* (Chapters 17 and 18 were the parentheses describing the fall of religious and commercial Babylon.) We had hit the pause button before Chapter 17, and now we are hitting the play button again; we are going forward. We have in vs. 11-13 the appearing of Christ, which starts with heaven being opened. This is the second time in The Revelation that heaven was opened. The first time was all the way back in Chapter 4, when John saw heaven opened and a voice said to him, **"Come up here"** (4:1). Heaven was opened so John could get *in.* Now, instead of someone going *in*, a door in heaven is opened for Someone to come *out.* We see a white horse; white is symbolic of victory, and the one who is seated on that horse is none other than the Lord Jesus Christ Himself. Notice that He is not riding a donkey; this is not the servant riding into Jerusalem to be killed, to give His life as a ransom for many. This is the returning, victorious, risen, glorified Lord Jesus Christ, riding on a white horse.

Jesus is given four names in this chapter. The first one is **Faithful and True** (v. 11). Faithful because He was faithful in fulfilling His mission to go to the cross to pay the price for sin; faithful in rising from the dead, just as He promised; faithful in sending the Holy Spirit just as He promised; and now, faithful in returning just as He promised. And True. Vernon McGee says (I love this): "He is the 'Bureau of Standards' of truth."[112] He is the yardstick of truth. He is *the* truth. He said, **"I am the way, and the truth, and the life"** (John 14:6). That is why He is called Faithful and True.

He judges and wages war in righteousness: perfect righteousness, perfect justice, no corruption in the way He judges. His eyes are a flame of fire, meaning that He sees even to the very heart and motives behind every action. Nothing is hidden from His eyes. He wore on His head many diadems. We sing the hymn, "Crown Him with Many Crowns...the Lord of love, the Lord of life, the Lord of heaven. Crown Him with many crowns."[113] These are the victor's crowns of the King, and He has many crowns.

He also has a *secret* name, the second name of this chapter. The second part of v. 12 says, **He has a name written upon Him that no one knows**

except Himself. What is that name? *No one knows.* Okay? I don't know and you don't know because it says **No one knows.** This is a secret name known only to Him. If you know anyone who says *I know what that name is,* he or she is lying! *No one* knows, so let's not speculate about that which is still secret. I did find one explanation, not for what the name is, but a good explanation for why this is stated to be secret. Those who practiced magic in the first century, and by magic I mean dark arts, believed that to know someone's name gave power over him whose name it was. John might be saying that no one has power over Christ. Certainly that makes sense. There is a *secret* name.

He has a robe dipped in blood. Whose blood? His blood, shed for us? Or the blood of those who are being judged? This chapter is about judgment, so certainly it must include that. However, the truth of the Lamb of God who shed His own blood for us could never be far from the mind of any writer, especially John, who was there at the cross when they pierced His side. So, it is likely both: His blood, and the blood of those who are about to be judged.

Then there is the third name that is given to Him: Word of God. He is, as John said in his Gospel, the One who was in the beginning with God. He is the One who became flesh as the living Word. He is the Word of God.

Armies of Christ (14)

This section is just one verse. The armies are clothed in fine linen, white and clean. We can't miss that, can we? Who is this? It's the Bride of Christ! It's the Church! Here they are, with the same adornment as v. 8! But since it says *armies*, it could possibly also include, along with the Church, Old Testament believers. About that we can only speculate. But it is the same description as in v. 8. They also ride white horses: the sign of victory. Dr. Merrill Tinney, wonderfully describes this entire picture, with Christ on a white horse and the armies behind Him on white horses, as follows:

> *It is the pattern of a Roman triumphal procession, when a general returned from a successful campaign, he and his legions were granted the right to parade up the Via Sacra, the main street of Rome that led from the forum to the temple of Jupiter on Capitoline Hill. Mounted on a white horse, the general rode at the head of his troops, followed by wagon loads of booty that he had taken from the conquered nation.*[114]

The people who read this in John's day could not have missed that when they saw Jesus riding on a white horse followed by His armies.

Authority of Christ (15-16)

John uses multiple metaphors. There was a sharp sword from His mouth. His speech is so strong that all He has to do is to speak a word, and it is as powerful as a sharp sword. His *speech* smites the nations. He rules with a *rod of iron*. That's easy to understand: a scepter, powerful, strong, and unbreakable. He treads the winepress of the fierce wrath of God the Almighty. A winepress was used to crush grapes. The winepress of wrath crushes the sinner.

Then we come to the fourth name for Jesus in this chapter: **King of kings, and Lord of lords** (19:16). Why the double name? It is possible that King of kings refers to rule over all human kings. King Artaxerxes and King Nebuchadnezzar in the Old Testament both used that first title for themselves (king of kings) because they ruled over everything they saw. They ruled over the known world. Jesus is the true King of kings, so He rules over all earthly kings. Lord of lords would then mean He rules over all of heaven. So he is King of heaven *and* Earth; He is King of kings, and Lord of lords. We see evidence of His humanity *and* His deity: the God-Man.

Avenging of Christ (17-21)

Curiously, this section starts with an invitation. Did you catch that? It is a loud voice (surprised?) giving an invitation to *birds*. The invitation is to come and dine on human and horse meat. *Birds, get ready!* The outcome is certain. There will be plenty to eat. You want a little bit of human filet mignon? You want a little bit of horse prime rib? You want a little bit of horse flank or horse sirloin? Human ribeye? Whatever you want, it will be available for you. You will be able to dine on all of it. The outcome is certain. It is called the great supper of God. Have we had a supper earlier in this chapter? Yes, it was the marriage supper of the Lamb, and blessed were those who were invited to that supper. But who is invited to this supper? The *birds*. What about the humans? They will not be in good shape at suppertime.

Now remember (back to Chapter 16) the beast and his armies gathered at Armageddon. They have gathered and are going to make war (19:19) against Christ. Ask yourself this: How could they be so stupid? Bad idea! But also remember, back in 16:13-14 there were three evil spirits: one from the dragon who is Satan, one from Antichrist, and one from the false prophet. They went out and they spoke to the kings of the earth, and they said, *Gather together, everybody come together, one big alliance against God.* It is the ultimate demonic influence on government. I know that exists today; it has existed for all the time there have been kings and governments. But this is the ultimate one. Charles Swindoll says:

How foolish it will look when those rulers point their guns and missiles at the all-powerful Creator, who spoke the entire universe into existence! How foolish, but how like fallen humanity! Always overestimating their abilities, forever proud of their technology, yet never coming to terms with their own weakness before the all-powerful, all-knowing Lord of the universe.[115]

Now watch what happens. The beast and the false prophet are seized and are thrown alive into the lake of fire. And the rest are killed with the sword. What is that sword? Remember: His speech smites the nations. And the birds, at the end of the chapter, (v. 21), have their fill. Not much of a battle, was it? People talk about the Battle of Armageddon? What battle? John Phillips says it this way:

Suddenly it will all be over. In fact, there will be no war at all, in the sense that we think of war. There will be just a word spoken from Him who sits astride the great white horse. Once He spoke a word to a fig tree, and it withered away. Once He spoke a word to howling winds and heaving waves, and the storm clouds vanished and the waves fell still. Once He spoke to a legion of demons bursting at the seams of a poor man's soul, and instantly they fled. Now He speaks a word, and the war is over. The blasphemous, loud-mouthed Beast is stricken where he stands. The false prophet, the miracle-working windbag from the pit is punctured and still... Another word, and the panic-stricken armies reel and stagger and fall down dead. Field marshals and generals, admirals and air commanders, soldiers and sailor, rank and file, one and all— they fall. And the vultures descend and cover the scene.[116]

Did you notice that no army weapons were even mentioned? Nowhere does it say that the army even has to fight. The only weapon mentioned is the sword: the word that comes from the mouth of the King of kings and Lord of lords. It happens just as Jesus predicted in Matthew 24:27-28:

Just as the lightning comes from the east and flashes even to the west, so will the coming of the Son of Man be; wherever the corpse is, there the vultures will gather.

Supplemental (v. 10)

You might have noticed that I skipped v. 10. That is because it is somewhat separate from the overall flow of the chapter, so I have saved it until here at the end. It is about whom to worship. John is so overwhelmed by all this that he gets confused and mistakenly falls down at the feet of the angel to worship him. The angel says, *Don't do that! Worship is for God alone. Don't worship me!* He adds: **"The testimony of Jesus is the spirit of prophecy."** Leon Morris explains this well:

> *The true spirit of prophecy always manifests itself in bearing witness to Jesus [not to an angel, in other words]. The Old Testament prophets, New Testament prophets such as John, and the angels, all alike bear their witness to the Son of God.*[117]

Don't worship the angel. This is one more evidence of the deity of Christ. Why do I say that? Do you remember that following Jesus' resurrection the apostles were gathered together, but there was a man by the name of Thomas who wasn't with them? All the rest of them got to see the risen Lord, and they told Thomas about it. And Thomas said, *I won't believe it until I see it for myself...until I put my finger in His hand and my hand in His side. Then I will believe.* About a week later, they are together again and Thomas is with them. Jesus appears and says to Thomas, **"Reach here your finger, and see my hands, and reach here your side, and put it into my side. And be not unbelieving, but believing"** (John 20:27). Thomas answers and says to Him, **"My Lord and my God"** (John 20:28). Does Jesus rebuke him? No, he does not. Because He is God, and He accepts worship as God. This is not the only place in the Gospels where He accepts worship as God, but it is the clearest. Jesus accepted worship; the angel did not.

The Rapture (One Last Time)

Before we end this lesson I want to discuss, for the third and last time, these two verses in I Thessalonians 4:16-17:

The Lord Himself will descend from heaven with a shout, with the voice of the archangel, and with the trumpet of God. And the dead in Christ shall rise first, then we who are alive and remain shall be caught up together with them in the clouds to meet the Lord in the air, and thus we shall always be with the Lord.

Caught up means raptured. We have looked previously at two different perspectives from scholars as to when in The Revelation this occurs. We must admit that we don't find a description like this in The Revelation, so we have previously asked the question, *When does this event occur?*

Some say it is Revelation 4:1. It is the first time the door in heaven is opened, and John is told, **"Come up here."** The people who hold to the view that that is symbolic of the entire church being raptured (caught up) are people who believe in a pre-tribulation rapture. When heaven opened and John was told to come up, John represented the Church. In support of this view is the fact that no mention of the Church is made again until right here in Revelation 19, where the Church appears as the Bride of Christ. Through all of the seven seals and the seven trumpets and the seven bowls and all of the interludes, this is the first time after Chapter 4 that we see the Church, and Chapter 4 comes after we just had two entire chapters of Church…to the church in Thessalonica, to the church in Laodicea, to the Church in Philadelphia…the seven churches. Church, church, church, church, church, church, church! Lesson 4 was an entire study of how the letters were possibly written not just to those seven literal churches, which they were, but also to seven church ages throughout history. Then we get to Chapter 4, John is told to come up, and we don't hear from the Church again until Revelation 19.

Some have speculated that the rapture comes here at the end of the tribulation (a post-tribulation view). I can tell you that vs. 11, 12, 13, 14, 15, and 16 are *not* the rapture, however. Heaven is opened and there is *a white horse*; if this is the rapture, what happened to the shout, and the voice of the archangel, and the trumpet of God (from I Thessalonians)? These verses do not describe the rapture. I can also tell you this: the rapture, whenever it happens, must happen *before* the marriage. Christ cannot have the marriage to His Bride, the Bride of Christ, in heaven while some are still on Earth. So the very latest the rapture could possibly happen is immediately before the marriage described here, starting with v. 7. Is there anything here in vs. 4-7 or anywhere in this chapter that resembles I Thessalonians 4? No, but that doesn't mean it can't happen here, because there is nothing in the entire Book of The Revelation that describes anything like I Thessalonians 4, as we have previously noted. You see, what we wish is that John had repeated Paul's words at some point and said, *Here it is!* But he didn't do that. So the post-tribulation supporters believe it happens in this chapter, probably just before 19:7.

What about the mid-tribulation view? The closest event in The Revelation to a catching up or a rapture is in Chapter 14, and we looked at I Thessalonians when we studied that chapter. There is an angel reaping the Earth because the Earth is ripe. The Church is fully developed, and therefore the angel reaps and the Church is raptured. But we also mentioned that right after that there is a second angel who reaps for judgment. There is a possibility that this is just a double metaphor; that all of that is a reaping of judgment on sinners and it doesn't have anything to do with the rapture. I am of the opinion that what is described in Revelation 14 probably *is* the rapture, the reaping of the saints, and that would seem to be evidence for a mid-tribulation rapture. However, remember what we said about Chapters 12, 13, and 14: they are not chronological. Some of that material looks back to the fall of Satan before the foundation of the world. Some of it looks back to the Old Testament…the woman, who is a symbol of Israel, who gives birth to the Messiah, and how Satan tries to prevent that from happening. Some of it looks forward to the very end of the tribulation. That means that even if the event in Revelation 14 does describe the rapture, it could come at any time. It could be at the beginning of the tribulation, it could come at any point during the tribulation, or it could be here at the end. The fact that a possible description of it is contained in Chapter 14 does not give us a chronology, because those chapters are not chronological.

So, what are we to conclude? Will the rapture come before the tribulation, sometime during the tribulation, or at the end of the tribulation? Yes! I know that some of you have strong opinions, and I respect you for that. Believers come from many different denominational backgrounds, and I'm sure many of my readers have been taught different viewpoints. Scholars have not agreed for centuries. I don't want to say that a particular view is the way it must be, that I'm right and everyone else is wrong. Others will stand in pulpits or write books saying something else, telling you they are right and I am wrong. I ask for humility and grace from all, beginning with myself.

I do want to add one more thing, because some people have said, *Well, I don't understand how there could be two second comings!* There is the rapture; that is the "first" second coming. And then there is this event in Revelation 19, and that is the "second" second coming. Let me ask you, when Jesus came the first time, was that just one moment? His first coming involved His miraculous conception, His virgin birth, a little bit that we know about His childhood, and His public ministry which included His teaching, His healing, His casting out of demons, His triumphal entry into Jerusalem, His arrest and trial, His death on the cross, His resurrection, and His ascension. That was His first coming. Do we say that He came 10 or 11 or 12 times? No, He came once. All of that was part of His first coming. So here, in the entire Book of The Revelation, and including prophecies from Daniel and I Thessalonians, we see all that is involved in His second coming. We know that there are seven years of tribulation leading up to His appearing. At some point there is the rapture, but it is all part of His coming the second time. He comes again once. In Lesson 5 I shared what my church's doctrinal statement says about Christ's return. I want to repeat it here:

We believe in the personal, bodily return of our Lord Jesus Christ at a time known only to God. We believe in the final judgment of all people. Those who do not know Christ will be condemned to eternal separation from God, and those who do know Christ will enjoy the glory of God with Christ in His Kingdom forever.[118]

The point of unity is that Jesus is coming again, personally, visibly. I reject the heresy that He came again when the Holy Spirit came, or He comes again when we experience Him anew. No, He is literally coming again. That is the point of unity for all believers. Whatever your view on the rapture, we are in agreement that the Lord is coming again. Hallelujah! Amen!

ATM (Apply to Me)

1. Have I made Jesus in my image? What I mean by that is being like the Laodicean church, the lukewarm church, that followed the gentle Jesus, meek and mild, and made Him their "Lord." They actually made themselves Lord over Him. Thomas Torrance says this:

    The world likes a complacent, reasonable religion. And so it is always ready to revere some pale Galilean image of Jesus, some meager anemic Messiah, and to give Him a moderate rational homage... The truth is that we have often committed adultery with alien ideologies, confounded the gospel with the religions of nature, and imbibed the wine of pagan doctrines and false principles and deceitful practices. We have sought to bend the will of God to serve the ends of man, to alter the gospel and shape the Church to conform to the fashions of the times.[119]

    That's what lukewarm churches have done. May your church never be a lukewarm church. May it always be a church that recognizes the risen Lord is *King of kings and Lord of Lords.*

2. The Word of God—the incarnate Word and the written Word—is always the final authority. Never put the authority of man over the authority of the Word.

3. In regard to John's mistakenly trying to worship an angel, is there a person, possession, or position challenging God's rightful place in my life? If there is, then I've made that person or possession or position my god. Whoever or whatever is most important in our lives...that's our god. If Jesus Christ is not Lord *of* all, He is not Lord *at* all. He must be Lord *of all.*

4. Which supper will you be a part of? The marriage and the marriage supper, or the supper of God? I have to tell you, if you choose the second option, you *are* the supper. That's not good. We want to be sure we know that we know that we know Jesus Christ.

5. Finally, am I ready? If you are a pre-tribulation rapture person, then you are waiting for the rapture. If you are a mid- or post-tribulation person, then you are waiting for the tribulation to start. Regardless of how all of that occurs, hear the words of Martha Snell Nicholson in a poem titled *If Christ Should Come Tonight*:

Is my house set in order, if Christ should come today?
What tasks would be unfinished if I were called away?

Suppose an angel told me at early morning light,
"Your Lord will come this evening; you shall go home tonight."

Would ecstasy be clouded by thought of work undone,
The seed I might have scattered, the crown I might have won?

The soul I meant to speak to, the purse I meant to share,
And oh, the wasted moments I meant to spend in prayer!

The weight of unsaved millions would press upon my heart,
In their death am I certain that I had not a part?

And such a few short moments in which to set things right!
How feverishly I'd labor until the waning light!

O slothful soul and careless heart, O eyes which have no sight,
—Work, lest you reap but vain regrets! Your Lord may come to-
night![20]

Lesson 19

Read 20:1 – 15

The Millennium and Beyond

Charles Swindoll wrote:

> *Sin spoils everything. It leads to physical and emotional illness, prompts addictions, and destroys marriages and families. No area of society or culture escapes its sinister influence. Sin corrupts the legal system, corrodes governments, encourages corporate greed, erodes economics, inspires wars, and promotes false religion. Just as sin destroys an individual's life, it also decimates communities, countries, and eventually the planet.[121]*

What we are seeing in this chapter is the end of sin and the end of the author of sin. Hallelujah! Let's review where we have come in the last few lessons. In the last lesson we looked at the marriage of the Lamb. The Lamb is the crucified, risen Son of God, and the bride is the Church. Scripture makes it clear that the Church is the Bride of Christ. We saw also the marriage supper. We saw that there were certain people who were *invited* to the marriage supper: a different group from the bride and groom. You do not invite the bride and groom to the marriage supper: it's *their* supper, and we believe that probably refers to Old Testament believers who were invited to the marriage supper. We saw Christ returning to Earth on a white horse; the white horse is symbolic of victory. One of the names we looked at in the last lesson was **King of kings and Lord of lords** (19:6). It is a fitting name for the returning, conquering King. We saw that He was followed by armies on white horses, and from the description of those armies it was clear that was the Church, following Him also on white horses. They face off against the beast, who is Antichrist, and his armies. Then we saw the "battle" of Armageddon, which didn't turn out to be much of a battle. The beast and the false prophet were seized and thrown into the lake of fire, and the rest of the armies of the beast were killed by the verbal sword of Christ. Then we saw, in contrast to the marriage supper, the great supper of God where the birds feasted on horse and on human flesh.

As we come to Chapter 20, I am pleased to tell you that it is pretty easy to understand the *what* of this chapter. Hurray! If you have read everything up to this point, you have engaged your brain in some very deep things as we have gone through The Revelation. This lesson is long, but it is pretty straightforward. There is a thousand-year period. It is the only time in the entire New Testament where a thousand years is mentioned, but it appears six times in this chapter. It's called the millennium because that's what 1,000 years is. We read about the millennium, and we read about what follows it. Later we will discuss some differing views about the meaning of the millennium, but it is still quite easy to understand what God is saying. What is harder to understand, and we will get to this toward the end of this lesson, is the *why* of the millennium.

So, let's look at the *what* first. There are five sections. In vs. 1-3 Satan is shut in the abyss for 1,000 years. In vs. 4-6 Christ and His followers reign for those same 1,000 years. In vs. 7-9, Satan is released and gathers an army, and the army is destroyed by fire from heaven. In v. 10 Satan is cast into the lake of fire, and in vs. 11-15, we read about the Great White Throne judgment. Let's examine those five sections individually.

Satan Chained

In vs. 1-3, Satan is chained in the abyss. This is the same abyss where demons begged Jesus not to send them. In Luke Chapter 8 there was a man who was possessed by a legion of demons. When Jesus gave the command to come out of the man, they begged Him not to send them to the abyss. They wanted to still have free reign to cause trouble on Earth, and they knew in the abyss they would be chained. This is the same abyss where disobedient spirits, who abandoned their proper abode (Jude 6), were imprisoned according to I Peter 3:19-20. They were not free as other fallen angels to roam the Earth and cause trouble. This special class of fallen angels, of disobedient spirits, was imprisoned in the abyss. We also saw the abyss in The Revelation, Chapter 9: the abyss where demonic locusts were released to cause a plague on the Earth. Now the devil is imprisoned there for 1,000 years, not free to cause any trouble.

Christ Reigns

In vs. 4-6, during those 1,000 years, thrones (plural) are set up. One throne, of course, is for Christ; the main throne, the highest and lifted up throne. But there are other thrones, and we are told in v. 4 that they are for tribulation martyrs: those who were martyred and had refused the mark of the beast and had given their lives in standing against Antichrist. They are raised to life and they also sit on thrones. I believe there are others not mentioned here who are also in some way part of this worldwide government. Those would be the armies of heaven that we read about in the last lesson that were following Jesus on white horses, i.e., the Church. I would assume that the Church is also in some way, while not on thrones, part of that government. In fact, Jesus told one specific group that they would sit on thrones. In Matthew 19:28, He said to His twelve apostles:

Truly I say to you, that you who have followed Me in the regeneration when the Son of Man will sit on His glorious throne; you also shall sit upon twelve thrones judging the twelve tribes of Israel.

So presumably not just the apostles, but the entire Bride of Christ which has returned following the Lord on white horses, are part of this millennial government. The twelve apostles of course have a *specific* mission to sit on twelve thrones, judging the twelve tribes of Israel. That's why it was so important that Judas be replaced in the Book of Acts (1:15-26). There are twelve thrones and twelve tribes of Israel, so Judas had to be replaced.

Explanation: Meaning of the Millennium

Before we go on to the next section, I want to say something about the meaning of this 1,000 years, where Satan is imprisoned and Jesus and these others sit on thrones, reigning. Christ returns to establish His millennial reign after the tribulation is over. That would be the view that I hold, and on which I have based all of these lessons. It is called the pre-millennial view. That is, first come the seven years of tribulation, and then Christ returns to Earth to establish His kingdom and reigns for 1,000 years. That sums up the pre-millennial view.

There is a second view, called the post-millennial view; it says the millennium will come because things will have gotten so good on Earth (say *what?*) that there will be righteousness and peace on Earth. Then Christ will reign for a thousand years. What will bring that about? The whole world will be evangelized, ushering in a millennium of peace and prosperity. Now, I obviously don't hold to that view. But I don't want to just create a straw man, and then shoot down the straw man. There are sincere Bible-believing Christians (who are in a shrinking minority, I might add) who still hold to this view. It was actually very popular at the end of the 19th century. The world *was* getting better and better; we had just had two centuries of great worldwide evangelism. The 18th and 19th centuries were the best centuries for worldwide evangelism since the first century. But then we came to the 20th century, and we had World War I, the Great Depression, World War II, nuclear weapons, and now global terrorism, and the post-millennial view fell out of favor. But for those who hold this view, let me tell you their argument, and not just give you something that you can instantly shoot down. They will rightly tell you that there are more Christians in the world than at any time in history, and that's true. Perhaps not proportionate to the world's population, but there are more Christians living in the world right now than ever. They will point out the fact that the Scriptures have been translated into thousands of languages, and more are completed every month. I heard recently that the estimated completion date for the work to get the Scriptures translated into every language has been moved 100 years sooner than originally thought because of technology, computer language software, etc. They also point out that through radio, TV, or any kind of way to broadcast or telecast information (like the internet) there are ways to reach into countries that previously were completely closed to the gospel. No missionary could get in to share the gospel, but now it can be shared electronically. So they say, *We are just getting started! We will be able to evangelize the whole world, and bring in the millennium.* I respect those who hold this view, but I do not accept it. It seems to me that the world is not getting better and better; it seems to me that the world is getting worse and worse. Maybe it's getting a little better during the day but it's getting a lot worse at night, and it's getting worse at night than it's getting better during the day! We are in a mess. The world is in a mess.

There is a third view, and that is called the amillennial view. The people who hold this view point out that the millennium appears only in this chapter. It is not mentioned anywhere else in the New Testament. (That is true, but it is mentioned here *six times*.) They say that because it is not mentioned anywhere else in the New Testament, the millennium is actually now. The millennium exists now as the Kingdom of Christ in the hearts of believers. You might ask, *Well, what about Satan being chained in the abyss?* They say that Satan is chained in the sense that his power is limited because he was defeated at the cross. (I once heard a scholar say, *If Satan is chained, it must be a very, very long chain.*) This view says that the thousand years is not literal but is symbolic of a very long period of time; that is, the church age when Christ reigns in the hearts of believers. This view is still widely held by many Bible-believing Christians.

I reject the amillennial position because of the answer to this question: What will the millennium be like? The Old Testament prophets, whether they were major prophets like Isaiah, Jeremiah, and Ezekiel, or minor prophets like Hosea, Micah, and so on, virtually every prophet had something to say when he looked forward to the millennium. We can't possibly cover all they said in this book; that would be an extensive study in and of itself. But except for Jonah, every prophet had something to say about what the millennium would be like. We will look at just some of those.

1. It will be a time of justice and peace. Micah wrote this (4:2-3):

Many nations will come and say, 'Come and let us go up to the mountain of the Lord into the house of the God of Jacob, that He may teach us about His ways and that we may walk in his paths. For from Zion will go forth the law, even the word of the

Lord from Jerusalem, and He will judge between many peoples and render many decisions for mighty distant nations. Then they will hammer their swords into plowshares and their spears into pruning hooks. Nation will not lift up sword against nation, and never again will they train for war.'

What a glorious, glorious description of this 1,000-year reign. Man's attempt to bring this in, the most recent *big* attempt, was in the 1940's following WWII: *Let's have a group of worldwide leaders and ambassadors of nations, and we will call it the United Nations. If we all just get together and talk, we will have peace on earth.* Do you know that there is a granite staircase in the northwest corner of the park across First Avenue in New York from the United Nations headquarters? It was built and dedicated in 1948 during construction of the U.N. headquarters, and has these words engraved on it: "They shall beat their swords into plowshares and their spears into pruning hooks. Nation shall not lift up sword against nation. Neither shall they learn war anymore." That is man's utopian dream of man trying to usher in peace on earth, but I am certain it will not happen through human efforts. Charles Swindoll says:

> *The light of justice will illumine every corner of the world. This condition will not be achieved through educational funding, political change, social programs, or cultural awakening. As promising as some of these things may seem in the short-term, fallen humanity ultimately foils all efforts at self-reformation.*[122]

The time of justice and peace will come because the King of kings and Lord of lords will be sitting on the throne.

2. It will be a time free from fear (Isaiah 11:6-9):

The wolf will dwell with the lamb, and the leopard will lie down with the kid and the calf and the young lion and the fatling together, and the little boy will lead them. Also, the cow and the bear will graze their young, and will lie down together, and the lion will eat straw like the ox. And the nursing child will play by the hole of the cobra, and the weaned child will put his hand on the viper's den. They will not hurt or destroy in all my holy mountain, for the earth will be full of the knowledge of the Lord as the waters cover the sea.

Even the little baby has nothing to fear from the deadliest animal. No animal need fear anything from any other animal. This is one of several reasons why I am a premillennialist. If we are living in the millennium now, do we see anything like this anywhere? No. Do you see mankind being able to usher in this kind of earth, even if the nations could get along? The only way this kind of change happens is if there is a *supernatural* change in the *natural* order of things, and that only happens when Christ comes and reigns on earth during his thousand-year reign.

3. It will be a time of abundance (Isaiah 35:1-2):

The wilderness and the desert will be glad, and the Arabah will rejoice and blossom. Like the crocus it will blossom profusely and rejoice with rejoicing and with shout of joy. The glory of Lebanon will be given to it the majesty of Carmel and Sharon. They will see the glory of the Lord, the majesty of our God.

Even the desert places will suddenly be filled with water, and there will be life in the desert. There will be abundance; no one will go hungry. It will be a time of great abundance. It will be a time of health and long life.

4. It will be a time of long life. I use the New Living Translation for this next Bible quotation because it helps us better understand exactly what this verse is saying. (Isaiah 65:20, NLT):

No longer will babies die when only a few days old. No longer will adults die before they have lived a full life. No longer will people be considered old at 100. Only the cursed will die that young.[123]

Doesn't that sound good? It will be a time of long life and health. Maybe you lost a child at childbirth or in infancy. That won't happen anymore. A hundred years won't even be considered old. People will obviously marry, they will have children, and they will live very, very long lives. Again, do we see this now, if this is the millennium? No. And no advances in medicine will change that. Do we see man being able to usher in an earth like that, destroying and beating all disease? My entire life I have heard, *Let's beat cancer, let's beat cancer!* Trillions of dollars have been spent worldwide in research, and every day people die from cancer. Mankind will not usher this in. Again, there must be a *supernatural* change in the order of things.

5. It will be a time of knowledge of the Lord. (Isaiah 31:34):

They shall not teach again each man his neighbor and each man his brother saying "Know the Lord" for they shall all know me, from the least of them to the greatest of them.

6. It will be a time of great joy! Can you imagine living on this kind of earth? We are so used to fallen earth and the mess that mankind has

made of it that we can't even imagine this. But it will be a time of *great joy* (Isaiah 30:29):

You will have songs as in the night when you keep the festival, and gladness of heart as when one marches to the sound of the flute, to go to the mountain of the Lord, to the rock of Israel.

There have been other things in The Revelation about which people don't agree, but this is probably the biggest of all--the meaning of the millennium. I believe the pre-millennial view: seven years of tribulation, followed by Christ returning to reign for a literal thousand years, is the one that conforms to Scripture. Satan will have no power, Jesus will take His rightful place as ruler of the Earth, the righteous will be in charge, and no one will be corruptible—not by money, by power, or by flattery. What a contrast with our present age, where all who desire to live godly in Christ Jesus suffer persecution. That is what the millennium will be like.

After the Millennium

After the 1,000 years Satan is released from the abyss, and he gathers an army like the sand of the seashore. They are said to come from Gog and Magog, which are symbolic of worldwide enemies of God. After all of this time and this wonderful 1,000 years of reign, here comes Satan and he is able to gather an army against Christ. How does he do that? First, we are told that he deceives them because he is the great liar—the father of lies. Second, do you believe everyone was content during the 1,000 years? Do you think the one who has wanted to be a thief has been happy? He has obeyed because he knows he has no other choice. He hasn't been able to steal, but he has wanted to. Do you suppose the loose woman who wants to be an adulteress has been happy? Oh, she has obeyed, because she knows she has had no other choice. Ah, but now, let's throw off the rules. We want to do our own thing! And thanks to Satan's deception, an army in numbers like the sand of the seashore is gathered. Charles Swindoll also notes that those who join in this rebellion will be "generationally removed from the tribulation."[124] A thousand years have passed. They will probably be geographically remote from the King's ruling city, which we will see in a moment is Jerusalem, and they will be spiritually distant from Christ in their hearts even though they have outwardly conformed. So what do they do? They surround the beloved city. What is the beloved city? It has to be Jerusalem, where Jesus apparently has set up His headquarters. But just like the battle of Armageddon, it is not much of a war, not much of a battle. Fire from heaven devours them. That's it. It's over. *Hey, I thought we were going to fight!* Nope. Fire comes down and destroys them.

Satan's Eternal Abode

Satan is cast into the lake of fire. He had started as the anointed cherub (Ezekiel 28), and now the enemy of our souls is gone *forever*, never to be heard from again. Hallelujah! We discussed this in Lesson 12, but I want to remind you of four falls from Lucifer to the lake of fire. Remember, the one we know as Satan was originally created with the name Lucifer, he was beautiful, and he was intended to give glory to God. But he said *I will be like God; I will take the throne.* And he went from glorified angel to demonic accuser. We read about that in Revelation 12:4. Isaiah and Ezekiel give great details about how Lucifer's power in heaven was taken away. But he was still able to come before God and accuse the brethren, as in Job. God asks Satan if he has seen God's servant Job. Satan says, *Well, he follows You because you have protected him with everything. Take away what he has and he will curse you to your face.* Of course, Satan was wrong. But he could still accuse before God. Then in Revelation 12:9, we saw that he couldn't even do that. He was restricted to activity on Earth, and he was very angry about that, so he did everything he could to cause trouble, especially for Israel. At the beginning of this chapter, we saw that he will be seized and put into the abyss for 1,000 years. His final fall, what we have read here in 20:7, is that he is released from the abyss for a short time before he is cast into the lake of fire *forever*.

Great White Throne

That brings us to the last section of this chapter, and that is the Great White Throne judgment. Notice those three words. THRONE: The one who sits on the throne is a King. GREAT throne: *Great* implies all power and all knowledge. WHITE: He judges in perfection, and in purity, and in holiness. All the dead are raised and they appear before this throne.

There is great agreement among scholars that of all of these dead who are raised for this judgment, none are believers. When the martyrs were raised to reign during the thousand years, we were told (20:6) **Blessed is he who shares in the first resurrection, because over him the second death has no power.** That was the first resurrection. Here is the second resurrection, and it leads to the second death, which will be the lake of fire for them also. Books are opened, and the books apparently record all of the deeds that they've done. How do I know that? They are judged according to their deeds (20:13). For example, here's Mortimer's book; it is opened, and we look at everything Mortimer did. (All the people who wanted to be judged according to their deeds, who thought they were going to be good enough to get into heaven...they will get their way.) Let's look at Mortimer's deeds; let's see how Mortimer did. The verdict for Mortimer, and for everyone standing before the Great White Throne, will be this: Guilty.

Guilty. Then is there no hope for anyone? Well, Mortimer, there is. There is this other book, the Book of Life. The Book of Life has in it *every* name of *every* person who has ever come to Jesus Christ as Lord and Savior. Mortimer, let's check to see if your name is in the Book of Life. But none of these people are believers, if the scholars are correct, so no. Mortimer's name is not there, and he is thrown into the lake of fire. Dante wrote about that. "Abandon all hope, ye who enter here."[125] Why open the Book of Life if none of these names are going to be there? The answer is to show this person fairly that he/she had a chance. That was the chance; if the name was in this Book, then he/she would not be here receiving this judgment.

Some have speculated that there will be degrees of punishment. Matthew 11:20-24 seems to imply different degrees of punishment for the wicked. We cannot say with certainty exactly what that means, but the end is the same: cast into the lake of fire.

Let me say one more thing about this judgment. The Great White Throne judgment is not the judgment seat of Christ. Believers must all appear before the judgment seat of Christ, *not to be judged for salvation.* Our salvation is secure in Christ in His blood. But believers' works will be judged for *reward.* That is not the same thing as the Great White Throne judgment.

We are also told something curious: death and Hades were cast *into* the lake of fire. That means Hades is *not* the lake of fire. Let's explain this. Think of the Old Testament. The place of the dead was called *Sheol.* Look at the following diagram.

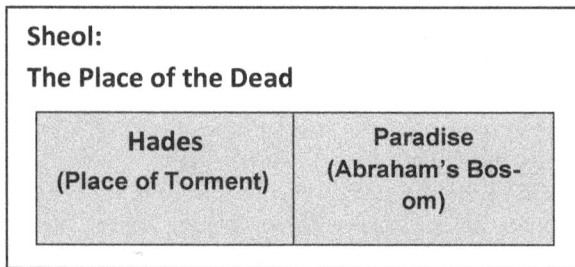

Sheol: The Place of the Dead	
Hades (Place of Torment)	**Paradise** (Abraham's Bosom)

Let's say this box represents Sheol. It apparently was divided into two sections. Part of it was Paradise; also called Abraham's Bosom. The other part was called Hades. It was a place of torment. You might remember the story of the rich man and Lazarus in the Gospel of Luke. Lazarus had nothing and the rich man had everything. The rich man was greedy and cared nothing for the things of the Lord. When they died, Lazarus went to Abraham's Bosom. The rich man was tormented in Hades, and he said, **"Send Lazarus over to dip some water for my tongue because I am in agony in this flame"** (Luke 16:24). The rich man was told that a great wall was erected between them, and that could not happen. What also did Jesus say to the thief on the cross? **"Today you will be with me [not in heaven but] in *Paradise*"** (Luke 23:43, my italic). Are you following me? That diagram is up until the cross. What happens after that? Jesus pays the penalty for sin, He is buried, He is raised from the dead, and then He ascends to heaven. When He ascended, he led a host of captives (Ephesians 4:8).

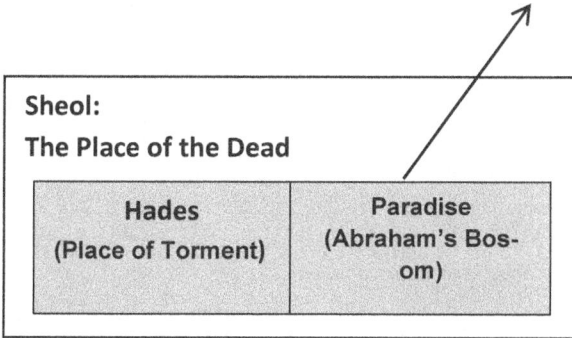

Sheol: The Place of the Dead	
Hades **(Place of Torment)**	**Paradise** **(Abraham's Bosom)**

Who were the host of captives? Those who were in Paradise. They were not in torment; they were happy and content. But heaven contained only two souls up until that time—Elijah and Enoch: two who were transposed to heaven without dying. All of the other Old Testament believers died and were in Paradise. When Jesus ascended, He led them to heaven, and now heaven is populated with all of the believers: Old Testament and New Testament believers. People who die now—where do they go? Paul wrote that to be absent from the body is to be present with the Lord (II Corinthians 5:8). So today it looks like this:

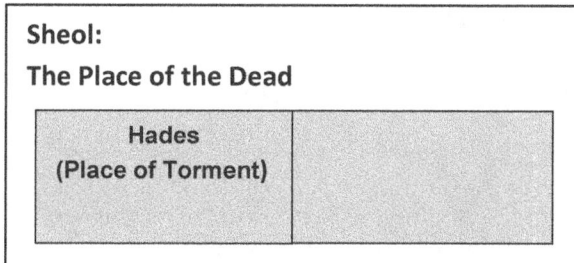

Sheol: The Place of the Dead	
Hades **(Place of Torment)**	

Paradise is empty, because all believers (OT and NT) are in heaven. That is how in Revelation 20 death and Hades are cast into the lake of fire. Does it make sense now? That's all that's left in Sheol that *can* be cast into the lake of fire.

Charles Swindoll[126] gives us five categories of those people who will stand at the Great White Throne judgment. First, there will be those who had the light of creation (that is, they never heard the Gospel), but they replaced worship of the Creator with worship of the creation. That's what mankind has done ever since the fall in the Garden. Second, there will be those who turned their backs on the free grace of God in favor of a works-based religion. It's everyone who ever said, *Yes, I'm going to be good enough. I'm going to do more good than bad. That will be enough to get me into heaven. I want to be judged by my works; let my works speak for me.* They will get their way, because they don't understand sin and a Holy God who must judge sin. Third, there will be those who heard the gospel of Christ but rejected Him. Fourth, there will be the people who thought they were so smart; those who concluded based on logic, reason, and experience, that God doesn't exist. The sad news is, for people who have chosen that path in life, at the Great White Throne judgment they will no longer be atheists. Finally, there will be those who lived out their depravity through selfishness, wickedness, and violence, as people have done for thousands of years.

All of these have *chosen* separation from God and, here at the end, at the final judgment, God gives them what they want. They have said *I don't want any part of God,* and God says, *I'm giving you exactly what you want; exactly what you have chosen.* Harry Ironside notes:

All of the lost, of all the ages, all who preferred their sins to His salvation, all who procrastinated until for them the door of mercy was closed, all who spurned His grace, and in self-will chose the way that seems right unto a man but was in truth the way of death, all such people are to be summoned to stand before that inexorably righteous throne.[127]

So there it is. The Great White Throne judgment.

Why the Millennium?

All of that is the *what* question. The *why* question requires more thought. Why the millennium? Why not just seize Satan and throw him into the lake of fire? End of story. Have you asked yourself that question before, or perhaps now? Even as we have gone through this chapter, why the millennium? Why put Satan in prison and then let him loose for a little while? Why not just throw him into the lake of fire and be done with him? Have you ever watched a television series where there is a recurring villain, and you've said, *Why doesn't someone just shoot that person and be done with it?* Why not just be done with it here? Why not just send Satan to the lake of fire? There are multiple answers to that question.

1. The millennium is an answer to the prayer, *Thy Kingdom come, Thy will be done on <u>Earth</u> as it is in heaven*. This is a prayer that believers, and even people who aren't believers, pray all the time. *Thy will be done on <u>Earth</u>...* Not the new heaven and the new Earth that we will learn about in our next lesson, but on *this* Earth. It will be an answer to that prayer. How will God's will be done during that millennium? Just like it is in heaven: perfectly.

2. Why the millennium? To reward those who have been faithful to Christ. They get to reign with Christ; particularly those who were martyred during the tribulation...those who refused the mark of the beast and who have surrendered their lives rather than bow down to Antichrist.

3. To redeem the Earth from its curse from back in Chapter 3 of Genesis. After the fall God cursed the ground, and it grows thorns and thistles. (I'm really good at that. It is hard to grow flowers and pretty things, but it is really easy for me to grow weeds. Every time I have to dig them out, I'm not so happy with Adam and Eve.) Romans 8:19-22 talks about how the whole creation groans waiting for redemption from the curse. This is it, right here in Chapter 20: redemption of the Earth from the curse.

4. To once again *prove* the depravity of man. Think about the history of man. It's not very pretty, is it? Just think about the Old Testament, and then on into the Gospels, and then into the Book of The Revelation. It starts with perfection in the Garden of Eden, and it led to the fall and the entry of sin and death. After that, rather than following conscience, mankind ignored conscience and every thought of mankind was always evil, which led to the waters of judgment in the days of Noah. Then God said He would tap one man on the shoulder; that man was Abram, later Abraham. There was a covenant with him. There was to be a nation of people devoted to the Lord, God's chosen people. After that nation developed, they were slaves in Egypt, and Moses led them out. What was the first thing they did? They disobeyed, and it led to that entire generation spending 40 years wandering and dying in the wilderness. Then they thought that once they got into the promised land, everything would be great, and everything would be righteous. They were governed by judges, and it led to this phrase, which is repeated in the book of Judges several times: **"Every**

man did what was right in his own eyes" (Judges 17:6, 21:25). *Well okay, the judge thing didn't work, but when we have a king, then things will be perfect!* A united kingdom with three kings: Saul, David, Solomon. Then a split into Israel and Judah, and most of the kings (including *all* of the northern kingdom kings [Israel]) were wicked: there was massive immorality and idolatry. The prophets warned people to repent, and they didn't. That led to exile in a foreign land. After exile, the leaders were so picky about not getting into idolatry again that *following the Lord* morphed into legalism, and that is what we find in the Gospels with the Pharisees. When the Messiah came, they crucified Him. Then in our last lesson, under Satan's influence, the nations gathered together at Armageddon to oppose Christ. And now, after a thousand years of peace and prosperity, people will still rebel against the Lord. They will obey during the millennium, but grudgingly. Jeremiah 17:9 is proved: **The heart is deceitful above all things, and desperately wicked. Who can know it?** The millennium proves the depravity of man one final time.

5. The millennium will show that utopia depends on God making things new: not on man being good enough.

6. This is just speculation, but some have suggested that perhaps the millennium is an opportunity for those who *couldn't* do so to receive Christ. Who would that be? Very young babies and children who passed into eternity before they were old enough to understand the gospel, or those who were never able to function well enough mentally to even grasp the concept of the gospel and of sin. *It doesn't say this in Scripture, and we must not read more into Scripture than what is there.* It's speculation, but it certainly makes sense to me that those who have never had the opportunity to make a moral choice as to whether to follow or reject Christ will have an opportunity to do so in the millennium.

So that is the why of *why* the millennium.

ATM (Apply to Me)

1. First is a quote from Warren Wiersbe: "The perfect environment cannot produce a perfect heart."[128] Think of all of the people who say if we could just fix all of the environmental things around us that are wrong, then we will have perfect kids growing up, and perfect students, with everybody educated, and everybody smart enough, and then we will have a perfect country or a perfect world. The perfect

environment cannot create a perfect heart. Only God can change the heart.

2. Is my name in the Book of Life? This is the most important point. Is your name in the Book of Life? Is your name in the Book of Life because you remember a specific time when you gave your heart to the Lord Jesus Christ? That is the only way to have our names written in the Book of Life. If you have never done that, do it right now. You don't want to stand before the Great White Throne judgment and be judged according to your works, because the standard is perfection, and the verdict will always be guilty. If your name is written in the Book of Life, you will not stand there. You will be free from sin and its penalty, and from its curse and its hold on you, through the shed blood of Jesus Christ.

3. Believers, brothers and sisters in Christ, are you weary? Are you weary of the world? You watch the news, and you are weary of the trouble? Remember this, there is a better day, not just a day but 1,000 years coming, and something even better after that. Hallelujah! Amen! Remember that when you get discouraged. Billy Graham was once asked if he is a pessimist or an optimist and he replied that he was an optimist. When asked why, he said that it was because he had read the last book of the Bible, and God wins. You see, God will win!

4. Finally, joy to the world, because the Lord is coming! Isaac Watts wrote words like that in a poem, and when he wrote them he didn't know he was writing a "Christmas carol." That's because he knew he was writing a poem, not about the *first* coming of Christ, but about the *second coming of Christ*. He was writing about the millennium:

Joy to the world, the Lord has come; let earth receive her King!

Joy to the earth, the Savior reigns.

No more let sins and sorrows grow, nor thorns infest the ground. He comes to make his blessings flow, far as the curse is found.

He rules the world with truth and grace, and makes the nations prove the glories of His righteousness and wonders of His love.[129]

Isaac Watts was writing about the millennial Kingdom, when Christ returns, and his hymn perfectly sums up this chapter of The Revelation. Why not sing it to yourself right now?

Lesson 20

Read 21:1 – 27

New Heaven and Earth

If you watch movies where there are scenes in heaven, you probably have seen people walking or floating in clouds, people walking around playing harps, and/or people like Clarence in *It's a Wonderful Life* who have finally gotten their wings and been promoted from Angel Second Class to Angel First Class, so now they can fly. The Scripture gives us a very different view of what eternity will be like after the return of our Lord Jesus Christ: a new heaven and a new Earth.

We will look first at v. 1, which is a general introduction to the entire chapter. We are told that the first heaven and Earth passed away, just as Jesus predicted in Matthew 24:35. **"Heaven and earth will pass away."** But scholars do not even agree about the meaning of that! Some say it means the Earth will be completely eliminated and God will start over with a new heaven and Earth. **The earth and its works shall be burned up** (II Peter 3:10). Others point to the fact that the word for making things new is a word that means renewal more than making from scratch. Like so many other things we have seen in The Revelation, we will not start a separate denomination over the meaning of new heaven and Earth. Whatever God chooses to do, everything will definitely be seen as new.

One very curious description of the new Earth in this verse is that there is no sea. Do you like the ocean? Many people dream of owning a house on the ocean, and some spend a large sum of money to obtain such a house. But here we read there will be no sea. Surprising? You must understand what the sea represented in John's day. Charles Swindoll tells us:

> *To people of the ancient world, the sea was a mysterious and dangerous place, characterized by brightening chaos and possessing the power to kill without warning. No fate could have been worse than to be swallowed up by the sea and have one's remains devoured by fish. Travel by sea was treacherous. Ships had to navigate within sight of land to avoid getting lost or caught in a sudden storm. At the same time, they couldn't sail too close to land, lest they strike a reef or be driven against rocks or jagged cliffs. Trading by sea was both a precarious and a lucrative business. If your ship made it back with goods from afar, you were rich; if it didn't, you lost everything, sometimes your own life.*[130]

Leon Morris adds: "In antiquity men did not have the means of copying successfully with the sea's dangers, and they regarded it as an unnatural element, a place of storms and danger."[131] So that is how people viewed the sea, and to be told that the new Earth would have no sea meant that the dangers of the sea would be eliminated.

There is one other thing about the sea that is often overlooked in Scripture. It concerns the ancient kingdom of Israel, specifically the southern kingdom known as Judah. There was a very, very good king who loved the Lord and followed the Lord. His name was Jehoshaphat. Sadly, he did something that was completely out of the will of God. Here is what we read in II Chronicles 20:35-37:

Jehoshaphat king of Judah allied himself with Ahaziah king of Israel. He acted wickedly in so doing. So he allied himself with him to make ships to go to Tarshish, and they made the ships in Ezion-geber. Then Eliezer...prophesied against Jehoshaphat saying, "Because you have allied yourself with Ahaziah, the Lord has destroyed your works." So the ships were broken and could not go to Tarshish.

Ezion-geber was apparently a place where ship building was well known; Solomon had had ships built there. Here Jehoshaphat makes an alliance with the wicked Ahaziah, King of Israel (the northern kingdom), an alliance he should not have made. Together they decide they want to have a fleet of ships. Because this alliance was not in God's plan, and because the idea of having a fleet of ships was not in God's plan, the ships were broken up at sea and lost. *That is the last time we read in the Bible about Israel having any ships.* The sea was not a friendly place, and this incident reinforces that.

So, when John says no more sea, people understood exactly what he meant, given the dangerous history Israel had with the sea. In any event, we know it was a very different kind of Earth that John saw in his vision—different from anything ever seen before.

The rest of Chapter 21 has two parts. Verses 2 through 8 are a preview of what will follow, and v. 9 through 27 give much greater detail about what John saw and summarizes in 2 through 8. Most of our lessons in this study have involved going through a passage from The Revelation in order by section. However, because the first and second sections overlap and because the second section reinforces and elaborates on the first section, we will look at this chapter thematically, rather than verse by verse.

Arrival of the New Jerusalem

In vs. 2, 9, and 10 John describes the new Jerusalem. We find out from v. 9 that John saw one of the angels who had the seven bowls of wrath (remember that seven angels had the seven last plagues, the seven bowls of wrath, and they poured them out on the Earth). Back in 17:1, when John was describing judgment on Babylon, he encountered one of these seven angels, using the same phrase: one of the seven angels who had the seven bowls of wrath. We don't know if this angel in Chapter 21 is the same angel as in Chapter 17, but they must have been very distinctive. When John encounters one again, as he does here in Chapter 21, he takes notice of the fact that it was one of those seven angels. This angel says to him in v. 9, **"Come here, I shall show you the bride, the wife of the Lamb."** John is carried away *in spirit* (not physically) to a high mountain from which he can observe the scene in front of him. In v. 2 and 10 he tells us he saw the holy city, Jerusalem (new Jerusalem in v. 2) **coming down out of heaven from God.** Those last seven words are identical in both verses.

The city is made ready as an adorned bride. You might remember in Lesson 18 we saw the Church, the Bride of Christ (the Bride of the Lamb). So how is it that the city is the Bride? That really tall skyscraper and that office building and that condominium tower are part of the Bride? No, that's not what John is saying. Vernon McGee helps us understand:

> *Certainly, we are not to infer that the empty city without the citizens is the bride. Although a distinction between the bride and the city needs to be maintained, it is the intent of the writer to consider them together.*[132]

The city and its inhabitants (the Church) together are the Bride of Christ. That is the New Jerusalem.

Presence of God

In vs. 3, 11, and 22-23 we see an important feature of the city: the presence of God Himself. John again heard a *loud voice* (this is the last of 20 uses of that phrase in The Revelation). I believe God did that here because when God makes everything new, when God puts an end to sin, when God casts Satan away from His presence, when everything is perfect, and when there is a new heaven and a new Earth, all those things deserve to be declared *loudly*, not whispered. The voice says, **"The tabernacle of God is among men."** (v. 3) You might remember in the Old Testament, before there was a temple, the central place of worship and sacrifice was the tabernacle. It was portable; it was used in the wilderness. Then it became the worship center in the promised land. Finally, David had the idea to build a temple for worship. God told him it would not be him, but rather his son Solomon who would build the temple. Here the tabernacle symbolizes God dwelling among His people. There is no temple building, but rather **the Lord God, the Almighty, and the Lamb, are its temple** (v. 22).

Verses 11 and 23 tell us the city has the glory of God Himself. For that reason there was no need for sun or moon. What does light come from? **Its lamp is the Lamb** (v. 23). Jesus had said symbolically when He was on Earth, "I am the Light of the world," referring to His message and His ministry and the sacrifice of Himself that He would offer for sin. But now, the light is literal. He will actually be the Light of the world, and there is no need for sun or moon.

Twice in v. 3 we are told that God shall dwell among His people, with repetition of the phrase emphasizing its importance. Do you understand how different that is? Do you remember when Moses asked God to show him His glory? God told him that he could see God's back, but you could not see God's glory and live (Exodus 33:18-23). How different this is because all sin is wiped away. There are no barriers; this is perfect fellowship like Adam and Eve had with God in the Garden before the fall. Now that is restored, and there is a wonderful, wonderful statement at the end of v. 3: **They shall be His people.**

Won't Be's

Verse 4 gives us a list of things that will exist no longer. The first is death; this enemy is destroyed. We saw in our last lesson that death and Hades were cast into the lake of fire. We've all experienced the loss of death in some way, the loss of a spouse, a parent, a grandparent. Some have sadly buried a child. There won't be death anymore. NO MORE DEATH. Think about that. Hallelujah! Because of that there will be no more mourning. When is it we mourn the most? Yes, we can mourn the loss of a job or a pet or financial resource, but most mourning is because of death, and there will be no reason to mourn any more. There will be no crying because there will be nothing to cry over. In particular John mentions pain. What is it that makes us cry? Physical or emotional pain. There will be no pain, so there will be no reason to cry. Remember that we live in an abnormal world. We were born into it. Many of us married and had children in it; we have jobs and careers in it. All that happened in an abnormal world. It's the only world we know, so we might think that's just the way it is. But this is not the world that God ever intended for people to live in—this sinful, fallen world. He created a perfect world, and one day things will be normal again, with no death, mourning, crying, or pain. And I love this next part. If you have ever shed a tear over anything: **He shall wipe away every tear from**

their eyes (v. 4). Isn't that an amazing promise? *All* these things have passed away. Charles Swindoll says:

> *Because of the abiding presence of God, it will not even be possible for death, mourning, crying or pain to make so much as a cameo appearance. Those former villains in the drama of human history will have been cut from the remake. No more terminal disease, breakdowns, or breakups. No more heart attacks, strokes, or debilitating illnesses. No more therapists, medications, or surgeries. No famines, plagues, or devastating disasters. He is making ALL things new!*[133]

Those are the things there won't be.

Description of the New Jerusalem

Then there is a detailed description of the New Jerusalem in vs. 11-21. So impressive was this sight when John saw it, he went to great pains to make sure he did his best to capture in words what could not possibly be described. He says the brilliance of the city was like a very costly stone. If you look at large cities from outer space, do you see brilliance? You probably see pollution. But this city was "like crystal clear jasper." However, jasper is not crystal clear, and because it is difficult to translate the words for various gems from ancient times into what we know today, many believe John was actually describing crystal clear diamonds. The foundation stones were beautifully adorned, and in vs. 19 and 20 John gives us names of the gems: jasper, sapphire, etc. The amount of discussion and commentary about the exact meaning of each gem and their colors uses much more ink than it should. I will allow Vernon McGee to sum it up succinctly: "A close examination of these twelve stones in the foundation reveals a polychromed paragon of beauty; varied hues and tints form a galaxy of rainbow colors."[134] Rather than spend our energy being concerned about the exact color of each gem, McGee's analysis is what we should remember. It is a true *rainbow* coalition of color!

We also learn the city is 1500 miles long, high, and wide. That's a long elevator to get from the bottom to the top! We can't fully understand this description. The distance from New York City to Houston is 1500 miles, so imagine a city that long, wide, and high. How would you get from the bottom to the top, unless the laws of gravity are completely different? Certainly, some things will be very different. Another question concerns a new Earth with a city coming down and landing on it. Does that mean there is a round Earth with a 1500-mile-high cubic protrusion bulging out of it? We don't know exactly. Perhaps the new Earth isn't round. Perhaps it's flat, like some people erroneously think of our present Earth. Then on that flat Earth there could be this kind of city. We simply cannot know right now.

There is something else that is puzzling. There is a great and high wall (vs. 12 and 18) made of jasper (diamonds?). The wall is 144 cubits, which is 72 years or 216 feet. There are unexplainable things concerning this wall. 216 feet high for a city 1500 miles high: what kind of a wall is that? If it refers to the wall's width, and the wall is as high as the city, how would that be possible? If you have studied architecture, you know it would take a wall much wider than 216 feet at its based to provide a foundation for 1500 miles of height. We don't know exactly what John saw. Additionally, why is a wall needed at all? There is no more death, mourning, crying, pain, sin. There are no more enemies, so why is there a wall? Although we have more questions than answers, we can say with certainty that the wall is symbolic of the fact that the city is secure in peace and safety because *God lives there*. Perhaps the wall is there simply to mark the boundaries of the city.

Verse 18 says the city is pure gold. Later on, we will see the streets described in the same way, but here it is the city itself. There is not enough gold in the whole world to build a city that big out of pure gold. Is that a problem? No. Who made the gold? If He needs more, can He make more? Of course! The streets are gold and look like transparent glass (v. 21). The gold we know isn't transparent, so this is a different kind of gold.

There are 12 gates, each being an opening in the wall, and there are 12 angels at those gates. Three gates each face east, north, south, and west. That's a curious order for those directions. Some scholars have looked at the way the twelve tribes of Israel camped around the tabernacle in the wilderness and attempted to apply that background. It does not, however, seem to make any difference to our study here. What *is* true is that the names of the twelve tribes of Israel are on the twelve gates. We also see the names of the twelve apostles written on the foundation stones that were so beautifully adorned. Think about that: twelve tribes of Israel and twelve apostles. What is the symbolism? In the new heaven and the new Earth Old Testament believers and New Testament believers will all be one. It will include those who looked forward to the coming of Christ in faith, and those who look back to the coming of Christ in faith. All who have put their trust in God will be one. Most of the Old Testament believers were Jews, but there were some from other nations who acknowledged the true God. (We can read about Nebuchadnezzar's conversion in the book of Daniel.) The point is there will no longer be a distinction; everyone will be one in Christ Jesus.

The gates had doors (which could be closed, but never were), with one pearl for each door. That's one really big and irritated oyster! Of course,

God doesn't need oysters to make pearls; He can make them any size He wants. Do you remember what Jesus said about pearls in Matthew 13:45-46? (This is a great life verse, by the way.) **"The kingdom of heaven is like a merchant seeking fine pearls, and upon finding one pearl of great value, he went and sold all that he had, and bought it."** He is referring of course to finding salvation through Jesus Christ. Harry Ironside tells us:

> *These pearls remind us at] every entranceway of that one pearl of great price for which our Lord, the heavenly merchantman, sold all the He had with which to buy the church because, although He was rich, yet He became poor that He might make it His own forever.*[135]

Charles Swindoll says:

> *The pearl represents pain resulting in beauty, suffering crowned with glory. When we read of this symbol of the pearl eternally embedded in the doorways of heaven, it should remind us that Christ's suffering had an eternal purpose and opened heaven for us.*[136]

Who Lives There

In vs. 7, 8, 26, 27 we get to see who's in and who's out. Who will be living in this city, and who will not? **He who overcomes** (v. 7) shall inherit these things. There is a promise: **I will be his God and he will be My son.** We are told of many nations. That's curious: will there still be countries? No. When you read nations here, read it as peoples or races. Everyone whose name is written in the Lamb's book of life will be there (v. 27). Is your name in the book of life because you have trusted Christ as your Savior? And what is that part about the overcomers? Does that mean now that if I have trusted Christ as Savior, I must also do something special in order to become an overcomer? Look at this promise from I John 5:4-5:

Whatever is born of God [whoever has been born again and whose name is in the Book of Life] overcomes the world; and this is the victory that has overcome the world—our faith. And who is the one who overcomes the world, but he who believes that Jesus is the Son of God?

The word overcome appears three times in those verses, and it describes one group of people—all who have put their faith and trust in Jesus Christ. They and we are overcomers.

Who's out? Verses 8 and 27: cowardly, unbelieving, abominable (the word means polluted), murderers, immoral, sorcerers, idolaters, liars. Nothing unclean will be there; all on that list will be out. Did you notice that cowardly is listed first? Think about every place and time in history except modern western countries. What has it meant to follow Jesus Christ? It has meant persecution: loss of job, loss of possessions, imprisonment, death. All of that was very clear to readers in John's day. We in the United States live in the exception. Leon Morris says:

> *To be cowardly before the enemies of God at the last is finally to lose the things of God. John is speaking not of natural timidity and fear, but of that cowardice which in the last resort chooses self and safety before Christ.*[137]

That is why cowardice is listed first.

All the people in that list will be in the lake of fire. We saw in our last lesson how that was labeled the second death. The second death is eternal death in the lake of fire. Notice also that a new heaven and new Earth in this chapter does *not* change their fate; the lake of fire is not temporary. It's permanent, it's *forever*. It has been rightly said that if you are born twice, you die once. If you are born physically and then born spiritually (i.e., born again), you will die physically one time, but you will not die spiritually, eternally. You will not die twice. But if you are only born once (physically) and are not born again spiritually, then you will die twice. You will experience first physical death, and you will experience eternal death (v. 8) in the lake of fire.

A Glorious Forever

What will it look like? God makes everything new, and it is done. Notice 21:6. **"I am the Alpha and the Omega,** [(first and last letters of the Greek alphabet, same as in 1:8), says Jesus]. **I am the beginning and the end. I will give to the one who thirsts from the spring of the water of life without cost."** John is told one more time to write these faithful and true words. Remember there was just one place he was told not to write; it was when the thunders spoke. But in multiple places he was told to write what he saw because these things are faithful and true.

The Light of the Lamb will be there to guide our paths. There will be no night because there will be no need for rest and sleep. Our bodies will not be weary after 16 or 17 or 18 waking hours.

The gates will never be closed (21:25). They, referring to nations and kings, will bring their glory into the city (21:24). You mean there will be nations? No, there will be one unified people from every tribe and tongue on Earth. Warren Wiersbe explains: "These verses reflect the ancient practice of kings and nations bringing their wealth and glory to the city of the greatest king."[138] Here the greatest King is the King of kings and Lord of lords, Jesus Christ, and He will be in charge.

Conclusion

There it is, the new heaven and the new Earth. Do you want to go there? We have a choice; we can choose there or we can choose the lake of fire. Be certain you have made the choice so that the new heaven and Earth will be your eternal abode.

ATM (Apply to Me)

1. Not the streets of gold, not the pearly gates, not all the treasures described in this chapter, but the greatest joy will be the presence of Christ with us for all eternity, the One who died for our sins.

2. Did you notice that right here in the midst of all this glorious description there is an invitation from Jesus (v. 6)? **"I will give to the one who thirsts from the spring of the water of life without cost."** The one who is thirsty for the things of God, who wants to know God, the one who recognizes his sin and learns how he can be saved, receives this great promise. How? By buying it with money? No, *without cost*. Salvation is a free gift. So, it has been offered since Calvary, since the empty tomb, through all the centuries since then, always without cost has come the invitation. There is coming a day when time's up, and that invitation will be closed. But right now it is open.

3. Have you struggled in life recently? In times past? Look forward to the day when God will wipe away every tear.

4. While we are on our journey toward the new heaven and the new earth, keep on doing your best to make its population as large as possible and the population of the lake of fire as small as possible. That's our task today. Warn people, encourage people, tell people that God loves them and sent His Son to die for them. Let people know there is a great, glorious end to sin and death, with a new heaven and Earth awaiting all who put their faith and trust in Christ.

I want to close with a lengthy quote from Charles Swindoll, who captures so beautifully what we look forward to:

No more sea: because chaos and calamity will be eradicated.

206

No more tears: because hurtful memories will be replaced.

No more death: because mortality will be swallowed up by life.

No more mourning: because sorrow will be completely comforted.

No more crying: because the sounds of weeping will be smoothed.

No more pain: because all human suffering will be cured.

No more thirst: because God will graciously quench all desires.

No more wickedness: because all evil will be banished.

No more temple: because the Father and the Son are personally present.

No more night: because God's glory will give eternal light.

No more closed gates: because God's doors will always be open.

No more curse [we will see this in our next lesson]: because Christ's blood has forever lifted that curse.[139]

God did all that for us because He loves us in Christ, and He loved us with a cross. What a future awaits us!

Lesson 21

Read 22:1 – 21

No More Night

If you could know that Jesus would appear
  Before another morn would give its light,
Oh, would your heart be filled with joy? or fear?—
  If you could know that He would come tonight!

The things you'd do, the words that you would say,
  Perchance the letter you had thought to write—
How many plans would have to change today?—
  If you were sure that Christ would come tonight!

How many acts would then remain undone?
  How many wrongs would have to be made right?—
If you should meet Him ere another sun;
  Could know for sure that He would come tonight!

How many things would you find time for then?
  Now crowded out or else forgotten quite—
The kindly deed, the hour of prayer again—
  Would aught be different, should He come tonight?

Soon that day will dawn, and make all time past;
  Then may we keep our lamps all trimmed and bright.
Oh, may we live each day as 'twere the last,
  And ready be if Christ should come tonight![140]

From the pen of Pearl Waggoner Howard comes this wonderful poem, a reminder that the things which we have been studying in this great book of The Revelation are certain to take place; Christ could return at any moment. We have come to the end of our study, and the last two chapters of this great book are filled with promise and joy and hope and power.

The first five verses of Chapter 22 actually go with Chapter 21. We saw a new heaven and a new Earth and the new holy city Jerusalem. John was describing in great detail in Chapter 21 the things that he saw in the Holy

City—in the new Jerusalem—and had we had time in our last lesson, I would have included these 5 verses with that study. But I have saved them here to study as part of Chapter 22. I want to review one thing from the last lesson. We noted from that the new Jerusalem was 1,500 miles long, 1,500 miles wide, and 1,500 miles high. To get a picture of how big that is relative to the earth, we have a little picture:

This is compared to the United States of America and the Earth. 1500 x 1500 x 1500 = 3,375,000,000 cubic miles. The actual Greek word gives the measurement in stadia or furlongs, and it is difficult to translate, so some scientists give a size 1,400 x 1400 x 1400 miles, which would be 2,744,000,000 cubic miles. Either way, it's really big! Now, as I said in our last lesson, we should not think of a new round Earth with this large projection sticking out of it. We do not know exactly what all this will look like. John is just telling us what he saw. I am certain that God has it all worked out. Perhaps, as I said last time, the new Earth will be flat; I don't know. But, in any event, the picture gives you an idea of the size.

Life in the New Jerusalem

We noted that John has been getting a tour of the new Jerusalem from an angel (this angel who has been giving him this tour is one who had one of those seven bowls of wrath, the final judgments; apparently, they are very distinctive angels). In the first five verses of the chapter, he describes what life is like in the new Jerusalem. The angel showed him the water of life which came from the throne of God and the tree or trees of life with leaves for healing. Now the tree is said to be on both sides of the river of water of life. I take that to mean more than one tree. The trees bore fruit, twelve kinds of fruit for the seasons, so apparently there is some way of marking time. The different fruits are born for different times of years or whatever periods of time there are. Then there is a curious statement about the leaves being for the healing of the nations. Healing of what??? There is no more sin, there is no more death, there is no more sorrow, there is no more suffering, there is no more war. What kind of healing of the nations is necessary? Leon Morris explains: "The leaves of the tree promote the enjoyment of life in the new Jerusalem, and are not for correcting ills which do not exist."[141] I thought that was excellent insight. So, we have these symbols of eternal life—the tree of life, the water of life—because there will be no more death.

We're also told in v. 3 that there will be no more curse, the curse going all the way back to Genesis 3. What was that curse that God pronounced on Adam and Eve after they sinned? One of the things was that women's pain would be greatly multiplied in childbirth. My understanding is that there is no marriage or procreation in eternity, so certainly that one would be done away with. If there is no procreation, there is no childbirth.

However, if we look at the rest of the curse, the ground was cursed with thorns and thistles. Have you ever tried to grow a garden? Did you ever have to pull any weeds out of it, or did they just stay away on their own? Just because you're a nice person, thorns and weeds and thistles, those things didn't grow in your flowerbed? If you managed to do that without any work, tell me because I want to know how you did it. The ground is cursed with things we don't want there and they show up whether we invite them or not. (By the way, if you have a flowerbed and you see something blooming, do you know how you can tell the difference between a valuable flower and a harmful weed? This is very important. You give it a little tug. If it comes out easily it was a valuable flower. If not, then it's a harmful weed!) So it is, those weeds have to be dug out. It takes great toil to grow things, but that will end. That's another part of what the curse meant.

In addition to that, physical death was always going to win. Everyone since Adam and Eve had to face physical death, and unless we live until the

Lord comes again, all of us will face that one day. But physical death will be done away with. There will be no more death. All of that gone—the curse no more. We're also told that God will live there and we will see His face. Why? Because we will be perfect in holiness, and there will be no barrier of sin. And His name will be on our foreheads. Isn't that a wonderful tattoo? Contrast that with those people back in Chapter 13 who received the mark of the beast: the name or the number of his name on their hands or on their foreheads. What an evil, evil thing that was. It meant certain condemnation to follow the beast. We will have the name of our Lord emblazoned on us for all of eternity.

There will be no night and there won't even be need of a sun or a lamp to make sure there is no night. We are told that God shall illumine us. No sun, no lamps. The light will come from God Himself. How is that possible without the sun? Let me ask you this question: which did God make first? Light, or sun and moon? Go back to Genesis; you will find that God made light *before* He made the sun and the moon. He doesn't need the sun and the moon. He Himself is able to be the light, and there will be *no more night*.

We are told in v. 3 that we shall serve Christ. If we have some vision of sitting around in eternity, just lounging around while angels wait on us, and we eat bonbons all day long, that is not an accurate picture of eternity. Eternity involves serving Christ. Eternity also involves reigning with Christ, which leads to the question "reigning over what?" Certainly not reigning over each other, not reigning over and judging sinners (there won't be any sin). Perhaps reigning over planets, maybe solar systems, galaxies? We don't know. Exactly what all that will be like is beyond our human comprehension. But I can tell you this: How long will we be there, in the new heaven, the new Earth, the new Jerusalem? Forever. I can tell you that it will never get boring. There will be the perfect balance of work, service, of taking breaks from work, there will be the right balance of fellowship, the right balance of worship of the Lord. It will all be perfectly balanced. Charles Swindoll says this about the *first* Earth:

> **In the beginning God created the earth to be perfectly suited for human life: security without locks, food without famine, work without toil, crops without weeds, relationships without conflict.**[142]

So, it will be in the new heaven and the new Earth. It will all be perfect, and the time will be perfectly balanced.

A.T. Pierson lists 6 rhyming perfections:

1. There shall be no more curse—that's perfect restoration.

2. The throne of God and of the Lamb shall be in it—that's perfect administration.

3. His servants shall serve Him—that's perfect subordination.

4. They shall see His face—That's perfect transformation.

5. There shall be no night there; and they shall need no candle, neither light of the sun;

for the Lord gives them light—that's perfect illumination.

6. They shall reign forever and ever—that's perfect exultation.[143]

That's what the new heaven and the new Earth will be like.

The Introduction to this Book Revisited

Before we move to the rest of the chapter, I want us to go back to the beginning of our study and the introduction to this book, which provided an overview of The Revelation. Let's see how the things I presented have played out. We said the book is about Jesus Christ. Have we seen Jesus Christ? He is the source of the Book, the theme of the Book, the main character of the Book, the climax of the Book. He is the Judge in the Book, the Victor in the Book, the Ruler in the Book. And we have seen how Jesus Christ is the Center of this Book.

I said that Jesus must return and gave reasons. The return of Christ is mentioned 318 times just in the New Testament. He must return to fulfill those prophecies. He must return to marry His bride, the Church, and we saw the marriage of the Lamb. He must return to judge the world; we saw that. He must return to rule the world; we saw that as well.

We also looked at some great contrasts between Genesis and The Revelation. Let's review those:

In Genesis we had creation; in The Revelation we have the consummation.

In Genesis we had the first heaven and Earth; in The Revelation we have a new heaven and Earth.

In Genesis we had the tree of life lost; in Revelation we have the tree of life returning.

In Genesis we saw the first Adam and his wife given authority over creation; in The Revelation we have the second Adam (Jesus Christ and His bride) ruling over a redeemed creation.

In Genesis we had the beginning of sin; in The Revelation we have the end of sin.

In Genesis we saw the serpent-devil active; in Revelation the devil is in the Lake of Fire.

In Genesis we had the first city of man; in The Revelation we have the city of God.

In Genesis we had the darkness called night; in The Revelation we have no more night.

In Genesis we had the curse pronounced; in The Revelation we saw the curse removed. In Genesis we had the beginning of sorrow and suffering; in The Revelation we have the end of sorrow and suffering.

In Genesis, we had the first death; in The Revelation we have no more death.

We mentioned that there are different ways of interpreting things by different scholars within the book of The Revelation. We rejected the idea that some put forth that this is a collection of myths, and we just sort of have to get some symbolism out of them about good triumphing over evil. Some have suggested that everything in this book was fulfilled during Roman times, that it is all past. I also reject that. This is a book about the future, of what is yet to come. Some have suggested (we discussed this in Lesson 19) that all of the things starting with Chapter 4 and going all the way through the book are being fulfilled now and will be fulfilled all the way through time. I do not accept that interpretation. I believe this is a prophetic book that primarily tells us what *will* happen. We studied the prologue, where John had a vision of the glorified Christ, and we examined the letters to the churches. Then we saw John taken up to heaven to witness worship there. Following that, in Chapter 6 we have things that are future, that have not taken place yet, but will happen as God brings judgment on the world.

We said at the start that some people believe the book is 100% chronological, while others believe it is only thematic. You have certainly seen that I believe it is chronological but that there are interludes, there is supplemental material, and there are parentheses, all with additional information. Sometimes we zoom out, sometimes we zoom in, but there is still an overall chronological flow to this book. To know what that chronological flow is, study the following chart.

Chronology of Revelation Judgments

6:1 – 17   **6 Seals**

> *7:1 – 17*   *Interlude*
> *(144,000 on Earth; great multitude in heaven)*

8:1 – 9:21, 11:14   **7th Seal**
                        6 trumpets (including woes 1 & 2)

> *10:1 – 11:13*   *Interlude*
> *(7 peals of thunder, little scroll, 2 witnesses)*

11:15 – 19   **7th trumpet**

> *Chapters 12 thru 14*   *Seven supplemental visions*
> *(Not chronological with the book or with each other)*

15:1 – 16:21   **7 bowl judgments (woe 3)**

> *17:1 – 19:6*   *Judgments on Babylon*
> *These summarize how (not when) these two evil*
> *systems are destroyed as part of God's judgments*
> *Chapter 17 = Religious Babylon*
> *Chapter 18 = Commercial Babylon*

19:7 – 20:15   **Marriage of the Lamb**
                        Return of Christ
                        Armageddon
                        Satan Bound/Millennium
                        Satan loosed/Final battle
                        Satan destroyed
                        Great White Throne Judgment

21:1 – 22:21   **New Heaven and Earth**
                        Epilogue of Warning & Invitation

Look at the left-hand column—the chapters and verses that are listed there. This is my best understanding of how everything flows together chronologically. Skip over the things that are in blue. Read what is there in black: Chapter 6, and then Chapter 8, and a little bit of Chapter 9, some of Chapter 11 and so on. Do it in one sitting if you have an opportunity. In less than 30 minutes, you can read all of that, and it will show you how we begin with seven seals, out of the seven seals come seven trumpets, from seven trumpets come seven bowls of judgment. Then we have the final consummation chapters, where all evil and every evil thing and person is in the lake of fire. We then have a new heaven and new Earth. There might be people who would disagree with the exact verses of this chronology, and that is fine. This is my best understanding. That does not mean that the other chapters are unimportant. Every chapter in book of The Revelation is important; every chapter in the Bible is important. But if you want to get a sense of the chronological flow and not be confused by the parentheses, the supplemental material, follow the left-hand column. Read it all the way through. Then you can go back later— right away, another day, or another week—and read the supplemental material to see what God has added about things that were happening simultaneously. You will also see some "zooming in" or "zooming out" of the big picture.

An Epilogue

What about the rest of Chapter 22? The last 16 verses, 22:6-21 (this is one of those few things in the book that scholars agree on), are the Epilogue. We have finished the chronological part of the book, and just as we had a prologue back in Chapter 1, we now have an epilogue. Like last lesson I want to look at the Epilogue thematically because some of the themes keep recurring.

How do we know this is the Epilogue? Chapters 1 and 22 of The Revelation are tied together in many ways. What God began to say in Chapter 1, He repeats and finishes saying here in Chapter 22:

1. The things in this book are from God. Notice 1:1: **The Revelation of Jesus Christ which God gave him to show to his bondservants.** Then look at 22:6:

   These words are faithful and true and the Lord, the God of the spirits of the prophets, sent His angel to show to His bondservants the things which must shortly take place.

In other words, John wasn't sitting around by himself on the island of Patmos bored and saying to himself, *Gee, I think I just want to write something fantastic, a fantasia book about—oh, the future. I'll just make up a whole bunch of stuff, people like to read that kind of stuff and they will love it.* The things in this book are not made up by John. The things in this book are The Revelation of Jesus Christ, which He gave to John. These things are from God.

2. John speaks as an eyewitness. Again, in Chapter 1 he said God communicated by His angel to his bond-servant John. In 22:8, John said, **"I, John, am the one who heard and saw these things."** *I didn't make it up; I heard it and saw it myself.* It took a great deal of courage on John's part to write all that down. Imagine what it was like to be the one who received all this revelation and then working to put it into words? Thankfully, he says, *I heard and saw. I am an eyewitness.*

3. The message is validated by an angel. In 1:1 **He sent and communicated it by His angel.** In 22:6, **the Lord, the God of the spirits of the prophets sent His angel to show to His bond-servants the things which must shortly take place.**

4. In both chapters there are blessings for heeding this book. **Blessed is he who reads and those who hear the words of the prophecy and heed the things which are written in it** (1:3). **Blessed is he who heeds the words of the prophecy of this book** (22:7). It's not just a book of information; it's not just for us to have our curiosity satisfied. It's not just to have knowledge of the future. We are to heed what is in this book and apply it to our lives.

5. These events will be quick. In 1:1 we see the phrase **the things which must shortly take place.** The exact same phrase is used in 22:6. When it happens, it will be quick.

6. Finally, in Chapter 1 and in Chapter 22, the eternal Lord Jesus Christ is at the center of everything. Jesus, speaking in 1:17 says, **"I am the first and the last."** In 22:13 He says, **"I am the Alpha and the Omega, the first and the last, the beginning and the end."** John

MacArthur says, "Christ is the supreme, sovereign alphabet."[144] 22:13 is a triple stating of it: Alpha and Omega (first and last letters of the Greek alphabet), first and last, beginning and end. What God started God will finish. We can be sure of it.

The Authority of Jesus

Besides the themes that return from Chapter 1, what else do we see in this Epilogue? We see the authority of Jesus. We already looked at 22:13 (the Alpha and the Omega, the fact that He is the first and the last). Then in 22:16, **"I am the root and the offspring of David, the bright morning star."** Think about what all that means. Do you remember when Jesus was debating with those wonderful Pharisee people, the ones who doubted who

He is and was, the Messiah? He said to them, **"Before Abraham was, I am"** (John 8:58). He could also have said, *Before David was, I am. I am the root; I am the One who made David. But miraculously I'm also the offspring of David.* Humanly speaking, He is descended from King David. What does that show? In those nine words, **I am the root and the offspring of David**, we see His Deity and His humanity. He is fully God and fully man, The God-man. That gives Him authority over all creation. The bright morning star also shows Deity, giving Him all authority.

Characteristics of Prophecy

In vs. 6, 9, 10, and 12 we see certain characteristics of prophecy. First, it is faithful and true. If something in the book of The Revelation is prophesied, then you know it will happen. It says that there is someone (Antichrist) who will rule the earth who will have everyone marked with the number of His name (666), and it will happen. He says there will be a great, white throne of judgment, so there shall be a great, white throne of judgment. He says there will be a massive earthquake such as has never happened before, and that means the Earth will get really shook up! Everything in this book is true. It will happen, and it will play out exactly as God has shown it to John. I know there are some things we aren't fully able to understand, but when they happen, we will understand them. Prophecy is to show us the future so we don't have to sit around wondering if sin will ever end. Will the strife between nations never end? Will the fighting between the parties in Washington never end? Will the pandemic never end? The future is bright. If we know the Lord Jesus Christ, it's brighter than we can ever imagine.

Reveal-ation

These things, according to verse 10, are not to be hidden. The angel said to John, **"Do not seal up the words of the prophecy of this book."** In other words, don't keep it hidden; write it down. There are many times in the book where John was told *write this, write this, write this, this is true, write it down.* You might also remember one place where John started to write and he was told *don't write that down; seal that one up.* It was when the thunders spoke; do you remember that? What did the thunders say? I don't know what the thunders said. Anyone who tells you they know is wrong. We don't know. But that's the only place. Everything else was *write it down, write it down, write it down.* These things aren't to be hidden. All of them are to be revealed, except for one little secret thing.

Obedience Must Follow

Remember also that what is revealed is to be followed and obeyed. I hope we have gained a new understanding of this book. We know how it fits together, the flow of it, the themes, the people, the main characters. I hope we have an understanding of its meaning. I hope this book no longer scares us. I hope we have a framework where we can read it and say, *Oh yes, I remember what such and such means.* That's great. But more important than we understand it is that we follow it and obey it. If this has only piqued our curiosity, then I have failed. It must have an impact on our lives. That includes how we think, how we act, how we live, how we have a sense of urgency for the lost who do not know Jesus Christ as Savior. It must impact our daily lives.

Rewards

This chapter reminds us (22:12) of rewards. **"My reward is with me to render to every man according to what he has done."** Keith, does that mean that what we have done earns us salvation? NO! Salvation is by grace through faith in Christ. We can never earn salvation. So what's this thing about rewards? Many places in Scripture, especially in the New Testament, rewards for believers are mentioned, which apparently are based on what we have done. This is not talking about getting into heaven, being part of the new eternal Jerusalem, it means rewards given out for faithfulness in service to the Lord. The way you serve faithfully and selflessly, the way you give of yourself in time, the way you give of yourself financially without being prodded, the way you love each other, the way you pray for each other, the way you do all this without wanting recognition for it. I've had people say, *I want to take care of such and such at the church, but don't tell anybody I'm doing it. I don't want anybody to know. I just want to do it because I love the Lord.* Those are all things that bring reward in heaven. If we want the praise of men, we can tell everybody, *Hey, look what I did for the Lord,* and we get only that praise as our reward. But he/she who serves quietly, without seeking reward here on Earth, will have great reward in heaven. And let's not be like the person who has this testimony: *You know when I was 12 (I'm 20 now), there was an invitation, I came down to an altar, and I knelt there and I accepted the Lord Jesus Christ as my Savior; I remember it well.* Then when that person is 40, he/she says *You know, when I was 12, I came down to the altar and I accepted Jesus Christ as my Savior.* When that person is 60, he/she says *You know, when I was 12, I came down to the altar and I accepted Jesus Christ,* and that's his/her entire testimony. What good is that? Yes, you're saved from sin, but you are supposed to be saved *to* (not by) good works. If that is your testimony, I hope you know you've got to do better than that. We need to be about the Lord's work, and we will be rewarded for it. This book reminds us of rewards.

Worship of God Alone

We're reminded that worship is for God alone. For the second time, John falls down at the feet of the angel, intending to worship the angel, because he is overwhelmed by everything he has seen and in vs. 8 and 9. He is told that angels are fellow servants. *Don't worship me* the angel said. The angel says to worship God. Worship is a theme that has not just shown up in reference to the mistake of worshiping an angel (Revelation 19:10 and 22:8-9); the theme of worshipping God alone impacts many things. In 16:2 people were warned not to worship the beast. The first angel went and poured out his bowl on the Earth and it became a loathsome sore and malignant sore on the men who had the mark of the beast and who *worshiped* his image. In Chapter 17 people were warned not to worship the god of the Babylonian religious system because it will be judged. In Chapter 18, people were warned not to worship the god of commercial Babylon because that will be judged. Worship is for God alone.

Quick

These events will be quick. In vs. 7, 12, and 20, we see the phrase 3 times, **"I am coming quickly."** Those 4 words *three times*. If something shows up three times in the same chapter, you'd better pay attention to it. **"I am coming quickly."** When all of this starts, it will be ZOOM—it will fly by. Seven years of tribulation. Even including a thousand years of Christ's reign on Earth before Chapters 21 and 22, when compared to all of eternity—do you know how short all this is? It's just a breath. It will be quick, and we need to be ready.

Invitations

This is also a chapter with great invitations. Let's look closely at 22:11, because it looks like it might be saying something that it certainly isn't. **Let the one who does wrong, still do wrong; and let the one who is filthy, still be filthy; and let the one who is righteous, still practice righteousness; and let the one who is holy, still keep himself holy.** It looks like it might be saying, *Hey, if you want to do wrong, just keep on doing wrong.* Does that sound like a right interpretation? No. **Let the one who is filthy, still be filthy.** *That's OK—you just keep on being filthy.* No, that's not what this is saying. This is an invitation to decide who we want to be. Do we want to be the one who starts out on the road to do wrong and just keeps on doing wrong and doing wrong, and doing wrong? Doing filthy things and keeping on and keeping on? Or do we want to be one who practices righteousness, who sets himself apart as holy. You see, decision determines character and character determines destiny. That's what this verse is saying. And the invitation to put aside, to repent of those things, is always there because character tends to permanence. Vernon McGee says, "The condition of the lost gets worse until each becomes a monster of sin. This thought is frightful!"[145] That's what the verse is talking about. You've got to make a decision; the invitation is open. You don't have to continue on that road of sin, but if you decide to, you will keep on going down that road.

Another invitation is in v. 14 (this is the last Beatitude, the last blessing of The Revelation). **Blessed are those who wash their robes**... (i.e., by the blood of Jesus Christ they've been cleansed from all sin). But **Outside are the dogs and sorcerers and immoral**... (v. 15) and a long list of people who are listed there. This invitation is saying is it's open to everybody. Anyone can be cleansed by the blood of Jesus Christ, but those who are outside, those who have spent their lives saying, *I don't want anything to do with God, I don't want God to be part of my life,* will get their wish, and they will get that wish for all eternity. They didn't want anything to do with God. God will say, *You will get exactly what you wanted.* You will be outside; you will have nothing to do with God for all of eternity.

Another invitation (v. 17): **The Spirit and the bride say, "Come." Let the one who hears say, "Come." Let the one who is thirsty come; let the one who wishes take the water of life without cost.** Some have suggested that the first part of this verse is perhaps referring to us saying, *Come, Lord Jesus; we want you to come.* But if you look at the whole verse together, the second part of the verse is clearly not saying that. The one who is thirsty (i.e., thirsty for salvation) may come; the one who wishes may take the water of life. That is the person who needs to be saved. This verse is an invitation from the Spirit (the Holy Spirit) and the Church saying, *Come to Jesus.* The first part of the verse is about one who hears; he/she should tell others to come to Jesus. This is all a verse of invitation to salvation. Notice, once again, what's the cost? How much does it cost? Nothing, it's free. Eternal life is free. Prophecy should bring people to Christ.

Warnings

There are solemn warnings in this chapter. *Don't add to this book, or its plagues will be added to you.* Would you like that? I don't think so. Verse 21 is the end. I shouldn't be adding a v. 22 that Keith wrote. I can't be adding anything to the book. Also, *don't take away anything from this book or God will take away your part in the holy city and access to the tree of life.* That's why I emphasized (when I was talking about the chronological chart) that the verses in blue are not unimportant. I don't want you to take them away or forget to read them. I was just providing a chronology to follow. Every part in this book is important. It's all true, and we can't take anything away from it. Now, of course this applies to the book of The Revelation, but for two millennia, the Church has also understood that in some way these verses also apply to all 66 books of Scripture. We should not take anything away from them or add to them. The Revelation is the last of the 66 books of the canon of Scripture, and this applies ultimately to all of Scripture.

There are four ways that people add to (or usually subtract from) Scripture. One way is they disobey: *You know, I don't like that part of Scripture, so I just won't follow that in my life.* Sometimes you hear celebrities talk about their faith in Christ. Then somebody asks them about their lifestyle, and you hear, *Well, Jesus loves everybody, so I can live however I want so long as I profess faith in Christ.* Those people need to read the book of Romans where Paul wrote **Are we to continue in sin that grace may abound? May it never be!** (Romans 6:1-2). *I'm just going to disobey because I feel like it.* Not a good idea. A second choice is to simply disregard portions of the Bible. That's taking away from Scripture. Third, sometimes people distort Scripture by taking a verse out of context and misapplying it. That's taking away from Scripture. That's why we should study in context; that's why we should study whole books of the Bible together. Fourth, they dilute it; they water it down. We saw that in a previous lesson concerning so many pastors who don't even believe in a literal hell. Those percentages were unbelievably high. *Oh, hell is just symbolic.* They've diluted Scripture.

Grace

Finally, I want us to notice that the chapter ends with a verse on grace. The book of The Revelation ends with grace (22:21). **The grace of the Lord Jesus be with all.** God is a God of grace. The gospel is all grace: Amazing grace, how sweet the sound that saved a wretch like me. And notice the two-word phrase **Lord Jesus.** It occurs in both of the last two verses (20 and 21), the only two times do we see it in the entire book of The Revelation. What does that emphasize? His Deity (Lord = God Incarnate) *and* His humanity (Jesus = Savior): the Lord Jesus. Right now, that invitation of grace is open to all. It's open to anyone who will surrender his or her life to Jesus Christ. No one can ever earn salvation, but it is offered to all as a free gift. But be warned, world, the day of grace will end. When it does, then comes judgment.

A Final Note About Current Events

Someone asked me when I was preaching this series, *How do current events fit into all this? Will you tie current events into this?* Well, no I'm not. I believe this is a book of prophecy. Yes, the letters to the churches apply to the Church today, but once you get to Chapter 6, it's all future. It's not current events; those things haven't happened yet. The tribulation hasn't started yet, and it starts in Chapter 6. For centuries people have been saying *Oh, so and so is Antichrist* or *Look at this great earthquake* or *Look at this huge war.* They start saying a particular event is in such and such a chapter. No, it's not. These events haven't started yet.

However, I want to say loudly (with a loud voice!) that prophecy casts a very long shadow, and when prophecy talks about evil running rampant on the earth, that shadow is present, is it not? When it talks about massive armies gathering for war, the shadow of war is present, is it not? It talks about a massive earthquake, such as has never been before. Do we see earthquakes all the time and other kinds of natural disasters? Yes, prophecy casts a very long shadow, which means that these *kinds* of events are occurring now, but we misinterpret Scripture if we say *Oh, well this event is such and such a verse in The Revelation.* Prophecy casts a long shadow, but actual events in The Revelation have not taken place yet.

ATM (Apply to Me)

1. I must believe what has been revealed in this book because it is faithful and true. I must believe it. Just like the rest of Scripture, I don't get to leave this book out, and now that we have studied it together, I don't get to say I don't understand it. I hope you have gained understanding of it. We know what it says, we know what it means, and we know how to ATM: Apply To Me.

2. Am I feeling attacked, discouraged, defeated, depressed? I must persevere and anticipate fulfillment of prophecy, bringing vindication. Two commentators by the name of Preston and Hanson encourage us to trust…

   …an active, living God, whose love and whose wrath are alike revealed in the events of human history, a God who has played the decisive part in that history when He sent Jesus Christ among us. Only if we hold this faith can we retain any real hope in this present world.[146]

3. This study has provided information, but more importantly, I must, as I have said before, heed the words. Knowing and obeying are different. It's the distance between the head and the heart. I must *heed* the words of this book.

4. Don't worship angels, don't worship things like the creation or money or objects, don't worship people. Don't worship a pastor and don't put him on a pedestal. That's one of the worst things you can do. Pastors sometimes like to put themselves on pedestals, by the way. Oh, there's always that one temptation. Have you ever heard a pastor say *I built this church*? No, they didn't. I just want to jump up and slap them

in the face when I hear that. If a church has grown and been blessed, God did that! I am a sinner, a sinner whom God chose by His grace to use in humble service for Him. Don't put pastors or anyone else on pedestals. Put Christ on the throne and worship Him.

5. Am I ready? One of the great commentaries on the book of The Revelation was written by Joseph Seiss. I want to close with this—it is symbolic of the Church—the bride waiting for her groom. Seiss says:

Fiction has painted the picture of a maiden whose lover left her for a voyage to the Holy Land, promising on his return to make her his beloved bride. Many told her that she would never see him again. But she believed his word, and evening by evening she went down to the lonely shore, and kindled there a beacon-light in sight of the roaring waves, to hail and welcome the returning ship which was to bring again her betrothed. And by that watchfire she took her stand each night, praying to the winds to hasten on the sluggish sails, that he who was everything to her might come. Even so that

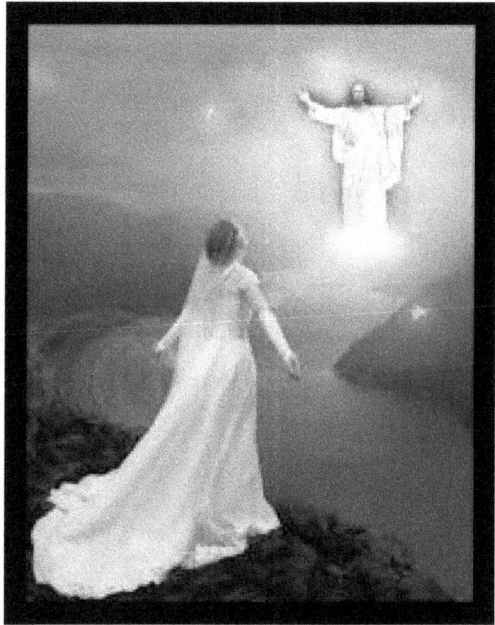

blessed Lord, Who has loved me unto death, has gone away to the mysterious Holy land of Heaven, promising on His return to make me His happy and eternal Bride. Some say that He has gone forever, and that here we shall never see Him more. But His last Word was, "Yea, I come quickly." And on the dark and misty each sloping out into the eternal sea, each true believer stands by the love lit fire, looking, and waiting, and praying and hoping for the fulfillment of His Word, in nothing gladder than in His pledge and promise, and calling ever from the soul of sacred love, "COME, LORD JESUS; COME QUICKLY." And one of these nights, while the world is busy with its gay frivolities, and laughing at the maiden on the shore, a form shall rise over the surging waves, as once on Galilee, to vindicate forever all this watching and devotion, and bring to the faithful and constant heart a joy, and glory, and triumph which never more shall end! Watch! Tis your Lord's command; and while we speak, He's near. Mark the first signal of His Hand, and ready all appear. O happy servant he, In such a pasture found! He shall his Lord with rapture see, and be with honor crowned[147]

ABOUT
KHARIS PUBLISHING

KHARIS PUBLISHING is an independent, traditional publishing house with a core mission to publish impactful books, and channel proceeds into establishing mini-libraries or resource centers for orphanages in developing countries, so these kids will learn to read, dream, and grow. Every time you purchase a book from Kharis Publishing or partner as an author, you are helping give these kids an amazing opportunity to read, dream, and grow. Kharis Publishing is an imprint of Kharis Media LLC. Learn more at: https://www.kharispublishing.com.

Cited Works

[1] Except as noted, all Bible quotations are from the New American Standard Bible. The Lockman Foundation, 1977.

[2] Swindoll, Charles. *Swindoll's Living Insights New Testament Commentary, Revelation*. Tyndale House Publishers, Inc., 2014.

[3] Ibid.

[4] Wiersbe, Warren W. *The Wiersbe Bible Commentary, New Testament*. David C. Cook, 2007.

[5] Ironside, H. A. *Revelation*. Kregel Publications, 2004 reprint of 1910 publication.

[6] Jeremiah, David. *Escape the Coming Night Study Guide*, published in 4 volumes.Turning Point, 2001.

[7] Talbot, David, quoted in Jeremiah.

[8] McGee, J. Vernon. *Thru the Bible with J. Vernon McGee, Volume 5*. Thru the Bible Radio, 1983.

[9] Ramsay, William. *The Letters to the Seven Churches*. Baker Book House,1963.

[10] Wiersbe.

[11] McGee.

[12] Jeremiah

[13] https://en.wikipedia.org/wiki/Polycarp.

[14] Ibid.

[15] McGee.

[16] Lyte, Henry F. P*raise, My Soul the King of Heaven*. 1834.

[17] Swinoll.

[18] https://edtaylor.org/2018/05/16/5-steps-toward-the-death-of-a-movement-of-god/.

[19] Swindoll.

[20] Jeremiah.

[21] Swindoll.

[22] McGee.

[23] Ironside.

[24] McGee.

[25] Jeremiah.

[26] https://edtaylor.org/2018/05/16/5-steps-toward-the-death-of-a-movement-of-god.

[27] https://en.wikipedia.org/wiki/In_hoc_signo_vinces.

[28] Jeremiah.

[29] https://www.studylight.org/commentaries/eng/isn/revelation-18.html.

[30] Jeremiah.

[31] McGee quoting High, source unknown.

[32] An actual church in Newark, Delaware.

[33] Ironside.

[34] https://www.lightsource.com/devotionals/bible-studies-for-students/bible-studies-for-students-week-of-august-13-11674108.html.

[35] Swete, Henry B. *The Apocalypse of St. John*. Macmillan, 1911.

[36] Wiersbe.

[37] Ironside.

[38] Ibid.

[39] Legacy Bible Church Statement of Faith, Noblesville, IN, adopted 2016, revised 2018.

[40] Swindoll.

[41] Wiersbe.

[42] Morris, Leon. *Tyndale New Testament Commentaries, The Revelation of St. John*. Eerdmans, 1969.

[43] Jeremiah.

[44] McGee.

[45] Swindoll.

[46] Ironside.

[47] Swindoll.

[48] Jeremiah.

[49] Wiersbe.

[50] Ibid.

[51] https://www.goodreads.com/quotes/7752737-independence-day-will-be-the-most-memorable-epocha-in-the.

[52] United States of America Declaration of Independence.

[53] Morris.

[54] Torrance, Thomas. *The Apocalypse Today*, James Clarke & Co Ltd, 1960.

[55] Swindoll.

[56] Jeremiah.

[57] McGee.

[58] Swindoll.

[59] Ibid.

[60] Wiersbe

[61] Peterson, Eugene H. *The Message*. Navpress, 2002.

[62] Ironside.

[63] Morris

[64] Jeremiah, quoting Scott, source unknown.

[65] Morris.

[66] Swindoll

[67] Ironside.

[68] Swindoll.

[69] Ibid.

[70] Ironside.

[71] McGee.

[72] Swindoll.

[73] Jeremiah, quoting Barnhouse, source unknown.

[74] Wesley, Charles. *Rejoice, the Lord Is King.* 1744.

[75] https://www.studylight.org/commentaries/eng/isn/revelation-13.html.

[76] Wiersbe.

[77] McGee.

[78] Ironside.

[79] Morris.

[80] Phillips, John. *Exploring Revelation.* Kregel Publications, 2001.

[81] Swindoll.

[82] Ironside.

[83] Swindoll.

[84] Ibid.

[85] Ibid.

[86] Wiersbe.

[87] Survey cited by Jeremiah.

[88] https://asburyseminary.edu/about/global-reach/global-history/.

[89] McGee.

[90] Swindoll.

[91] Morris.

[92] Jamieson, Robert et al. *Commentary Critical and Explanatory on the Whole Bible.* 1871.

[93] Morris.

[94] Swindoll.

[95] McGee.

[96] Ironside.

[97] Swindoll.

[98] Morris.

[99] Ironside.

[100] Swindoll.

[101] Ibid.

[102] Wiersbe.

[103] Morris.

[104] Thrupp, Adelaide. *Lord, Who at Cana's Wedding Feast.* 1873.

[105] Jeremiah, quoting Barnhouse, source unknown.

[106] Ironside.

[107] Swindoll.

[108] Wiersbe.

[109] Toplady, Augustus. *Rock of Ages.* 1776.

[110] McGee.

[111] Ibid.

[112] Ibid.

[113] Bridges, Matthew. *Crown Him with Many Crowns.* 1851.

[114] Tenney, Merrill. *Interpreting the Revelation*. Eerdmans Publishing, 1988.

[115] Swindoll.

[116] Phillips.

[117] Morris.

[118] Legacy Bible Church, Noblesville, IN Statement of Faith.

[119] Torrance.

[120] Nicolson, Martha Snell. *If Christ Should Come Tonight*. Poem, date unknown. She lived from 1886 to 1957.

[121] Swindoll.

[122] Ibid.

[123] *The New Living Translation*. Tyndale House Foundation,1996.

[124] Swindoll.

[125] Dante Alighieri. *Inferno*. 14th century epic poem.

[126] Swindoll.

[127] Ironside.

[128] Wiersbe.

[129] Watts, Isaac. *Joy to the World*. 1719.

[130] Swindoll.

[131] Morris.

[132] McGee.

[133] Swindoll.

[134] McGee.

[135] Ironside.

[136] Swindoll.

[137] Morris.

[138] Wiersbe.

[139] Swindoll.

[140] Howard, Pearl Waggoner. *If You Could Know*. Poem, date unknown. She lived from 1885 to 1969.

[141] Morris.

[142] Swindoll.

[143] garymitchell.net/BIVO/SermonArchives/LowellJohnson/Revelation/Revelation-37.htm

[144] MacArthur, John. The MacArthur Bible Commentary. Thomas Nelson, 2005.

[145] McGee.

[146] Preston, Ronald H. & Hanson, Anthony T. *The Revelation Of Saint John The Divine Introduction And Commentary*. Franklin Classics Trade Press, 2018.

[147] Seiss, Joseph A. *Apocalypse: An Exposition of the Book of Revelation*. Kregel Publications, 2000.

www.ingramcontent.com/pod-product-compliance
Lightning Source LLC
Chambersburg PA
CBHW062053080426
42734CB00012B/2638